The Complete Guide to Investing in Rental Properties

STEVE BERGES

McGraw-Hill

New York   Chicago   San Francisco   Lisbon   London
Madrid   Mexico City   Milan   New Delhi   San Juan
Seoul   Singapore   Sydney   Toronto

ISBN 0-07-143682-0

This publication is designed to provide accurate and authoritative information in regard to the subject matter covered. It is sold with the understanding that neither the author nor the publisher is engaged in rendering legal, accounting, or other professional service. If legal advice or other expert assistance is required, the services of a competent professional person should be sought.

—From a declaration of principles jointly adopted by a committee
of the American Bar Association and a committee of publishers

McGraw-Hill books are available at special quantity discounts to use as premiums and sales promotions, or for use in corporate training programs. For more information, please write to the Director of Special Sales, Professional Publishing, McGraw-Hill, Two Penn Plaza, New York, NY 10121-2298. Or contact your local bookstore.

 This book is printed on recycled, acid-free paper containing a minimum of 50% recycled, de-inked fiber.

In recent years I have had the good fortune of being blessed with wealth beyond measure. The source of my wealth does not stem from the riches of the world but rather from the riches of my family and, more particularly, my children. This book is dedicated to my three handsome young sons—Philip, age 7, who is full of boundless energy and a zeal for life; Samuel, age 5, whose gentle nature and carefree spirit bring much happiness to others; and my little Benjamin, age 1, whose eyes sparkle with joy and laughter and whose spirit radiates with purity and virtue and reminds me from whence I have come. My heart overflows with love for each of them. My family is my greatest treasure here on the earth, and I thank God for this precious and most wonderful gift he has given me. Truly they are my pearls of great price.

Contents

Contents

Section 2 How to Manage Rental Properties the Smart Way

Contents

Contents

SECTION 1

How to Buy Rental Properties the Smart Way

1

Real Estate for the Smart Investor

Buying, managing, and selling real estate can be one of the most profitable and rewarding investment activities you can participate in. There are as many ways to invest in real estate as there are people. Most investment strategies center around diverse time horizons. Whereas some investors, for example, prefer to adopt a short-term approach by "flipping" or "rehabbing" houses, other investors prefer to adopt a longer-term approach that includes buying, managing, and holding rental houses for several years. Volume is a significant factor that affects both strategies. For example, increasing the volume of units bought and sold, or flipped, increases the investor's opportunity to generate profits. By the same token, increasing the volume of units bought, managed, and held in a portfolio increases the investor's opportunity to generate income.

In a recent book I wrote entitled *The Complete Guide to Flipping Properties*, I focused on the advantages of flipping or rehabbing houses. The focus of this book, however, is an exploration of the advantages of buying, holding, and maintaining rental houses in a portfolio over an extended period of time. This book is intended for individuals who already consider themselves to be smart in their approach to investing in real estate, as well as for those who want to become smart in their approach to investing in real estate.

This book is organized into three sections that correspond directly with the three phases of real estate. Section 1 focuses on the process of purchasing rental houses and includes such topics as what types of houses to buy, various ways to locate houses, financing techniques, and the closing process. Section 2 centers on the management of rental units once acquired and includes such topics as how to find qualified tenants, what specific clauses your lease agreement should contain, how to increase rents while decreasing expenses, and how to reduce headaches by managing your tenants the smart way. Section 3 focuses on the final phase of real estate, which is the process of selling your rental houses. This section includes such topics as how to improve the marketability of your houses, the smart way to sell your houses, and how to negotiate for top dollar. The focus of the last chapter of this book shifts from real estate to the five cardinal laws for success. When applied properly, these five laws can help to propel you to achieve extraordinary success in real estate or in any other endeavor you choose to pursue.

Historical Performance

The housing market has performed quite well historically. When compared with other asset classes, such as stocks or commodities, it has been much more predictable and not nearly as volatile. While there have been some flat years of increasing home values and even some declining years, home values in general have risen year after year. According to the U.S. Census Bureau, new home prices have risen from an average sales price of $19,300 in 1963 to $228,300 in 2002 (see Exhibit 1-1). This is a total increase in value of 1082.9 percent over a 40-year period, which represents a very respectable annualized growth rate of 6.37 percent. Thus, if you were fortunate enough to acquire a small portfolio of only five rental houses back in 1963, their aggregate value today would be worth, on average, an estimated $1,141,500.

Exhibit 1-1   Historical new home sales: average sales price and percent growth, 1962–2003

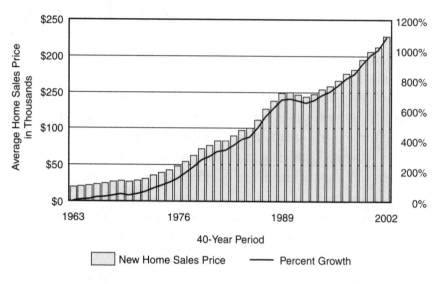

New Home Sales Price   —— Percent Growth

Four Ways to Benefit from Owning Real Estate

The historical performance of real estate as an asset class captures only one portion of the gains available to investors and results from an increase in value that can be attributed to price appreciation. There are three additional ways inherent in real estate on which investors can capitalize as well. Benefits accrue through reductions in the principal of a loan, through tax savings, and through net positive income generated from rents.

Changes in real estate values that precipitate through appreciation, or increases in price, primarily are due to two factors—increases in the money supply and increases in demand. The Federal Reserve Board (Fed) is responsible for changes in the nation's supply of money. Increases in the money supply result in devaluation of the dollar and, conversely, cause prices to increase, or inflate. As more dollars flood the market and become available to purchase goods, they begin to diminish in value. For example, without dating myself too much, I can remember as a child when it only cost 25 cents to go to the movies. The going rate now ranges anywhere from $6 to $10 a ticket depending on where you live. Not only did it cost less to get into the movies, but the costs of food, gasoline, and housing, as well as all other goods, also were much less then. The subsequent rise in prices is a result of increases in the supply of money, otherwise known as *inflation*. The second component of price appreciation reflects changes in the demand for housing. Positive changes in economic conditions for many families over the last few decades have made the possibility of home ownership a reality, thereby resulting in an increase in demand. Other significant factors that have contributed to the demand for housing are the growth in the nation's population from two primary sources. The first occurs quite naturally through the birth of children, whereas the second stems from a steady flow of immigrants into the country.

The second benefit to owners of investment rental property accrues through reductions in loan principal. Each month as the mortgage payment is made, a portion of the payment is applied to both the interest and the principal. Since reducing the principal means reducing the loan balance, as the payments are made month after month and year after year, the balance eventually will be paid in full. In the early years of repayment, most of the payment is applied to the interest, with very little being applied to the principal. Over time, however, the respective proportions begin to reverse gradually as the interest portion decreases and the principal portion increases. A loan with a 30-year amortization period, for example, will be paid down completely in exactly 360 months if equal payments are made over the duration of the loan. The beauty of this benefit is that it is the tenants who are making the monthly payments and subsequently reducing the loan balance.

The third benefit to owners of investment rental property is derived from a reduction in their tax liability. The Internal Revenue Service (IRS) mandates that rental property be depreciated over a specific time horizon. Depreciation can be a little confusing to investors who are new to the concept. The important thing to understand is that it is a calculation made primarily for tax purposes and has no bearing on the cash flow from operations. The calculation is made for income tax reporting purposes and should not be considered when estimating the cash flow from a rental property because this is an annual event and cannot be applied effectively to ongoing monthly expenses. Make no mistake, though, a reduction in one's tax liability is a very real benefit, and depending on how many properties are owned and the profitability of each one, an investor's tax liability can be reduced to zero.

The fourth benefit to owners of investment rental property arises from the net positive cash flow produced from the monthly payments made by the tenant. It is the portion remaining after taking the difference of the monthly rental income less all expenses. Investors of rental houses should strive to purchase only properties that meet two tests. The first test is to locate a rental property that is priced at or below fair market value, and the second test is to make sure that the property cash flows properly. This will be covered in much greater detail in Chapter 4. For a rental property's cash to flow properly, it should be sufficient to produce a residual on a continuing basis. This means that at the end of the day, after all expenses for the month have been paid, including principal, interest, taxes, and insurance (PITI), an investor should have something left over. A net positive cash flow from the property is just one more way investors can benefit by owning rental properties.

Economic Housing Outlook for the Coming Decade

There has been a great deal of speculation about the so-called real estate bubble. After attending the American Housing Conference in Chicago recently, I am more convinced than ever that there is no real estate bubble. This is not to suggest that the pace of growth in the real estate market will not slow, for surely it will. There may even be some periods of softness with flat to declining home values just as there have always been. The last 40 years of growth at an average annual rate of 6.37 percent, however, should prove to be a reliable indicator of what we can expect in the future.

Dr. David Berson, vice president and chief economist for Fannie Mae, attended the American Housing Conference in Chicago to present a paper entitled, "Long-Term Economic, Housing, and Mortgage Outlook to 2010." In his presentation Dr. Berson focused on several key points regarding a favorable outlook for the national housing industry over the next decade. The first of these is a forecast that calls for average real gross domestic product (GDP) growth of 3.4 to 3.5 percent, versus 3.2 percent during the 1990s (see Exhibit 1-2). In addition, Dr. Berson's forecast for fixed-rate mortgages is 7.2 to 7.5 percent, versus 7.9 percent during the 1990s. A more favorable interest-rate environment for housing is almost always a bullish indicator. Furthermore, according to Dr. Berson, Census data for 2010 projects a total population of 315 million, representing an increase of an additional 35 million residents (see Exhibit 1-3). The increase in residents stems from two primary sources—the natural growth in population due to the birth of children and the nation's immigration policy, which provides for liberal entry into our country. Lastly, the national average of unsold homes is at historically low levels, providing for a tight supply and demand relationship (see Exhibit 1-4).

The culmination of these different factors presents an exceptionally positive outlook for real estate investors. If Dr. Berson's forecasts prove to be even remotely accurate, you should be able to enjoy many opportunities over the next decade to participate successfully in one of the

Exhibit 1-2   Historical and projected economic and housing activity

	1980s	1990s	2000s
Real GDP Growth	3.2%	3.2%	3.4%–3.5%
30-Year FRM Rates	12.3%	7.9%	7.2%–7.5%
Housing Starts	1.48 million	1.41 million	1.64–1.68 million
New Home Sales	0.61 million	0.73 million	0.91–0.93 million
Existing Home Sales	2.98 million	4.21 million	5.50–5.64 million
Mortgage Originations	$325.5 billion	$934.6 billion	$1599.4–$1808.1 billion

(Commerce Department, Federal Reserve Board, Housing and Urban Development, National Association of Realtors, and Fannie Mae Economic Projections.)

Real Estate for the Smart Investor

Exhibit 1-3 The population is likely to continue to grow at 1990s rates

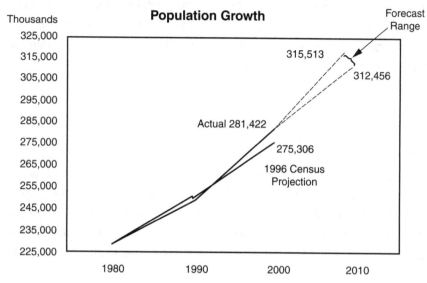

(Bureau of the Census and Fannie Mae.)

Exhibit 1-4 The unsold home inventory is historically low

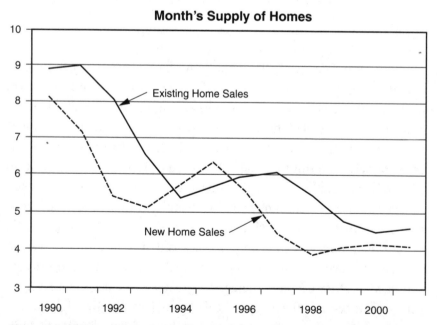

(Existing housing: National Association of Realtors; new homes: Bureau of the Census.)

most exciting industries of all—the real estate industry. The techniques outlined in this book will provide you with the tools needed to capture a generous portion of the many profits that will be generated over the coming years in the rental house industry. It will be up to you to implement the techniques outlined herein so as to maximize your opportunities for success.

The Lever and the Fulcrum

One of the first real estate books I ever read was entitled *How to Wake Up the Financial Genius Inside You* (New York: Bantam Books, 1976). It was written by Mark O. Haroldsen. Mr. Haroldsen had joined the ranks of notoriety by achieving the status of millionaire at the early age of 31 through a series of successful real estate investments. It was here that I learned about the dynamic forces of leverage. In Chapter 6 of his book, Haroldsen wrote

> Archimedes, the Greek mathematician and physicist, calculated the law of the lever. He is reported to have said that if he had a lever long enough and a place to stand, he alone could lift the world. In real estate the same principle applies. If you have a long enough lever, you can lift or buy properties that are so large that you heretofore have not even dreamed of such purchases. The OPM formula— Other People's Money—is the formula for using leverage. [p. 59]

A *fulcrum* is defined as the support on which a lever turns. In the case of real estate, the fulcrum represents the use of other people's money. On one end of the lever is your initial investment, however small it may be, and on the other end of the lever is the real estate you are levering up. It is the fulcrum that enables you to apply the law of leverage. Leverage is an extremely powerful tool that, when used properly, can enable you to quickly magnify the return on your investment. The other people's money (OPM) principle allows you to maximize the use of leverage. Your purpose is to control as much real estate as possible while using as little of your own money as you can. This means that to be a smart investor, you have to maximize the use of other people's money. The more access you have to other people's money, the greater is the degree of leverage you can achieve, and the greater the degree of leverage, the higher is the potential return on your investment. For those of you who may be first-time investors, leverage can be especially important because often individuals just getting started have the least amount of cash to work with. Constraints on the availability of your personal cash need not prevent you from becoming a successful real estate investor. Rather, the lack of capital when just getting started actually can benefit you by forcing you to seek alternative means of financing.

Other people's money can be provided to you in one of two forms— either debt or equity. The most common type of financing is debt. Debt is provided most often in the form of some type of loan that can come from any number of sources, including banks, mortgage companies, family members, friends, credit cards, and home equity loans, to name a few. Financing with debt typically requires that you repay a loan with predetermined terms and conditions, such as the repayment term (number of years to repay the loan), the interest rate, and any prepayment penalties that may be imposed for paying off a loan early.

One primary advantage of using debt is its lower cost of capital than other forms of financing such as equity. Another advantage of using debt is that typically it is more readily available than equity. One key disadvantage of using debt is that the debt must be serviced. In other words, you have to make periodic payments on the loan. Using debt as a source of financing usually will have a direct negative impact on the cash flow from your rental house because loans usually require monthly payments. It should be obvious to you that the more you borrow for a particular investment, the greater your monthly payment will be, and the greater your monthly payment, the less remaining there will be of the property's after-tax cash flow. As a smart investor, you must be sure that you have structured the purchase of your rental house in such a manner that will allow you to service the debt on it, whatever the source of that debt is, without a negative cash flow. This is after all expenses have been accounted for. You should have a minimum of a 1:1 to 1:2 ratio of free cash flow left over after all expenses have been paid to ensure that you can meet the debt requirements adequately. Debt is a wonderful tool, but like any tool, you must exercise caution and respect when using it. Otherwise, you can quickly find yourself in trouble. You must be in control of your debt. Do not allow your debt to control you.

An alternative to using debt financing is to use equity financing. While debt represents money that is borrowed, equity represents money that is invested. Equity financing can be provided from any number of sources and commonly involves the formation of a legal partnership such as a limited-liability corporation (LLC). Family, friends, business associates, and private investors all can be good sources of equity financing. Whereas debt financing is repaid at specified periodic intervals, equity financing often is not. Equity investors most often participate in the profits of a business enterprise, such as rental houses. Thus, while lenders providing debt financing enjoy the security of fixed periodic payments, investors providing equity financing enjoy the opportunity to earn a higher rate of return on their invested capital.

A primary reason for using equity financing is to minimize the cash flow out of your rental properties. The repayment of equity financing can be structured in any number of ways. For example, you can agree with the investor to pay him or her a specified percentage of the profits at the end of each quarter, semiannually, or even annually. You also could agree to pay the investor a predetermined percentage of the gain on sale when the property is eventually sold. Preserving as much cash as possible, especially in the early years, can mean the difference between success and failure in your real estate business.

Whatever the source of your funding, the idea is to use as little of your own money as possible because that is what your returns are based on. Your *return on investment,* or *cash on cash return* as it is also sometimes referred to, is derived from the simple ratio of the net cash left over after all expenses have been paid divided by the amount of your original investment plus any out-of-pocket improvements or expenses that require an additional owner's contribution. So in a simplified example, if you paid all cash for a $100,000 house that required no improvements and that appreciated at an annual rate of 5 percent, the $5000 of increased value would represent a return on investment of 5 percent after the first year. For a meager return of only 5 percent, you may as well leave your money invested in certificates of deposit (CDs) and save yourself the time and trouble of managing rental houses. On the other hand, if you invested only $10,000 in the deal and borrowed, or leveraged, the remaining

$90,000, assuming the same $5000 in appreciation, your return on investment now jumps to 50 percent. This simplified example does not even take into consideration the effect of income generated from the rents, the reduction of the principal loan balance through monthly payments, or the tax benefits derived through depreciation. This is how the power of leverage works. It allows you to use a little bit of your own money, invest it in real estate or any other income-producing asset, and maximize the return on it.

Take a minute to study Exhibit 1-5. It illustrates the effect of price appreciation on leverage using an initial investment of $10,000, or 10 percent of the purchase price, using different growth rates over a period of 25 years. Notice that when using a growth rate of 5 percent, the value of your $10,000 investment has earned a phenomenal 2386 percent rate of return. Think you can get that kind of return in the stock market? Maybe, but not likely. Once again, this simple chart does not even take into consideration the effect of income, taxes benefits, or principal reduction.

Now take a moment to review Exhibit 1-6. It illustrates the effect of price appreciation with no leverage using an initial investment of $100,000, or 100 percent of the purchase price, using different growth rates over a period of 25 years. Notice that when using a growth rate of 5 percent, the value of your $100,000 investment has earned a respectable 238 percent rate of return. I think that you would agree with me that the unleveraged returns in Exhibit 1-6 pale in comparison with the leveraged returns in Exhibit 1-5.

In *The Complete Guide to Flipping Properties*, I addressed the issue of the favored and much-touted "nothing down" methods. I wrote

There are a number of popular books about how to apply no money down techniques. Many of them are well written and have sound principles. While I am a firm believer in the use of other people's money, in my opinion these methods carry the concept of leverage to an extreme. That's not to say that they don't work. I'm sure in many cases they do. By relying solely on these techniques, however, you are restricting yourself to a much more limited pool of available properties to choose from. Let's face it. You are in the real estate business to make money, and time is money. Why spend all of your time trying to find a no money down deal when there are far more houses that can easily be purchased with 5 to 10 percent down? I realize that some of you may not have even that to start with, and if that

Exhibit 1-5 Effect of price appreciation on leverage using an initial investment of 10 percent of purchase price

Purchase Price:	$100,000
Percent Down:	10.0%
Down Payment:	$10,000

Number of Years	Annual Appreciation Rate					
	2.5%	Ret on Inv	5.0 %	Ret on Inv	10.0 %	Ret on Inv
1	102,500	25.0%	105,000	50.0%	110,000	100.0%
2	105,063	50.6%	110,250	102.5%	121,000	210.0%
3	107,689	76.9%	115,763	157.6%	133,100	331.0%
4	110,381	103.8%	121,551	215.5%	146,410	464.1%
5	113,141	131.4%	127,628	276.3%	161,051	610.5%
6	115,969	159.7%	134,010	340.1%	177,156	771.6%
7	118,869	188.7%	140,710	407.1%	194,872	948.7%
8	121,840	218.4%	147,746	477.5%	214,359	1143.6%
9	124,886	248.9%	155,133	551.3%	235,795	1357.9%
10	128,008	280.1%	162,889	628.9%	259,374	1593.7%
11	131,209	312.1%	171,034	710.3%	285,312	1853.1%

12	134,489	344.9%	179,586	795.9%	313,843	2138.4%
13	137,851	378.5%	188,565	885.6%	345,227	2452.3%
14	141,297	413.0%	197,993	979.9%	379,750	2797.5%
15	144,830	448.3%	207,893	1078.9%	417,725	3177.2%
16	148,451	484.5%	218,287	1182.9%	459,497	3595.0%
17	152,162	521.6%	229,202	1292.0%	505,447	4054.5%
18	155,966	559.7%	240,662	1406.6%	555,992	4559.9%
19	159,865	598.7%	252,695	1527.0%	611,591	5115.9%
20	163,862	638.6%	265,330	1653.3%	672,750	5727.5%
21	167,958	679.6%	278,596	1786.0%	740,025	6400.2%
22	172,157	721.6%	292,526	1925.3%	814,027	7140.3%
23	176,461	764.6%	307,152	2071.5%	895,430	7954.3%
24	180,873	808.7%	322,510	2225.1%	984,973	8849.7%
25	185,394	853.9%	338,635	2386.4%	1,083,471	9834.7%

Exhibit 1-6 Effect of price appreciation with no leverage using an initial investment of 100 percent of purchase price

Purchase Price:	$100,000
Percent Down:	10.0%
Down Payment:	$10,000

Number of Years	Annual Appreciation Rate							
	2.5%	Ret on Inv	5.0 %	Ret on Inv	10.0 %	Ret on Inv		
1	102,500	2.5%	105,000	5.0%	110,000	10.0%		
2	105,063	5.1%	110,250	10.3%	121,000	21.0%		
3	107,689	7.7%	115,763	15.8%	133,100	33.1%		
4	110,381	10.4%	121,551	21.6%	146,410	46.4%		
5	113,141	13.1%	127,628	27.6%	161,051	61.1%		
6	115,969	16.0%	134,010	34.0%	177,156	77.2%		
7	118,869	18.9%	140,710	40.7%	194,872	94.9%		
8	121,840	21.8%	147,746	47.7%	214,359	114.4%		
9	124,886	24.9%	155,133	55.1%	235,795	135.8%		
10	128,008	28.0%	162,889	62.9%	259,374	159.4%		

11	131,209	31.2%	171,034	71.0%	285,312	185.3%
12	134,489	34.5%	179,586	79.6%	313,843	213.8%
13	137,851	37.9%	188,565	88.6%	345,227	245.2%
14	141,297	41.3%	197,993	98.0%	379,750	279.7%
15	144,830	44.8%	207,893	107.9%	417,725	317.7%
16	148,451	48.5%	218,287	118.3%	459,497	359.5%
17	152,162	52.2%	229,202	129.2%	505,447	405.4%
18	155,966	56.0%	240,662	140.7%	555,992	456.0%
19	159,865	59.9%	252,695	152.7%	611,591	511.6%
20	163,862	63.9%	265,330	165.3%	672,750	572.7%
21	167,958	68.0%	278,596	178.6%	740,025	640.0%
22	172,157	72.2%	292,526	192.5%	814,027	714.0%
23	176,461	76.5%	307,152	207.2%	895,430	795.4%
24	180,873	80.9%	322,510	222.5%	984,973	885.0%
25	185,394	85.4%	338,635	238.6%	1,083,471	983.5%

is the case, then you may have to search for that nothing down deal. I would encourage you to build as large of a capital base as possible so that you can quickly and easily purchase some of the more attractive opportunities as they become available. For every one or two nothing down deals that are available, there are at least a hundred deals that can be purchased with 10 percent down. The pool of investment properties available to choose from is much larger at this level. In the end, more choices mean greater opportunity, which can potentially mean much more money, and that's what you're in the real estate business for, right?

In summary, you must seek to maximize the power of leverage in all your real estate transactions. Remember, you need both a lever and a fulcrum (other people's money) to apply the law of leverage. In order to increase the pool of available rental houses to purchase, don't get carried away with the nothing down approach. Instead, build up your base of investment capital and have it readily available to take advantage of some of the more attractive opportunities that surely will come your way.

The Magic of Compound Interest

Interest as it applies to money is simply the cost of money if you are the borrower or the income if you are the lender. *Compound interest* is interest paid on interest if you are the borrower or interest earned on interest if you are the lender. Another section that I found particularly fascinating in Mark O. Haroldsen's book explained just how significant the principle of compound interest is as it pertains to real estate. Mark illustrates this principle by using the following example. He writes

> If I gave you a choice of working for me for $1000 a day for a period of thirty-five days, versus working for yourself for 1 cent the first day and doubling the amount each day for thirty-five days, which job offer would you take?
>
> Obviously, if you were to take the first choice, at the end of thirty-five days you would have $35,000. A wage of $35,000 in thirty-five days is phenomenal. Had you chosen the alternative of working for 1 cent the first day and doubling the amount each day for thirty-five days, you would be compounding your money at 100 percent per day.
>
> When I use this example in lectures, usually about half the people prefer the first job offer and half the second. Without the aid of a pencil or calculator, decide which choice you would make. [p. 1]

Offer 1	Dollar Amount	Offer 2	Dollar Amount
Day 1	1,000.00	Day 1	0.01
Day 2	1,000.00	Day 2	0.02
Day 3	1,000.00	Day 3	0.04
Day 4	1,000.00	Day 4	0.08
Day 5	1,000.00	Day 5	0.16
Day 6	1,000.00	Day 6	0.32
Day 7	1,000.00	Day 7	0.64
Day 8	1,000.00	Day 8	1.28
Total	8,000.00	Total	2.55

After reviewing the preceding table, Offer 1 looks pretty good, especially when compared with Offer 2. So what do you think? Would you take the guaranteed $1000 per day, or would you choose the 1 cent compounded at a rate of 100 percent? Let's examine the next eight days, and we'll reassess our decision.

Offer 1	Dollar Amount	Offer 2	Dollar Amount
Days 1–8 total	8,000.00	Days 1–8 total	2.55
Day 9	1,000.00	Day 9	2.55
Day 10	1,000.00	Day 10	5.10
Day 11	1,000.00	Day 11	10.20
Day 12	1,000.00	Day 12	20.40
Day 13	1,000.00	Day 13	40.80
Day 14	1,000.00	Day 14	81.60
Day 15	1,000.00	Day 15	163.20
Day 16	1,000.00	Day 16	326.40
Total	16,000.00	Total	652.80

Okay, so now what do you think? Offer 1 still looks pretty good compared with Offer 2. Let's look at the next eight days, and again reassess.

How to Buy Rental Properties the Smart Way

Offer 1	Dollar Amount	Offer 2	Dollar Amount
Days 1–16 total	16,000.00	Days 1–16 total	652.80
Day 17	1,000.00	Day 17	652.80
Day 18	1,000.00	Day 18	1,305.60
Day 19	1,000.00	Day 19	2,611.20
Day 20	1,000.00	Day 20	5,222.40
Day 21	1,000.00	Day 21	10,444.80
Day 22	1,000.00	Day 22	20,889.60
Day 23	1,000.00	Day 23	41,779.20
Day 24	1,000.00	Day 24	83,558.40
Total	24,000.00	Total	167,116.80

Wow! Look at the difference now. Suddenly Offer 2 is starting to look pretty good. In fact, my guess is that any of you who may have initially chosen Offer 1 surely will have switched to Offer 2 by now. Just for fun, let's see what the effect of compounding at a rate of 100 percent for 11 more days does to our earning potential.

Offer 1	Dollar Amount	Offer 2	Dollar Amount
Days 1–24 total	24,000.00	Days 1–24 total	167,116.80
Day 25	1,000.00	Day 25	167,116.80
Day 26	1,000.00	Day 26	334,233.60
Day 27	1,000.00	Day 27	668,467.20
Day 28	1,000.00	Day 28	1,336,934.40
Day 29	1,000.00	Day 29	2,673,868.80
Day 30	1,000.00	Day 30	5,347,737.60
Day 31	1,000.00	Day 31	10,695,475.20
Day 32	1,000.00	Day 32	21,390,950.40
Day 33	1,000.00	Day 33	42,781,900.80
Day 34	1,000.00	Day 34	85,563,801.60
Day 35	1,000.00	Day 35	171,127,603.20
Total	35,000.00	Total	342,255,206.40

If the choice wasn't obvious before, it sure is now. At the rate of $1000 per day, Offer 1 resulted in a grand total of $35,000. This figure pales in comparison with Offer 2 in what started out as a meager 1 cent. By day 35, that penny, compounded at a rate of 100 percent grew to an amazing $342,255,206. Although compounding at a daily rate of 100 percent is highly unlikely, this simple example is used to illustrate just how powerful the magic of compounding can be. I encourage you to join the ranks of smart investors by taking full advantage of this vital tool, for by doing so you will be able to quickly accelerate the value of your real estate portfolio.

How to Build a $10 Million Retirement Portfolio

The process of buying, managing, and selling real estate properties is undeniably one of the surest means for building a sizable retirement portfolio. Amassing a $10 million real estate portfolio is a process that can take anywhere from a few years to many years depending on your ability to purchase rental houses. The patient and diligent investor who applies a well-defined and systematic approach over time, however, will be able to retire with more than enough to enjoy a very comfortable lifestyle.

In *The Complete Guide to Flipping Properties*, I used the following analogy to describe the investment process an individual must be willing to undergo in order to be successful:

> Just as a beautiful and healthy tree requires sunlight, food, and water for proper nourishment, so does the process of building wealth. Leave your fortune to chance, and chances are you will have no fortune to leave. To build wealth, you must plant the proper seeds, and then nourish them with food and water over time. An occasional pruning will also be required. Almost before you realize it, a strong and magnificent tree will begin to take shape right before your very eyes. Although the grand and noble oak tree exhibits towering beauty and strength above the surface of the earth, it is the tree's root system that extends deep beneath the surface, unseen by human eyes, which give it force and stability allowing it to withstand the mighty forces of nature. Like the oak tree, you too, must be well rooted in fundamentally sound principles of real estate before your branches can grow. As you apply the principles learned from this book, you will eventually be able to enjoy a sweet comfort from the shade that your branches will provide. Although the winds of adversity may descend upon you with great force and vigor, if you are prepared, they shall not prevail.

How to Buy Rental Properties the Smart Way

To be successful in real estate does not happen by chance. You must have a well-defined plan outlining your specific objectives. Determine exactly what it is you want out of your real estate investment activities, and identify your time horizon for accomplishing your goals. Be realistic as well as specific with your objectives. You must begin with the end in mind. In other words, you must know where it is you are going before you can begin the journey to your destination. Otherwise, if you don't know where you are going, how will you know when you get there? Only you can determine your destination in life. If you don't have one, then you'll end up exactly where you intended to go, which is nowhere.

I think that you will agree with me that building a $10 million real estate portfolio will not happen all by itself. It will require some degree of effort on your part. Not a whole lot, but some. Take a moment to study Exhibit 1-7. The investor in this example simply buys $200,000 worth of rental property each year for 10 years and then stops. Depending on where you live, the average rental house may sell for only $100,000. This means that you need to buy two houses instead of one. Rental houses in your market may sell instead for closer to $65,000. If this is the case, then you will need to purchase three rental houses. You get the idea—$200,000 worth of rental property each and every year for a total of 10 years. That's it! After accumulating investment property for a period of only 10 years, you can stop. That is, if you want to. This example also assumes an average annual rate of price appreciation of 6.37 percent, which is the historical average for the 40-year period from 1963 to 2002 we discussed earlier.

Now look at the results in Exhibit 1-7. If you do nothing more than just maintain your properties, by year 12 your minimum net worth will be in excess of $1 million. This net worth reflects only the value accumulated through the increase in property values and does not capture the income generated from the houses, the reduction of debt by paying down the loans, or the tax benefits attributed to the portfolio. If you are patient and wait another 5 years, your net worth will have increased to over $2 million by year 17. Wait an additional 7 years, and your net worth doubles again. By year 24 it has grown to $4.4 million. If you can

Exhibit 1-7   Ten-million-dollar retirement portfolio

| | Investor A—Buy and Hold Strategy | | | | | | | | | | |
Year	Rental House 1	Rental House 2	Rental House 3	Rental House 4	Rental House 5	Rental House 6	Rental House 7	Rental House 8	Rental House 9	Rental House 10	Increase in Value
1	200,000										0
2	212,740	200,000									12,740
3	226,292	212,740	200,000								39,032
4	240,706	226,292	212,740	200,000							79,738
5	256,039	240,706	226,292	212,740	200,000						135,777
6	272,349	256,039	240,706	226,292	212,740	200,000					208,126
7	289,698	272,349	256,039	240,706	226,292	212,740	200,000				297,824
8	308,151	289,698	272,349	256,039	240,706	226,292	212,740	200,000			405,975
9	327,781	308,151	289,698	272,349	256,039	240,706	226,292	212,740	200,000		533,756
10	348,660	327,781	308,151	289,698	272,349	256,039	240,706	226,292	212,740	200,000	682,416
11	370,870	348,660	327,781	308,151	289,698	272,349	256,039	240,706	226,292	212,740	853,286
12	394,494	370,870	348,660	327,781	308,151	289,698	272,349	256,039	240,706	226,292	1,035,040
13	419,624	394,494	370,870	348,660	327,781	308,151	289,698	272,349	256,039	240,706	1,228,372
14	446,354	419,624	394,494	370,870	348,660	327,781	308,151	289,698	272,349	256,039	1,434,020
15	474,786	446,354	419,624	394,494	370,870	348,660	327,781	308,151	289,698	272,349	1,652,767
16	505,030	474,786	446,354	419,624	394,494	370,870	348,660	327,781	308,151	289,698	1,885,448
17	537,201	505,030	474,786	446,354	419,624	394,494	370,870	348,660	327,781	308,151	2,132,951
18	571,420	537,201	505,030	474,786	446,354	419,624	394,494	370,870	348,660	327,781	2,396,220
19	607,820	571,420	537,201	505,030	474,786	446,354	419,624	394,494	370,870	348,660	2,676,259
20	646,538	607,820	571,420	537,201	505,030	474,786	446,354	419,624	394,494	370,870	2,974,137
21	687,722	646,538	607,820	571,420	537,201	505,030	474,786	446,354	419,624	394,494	3,290,989
22	731,530	687,722	646,538	607,820	571,420	537,201	505,030	474,786	446,354	419,624	3,628,025

Exhibit 1-7   Ten-million-dollar retirement portfolio (*Continued*)

	Investor A Buy and Hold Strategy										
Year	Rental House 1	Rental House 2	Rental House 3	Rental House 4	Rental House 5	Rental House 6	Rental House 7	Rental House 8	Rental House 9	Rental House 10	Increase in Value
23	778,129	731,530	687,722	646,538	607,820	571,420	537,201	505,030	474,786	446,354	3,986,531
24	827,696	778,129	731,530	687,722	646,538	607,820	571,420	537,201	505,030	474,786	4,367,873
25	880,420	827,696	778,129	731,530	687,722	646,538	607,820	571,420	537,201	505,030	4,773,506
26	936,503	880,420	827,696	778,129	731,530	687,722	646,538	607,820	571,420	537,201	5,204,978
27	996,158	936,503	880,420	827,696	778,129	731,530	687,722	646,538	607,820	571,420	5,663,936
28	1,059,613	996,158	936,503	880,420	827,696	778,129	731,530	687,722	646,538	607,820	6,152,128
29	1,127,110	1,059,613	996,158	936,503	880,420	827,696	778,129	731,530	687,722	646,538	6,671,419
30	1,198,907	1,127,110	1059,613	996,158	936,503	880,420	827,696	778,129	731,530	687,722	7,223,788
31	1,275,278	1,198,907	1,127,110	1,059,613	996,158	936,503	880,420	827,696	778,129	737,530	7,811,343
32	1,356,513	1,275,278	1,198,907	1,127,110	1,059,613	996,158	936,503	880,420	827,696	778,129	8,436,326
33	1,442,923	1,356,513	1,275,278	1,198,907	1,127,110	1,059,613	996,158	936,503	880,420	827,696	9,101,120
34	1,534,837	1,442,923	1,356,513	1,275,278	1,198,907	1,127,110	1,059,613	996,158	936,503	880,420	9,808,261
35	1,632,606	1,534,837	1,442,923	1,356,513	1,275,278	1,198,907	1,127,110	1,059,613	996,158	936,503	10,560,448

Investor Assumptions
1. Purchases one or two rental houses per year totaling $200,000 each year for 10 years.
2. Holds all 10 houses through desired period.
3. Assumes annual growth rate of 6.37 percent.

hold out a few more years, you will have amassed a fortune that even Donald Trump would be envious of. By year 35, your wealth will have grown to well over $10 million.

Remember to follow the guidelines mentioned previously in this chapter. As a smart investor, you must be willing to apply a systematic approach over time to accumulate a fortune such as this. Take the time to establish a well-defined business plan that will allow you to implement your investment strategy, and then be willing to stick with it. This is not to imply that you must be rigid and immovable in your approach. Even the captain of a large ship must adjust the rudder from time to time as unanticipated winds and oceanic currents attempt to push the ship off course. You, too, will have to adjust the rudder from time to time as unanticipated events occur. This is okay. Make the necessary adjustments and then continue on your journey to success.

I hope that I shall always possess firmness and virtue enough to maintain what I consider the most enviable of all titles, the character of an honest man.

—GEORGE WASHINGTON

2

Selecting Great Rental Houses for the Smart Investor

Smart investors understand that to be successful in the rental house business, they have to offer the right type of product in the right location and at the right price. If you are just getting started in the real estate business, you are likely to have lots of questions. One of the first questions that naturally comes to mind is, "What type of house should I buy?" There are so many choices available that for the first-time investor it can seem overwhelming. If you feel overwhelmed, don't despair! What you are feeling is perfectly normal. There are many decisions to make, and as a future owner of rental houses, one of the biggest decisions to make will be the type of house to purchase. Your selection process will include several important factors. You must consider the house's location, the type of neighborhood it is in, and the type of house it is. You also will need to consider the age of the property and its physical condition. In addition, you must consider the purchase price and the terms. The price and terms of the house are important for two reasons. The first reason is that your tenants have to be able to afford it, and the second reason is that it has to have a cash flow that makes sense as an investment for you. Before you can determine if the rental unit will provide enough cash flow, you'll need to know how much rent to charge. Once you have narrowed down the selection to two or three candidates, you can analyze the income and expenses and measure their returns against the investment criteria you have set for yourself.

One significant factor to keep in mind throughout the selection process is to be patient. If you are anything like me when I bought my first rental house, you are most likely to be eager, excited, and ready to get started. This is great. Just remember that your primary reason for getting into this business is to make money, so be smart and take your time before jumping into anything. Smart investors are patient, and patient investors are smart.

How to Choose the Right Location

As a smart investor who is in the rental house business, you want to be very careful about where your units are located. The type of location best suited for rental houses is typically in a neighborhood that is between 10 and 35 years old. These neighborhoods represent areas where the average middle-class citizen lives. Neighborhoods younger than 10 years old tend to have larger and more expensive homes, whereas neighborhoods older than 35 years old are often run down and in declining areas of town. This is not always the case, of course, since I have seen some areas 40 or more years old that continue to be well maintained and where pride of ownership exists. The 35-year age rule is a generalization where the tendency for homes and neighborhoods older than that are likely to be declining in value.

One important factor to consider when choosing a location is your holding period. In other words, how long do you intend to keep the house? If you are going to keep a rental unit until the mortgage is paid off, say, 25 or 30 years, and the house you are considering is already nearing the end of its economic life span, you may want to reconsider. Purchasing a rental house that you intend to hold for 30 years that is already 30 years old may not be in your best interest. Simple addition tells us that the house will be 60 years old when you get ready to sell it, and by then it may well be considered functionally obsolescent, which is a polite way of saying that it is not worth anything to anyone. On the other hand, if you intend to keep the house for only 5 to 10 years, your decision to purchase an older house is probably okay.

The ideal location for investors is one in which the majority of houses are well kept and in an area that is not declining. The area should be well established, have good schools nearby, and be in a moderately strong resell market. Communities of this type often exhibit such characteristics as mature landscaping, plush lawns, and homes that are in relatively good condition. The following box features a handy 10-point checklist for identifying suitable locations with which you'll want to become familiar.

Ten-Point Property Location Checklist

____ The neighborhood is between 10 and 35 years old.

____ Home sales should be moderate to strong.

____ The neighborhood should consist of attractive homes that are well cared for and not run down.

____ Mature landscaping and well-maintained lawns are the norm for most homes in the neighborhood.

____ It is a reputable area with a low crime rate.

____ There are no junk cars, RVs, or trailers parked in the driveway, in front of the house, or worse yet, in the yard.

____ Boats are stored properly (if allowed).

____ The neighborhood is free of trash and debris.

____ The neighborhood is in close proximity to schools, churches, and shopping.

____ The neighborhood should not be located in a declining area of town.

How to Choose the Right Type of House

There are just about as many different types of houses as there are people, or so it seems. For example, there are one-bedroom efficiency units, there are slightly larger two-bedroom houses, and there are three- and four-bedroom houses as well. Some houses may have garages, whereas others may have covered carports. Some houses may have a patio, whereas others may have a deck. Some houses may be a one-story ranch, whereas others may be two-story colonials. With so many choices, it's sometimes difficult to determine which type is the best suited for your investment purposes.

The smart investor will evaluate the surrounding market that is most likely to affect her selection. In other words, you must ask yourself, "Who are my tenants most likely to be, and where will they come from?" For example, if you live in a college town or near a university, your tenants are most likely going to be young college students who are on a shoestring budget. This suggests that you should concentrate your efforts on finding housing that will best meet their needs. In my experience, since the average college student is operating on a tight budget, she is typically willing to sacrifice all the extras for a place that is cheap. This narrows your selection to affordable housing units such as one-bedroom efficiencies or small two-bedroom houses with very few frills. College students don't need a large place, they don't need a deck, they don't need a garage, and they don't even need covered parking. What they do need is cheap housing. For this particular market, you may even consider a small duplex or triplex building.

Suppose that you don't live in a college town or near a university. Then what? Again, examine the market surrounding your area and determine who your customers, or tenants, are most likely to be. The largest pool of prospective tenants in most areas consists of families with anywhere from one to as many as four children, with the average being about two. These families customarily require a two- or three-bedroom house with one or two baths and a one- or two-car garage. Remember that, as a general rule, people who rent cannot afford to buy for one reason or another. It may be that they don't earn enough or perhaps have a deficient credit history. Whatever the reason may be is not as important as to recognize that most families are on a limited budget. As a result, they typically seek basic living accommodations. This means that in your search to select the right type of housing, you want to keep these facts in mind. You typically should look for modestly sized houses with two to three bedrooms that are moderately priced relative to the market. The rents generated from these properties must be sufficient to cover all the expenses, service the debt, and still have something left over. The portion that is "left over" represents your return on investment (ROI), and that's why you're in the real estate business. At the end of this chapter we will explore more fully exactly how to properly analyze a rental house to determine if investing our capital in it makes sense.

Physical Condition: Inspecting Is Key

A rental house's physical condition can range anywhere from extremely poor, as in condemned, to very good, as in immaculate. The type of property to focus on will depend primarily on your investment objectives. Some investors prefer to buy rental properties that are well maintained, clean, and ready to go. On the other hand, some investors prefer to buy rental properties that are in need of some repair, often referred to as *fixer-uppers*. The reason that some individuals prefer fixer-uppers is that they can purchase them for less money than a house that is ready to go. These individuals often contribute their time and labor to add or create value in the property, or they may even hire a handyman to complete these tasks. In *The Complete Guide to Flipping Properties*, I have devoted an entire book to this strategy. The business of flipping, or rehabbing properties, for quick resell can be very profitable. You will have to decide for yourself if you want to spend the time and energy required to make repairs or if you just want to purchase a house that is ready to go.

If you're the type of person who doesn't mind taking on a little extra work, then your attention should center on houses that are in need of only minor repairs. Buying rental houses that fall into this category will prove to be the most profitable because you will be able to minimize the amount of money needed for the required improvements, thereby allowing you to maximize your ROI. Another concern is the time involved in making major repairs. The time needed for rental houses that require only minor repairs is much shorter than it is for those which require major repairs. If you are planning on renting the house out, then the more time you spend working on it, the more it will cost you in lost rents. Ideally, you want to begin collecting rent by the time your first payment is due. If you do decide to take on a fixer-upper, I recommend that you look for a house that looks a lot worse than it really is. In other words, you should look for a house that is in need of cosmetic-type repairs such as new paint, landscaping, and maybe a good cleaning. Cosmetic repairs are quick and easy to make and are often the least expensive type of repair.

The following inspection items provide an overview of things to look for in your assessment of a house's physical condition. Appendix C provides a more comprehensive checklist that can be used by you during your inspection of prospective rental houses to ensure that nothing is overlooked.

Houses with weak or bad foundations should be avoided entirely because repairing foundations can be both time-consuming and expensive. For example, if the house is built on a concrete slab and major settling has occurred, the house will have to be leveled. Leveling a house not only can be very costly, but it also can be time-consuming. This will cost you money in repairs as well as lost rents. In addition, houses with foundation problems are likely to have other structural damage caused by the settling. A close inspection of the interior walls almost always will show evidence of settling because the drywall will be cracked and separated. It is common in many houses to see hairline cracks in walls, especially around the seams, so don't be alarmed if you see small cracks such as these. Separation cracks can be repaired quickly and easily with a little filler such as caulk and a fresh coat of paint. If, on the other hand, you see large cracks running down the wall, you can almost bet that the house has a foundation problem. You also should inspect the exterior of the house. In particular, if the house has some brick on it, look for larger than normal separations in the mortar. Again, don't worry about hairline cracks. These are normal. If the house does not have brick, signs of a poor foundation can be seen around doorjambs and window frames that are out of alignment.

If the house was not built on a slab but was built with a basement foundation instead, you must be especially aware of moisture problems. This is fairly common, especially in older homes. Look for cracks in the basement walls that may have evidence of leaking around them, such as staining or mildew. Leaks in the walls also can create a buildup of mold in the basement area, a problem that is becoming a major liability for many property owners. It is not at all unusual to see small cracks in a basement floor or even in the walls. You don't need to be excessively concerned about these types of cracks because they are usually just surface cracks that do not go all the way through the floor or the wall. Just as houses built on slabs with foundation problems can be very expensive to repair, so can houses built on basements with similar problems. You best bet is to avoid basement and slab foundation problems entirely. There are too many other houses that are in better condition from which to choose.

Roofs also represent another area where major repairs may be required. The cost to repair a roof can vary widely with age and condition. Most composition shingles have a minimum life of 20 to 25 years, so if the existing shingles are less than 15 years old, it's a pretty safe bet that any repairs required would be minimal. After 15 years, the shingles can begin curling up and wearing to the point where leaks may begin to develop, so be sure to look for signs of this. One way to determine if the roof has been leaking is to look at the ceilings inside the house. If you observe water spots or stains, this is a very good indication that the roof has been and may be leaking. Wet spots or stains in the attic are also a good indicator.

Although older roofs often show signs of discoloration, it is not uncommon for newer roofs to become discolored as well. Discolored roofs can be cleaned easily and inexpensively by applying a chemical process. The discoloration typically is caused by a buildup of mildew that can be killed and removed with a solution of water, bleach, and other chemicals that is available at most hardware stores. If a new roof is needed, the cost to replace it may not be prohibitive. If, for example, a new layer of shingles can be applied over the existing layer, the cost and time involved are minimal. On the other hand, if two or three layers of shingles already exist, then a tear-off almost certainly will be necessary. This can increase the price of a new roof significantly because the labor required for the tear-off can be expensive due to the extra time involved. Furthermore, older homes that already have several layers of shingles on them may require still more work. The roof deck, which in newer homes is made of sheathing or plywood, may be damaged as a result of water leaks that have occurred over time. If the house needs to be completely redecked, this will certainly increase the repair cost due to the additional time and materials required for replacement.

Other repairs that may prove to be costly include replacing equipment, windows, and exterior surfaces such as brick or siding. If the furnace and air conditioner are worn out, replacing them can quickly add up. Costs can range anywhere from $1500 to $7500 depending on what needs to be done and the type of equipment you replace. Replacing all the windows also can be costly and can add thousands to the price you pay. Brick and siding repairs, depending on the extent of wear or damage, are another item that can add up fast. If only a few minor repairs are needed, such as replacing one or two windows or screen doors or applying fresh paint, then you are probably pretty safe with your decision to purchase the rental house, provided, of course, that the rest of your investment criteria are met.

The house's plumbing also should be checked carefully for proper operation. The plumbing can be inspected easily by flushing toilets, checking underneath sinks, and looking for leaky faucets. Be sure to check the age and condition of the home's hot water heater also. Leaky faucets and hot water heaters are fairly easy to repair and/or replace and can be done quickly and inexpensively. More expensive repairs that can add up quickly involve underground sewer lines, especially if they are embedded in a cement slab. These lines sometimes can get broken because of foundation problems such as settling. The separation in the line does not allow the sewage to drain properly and also can cause the line to back up. Smart investors will minimize dealing with the more severe types of plumbing problems such as broken underground lines. While leaky water faucets and hot water heaters are fairly easy to repair or replace, broken or damaged sewer lines can be harder to detect and cost much more to repair. A careful inspection of the plumbing system potentially can save you thousands of dollars.

As part of your inspection process, the home's electrical wiring also should be checked to ensure that it is working properly. A simple check of outlets and light switches throughout the house can tell you a great deal about its electrical condition. If they are working properly, chances are that the system is okay. Houses that are 30 to 40 years old or more may need to be checked more thoroughly because they tend to have more problems. For example, breakers and switches eventually wear out and need replacement. In some houses, the wiring may be so old that it will have to be replaced completely. Replacing the wiring in a house can be very costly because it is run behind the walls. An electrician likely will have to make cuts in the drywall to remove and replace the wiring. This means that when the electrician is done, the drywall will need to be repaired, and after that, the walls will need to be repainted. Do you see how quickly something like faulty wiring can add up? Unless you happen to be an electrician, avoid houses that have wiring problems.

If you lack experience or are not yet comfortable with the inspection process, I recommend that you hire a professional house inspection company. These companies perform a very thorough inspection and almost always find things wrong. Keep in mind that this is what they are getting paid to do. When they complete their inspection, you can expect to receive a comprehensive written report. The report documents everything the inspector finds and often contains things that are fairly minor. Unless you are prepared for this, you may be alarmed at all the items written on the report. Inspection companies document everything they find because that's what they are being paid to do, and they also do so to protect themselves. If something isn't documented, the buyer may come back to them after taking possession of the house and claim that the company overlooked the deficiency and consequently sue for damages. Inspection services usually cost anywhere from $150 up to $500 depending on the area of the country in which you live and the size of the house. I rarely use professional inspection companies anymore because more often than not they end up telling me what I already knew from my own inspection. A few years ago I had a house under contract that I was about to purchase. I had performed my own assessment of the house's physical condition and concluded that it needed new paint and a new roof. Although I had already examined the house, I decided to hire a professional inspector just to make sure that I hadn't overlooked anything. After he completed his assessment and filled out the report, he told me, "The house needs to be painted, and it needs a new roof." I suppose I got what you might call a "second opinion." After having spent $450 to have someone tell me what I already knew, I determined that for the most part, I could do just as good of a job inspecting as the inspector could. I have only used the services of a professional inspection company for a single-family house on one occasion since that time, and that was for a house built in 1903.

In summary, as you gain experience by inspecting more and more houses, you will be able to quickly assess a house's physical condition and know within a short time whether or not it meets your investment criteria. Investors should steer clear of larger and more costly repairs such as foundation or structural problems. There are too many other opportunities just waiting for your investment capital that won't require nearly as much time and money as these will.

How to Determine the Best Price Range for Your Area

Just as important as choosing the right type of house and the right location is choosing a house that falls into the right price range. A good rule of thumb to keep in mind for choosing a rental unit is to target houses that are at or below the median selling price of homes in your area. The median sales price means that half the houses sold are more expensive than a particular price and half the houses sold are below that price. For example, if the median sales price in your area is $112,000, then half of all homes sold are equal to or greater than $112,000 and half of all homes sold are less than $112,000. Median home prices for your area are not difficult to determine. Almost any real estate agent is likely to be familiar with median sales prices and can help you to determine that. Median selling prices vary widely and will depend on the particular region in which you live. For example, according to the 2000 U.S. Census, the median selling price of homes in Victoria County, Texas, is only $73,300, whereas in Richmond County, New York, it is $209,100. This is almost three times as much as Victoria County.

There are three main reasons for focusing your efforts on houses that fall below the median sales price. Houses in this price range are more affordable for your tenants, require less investment capital, and generate higher returns for you. It stands to reason that, as a general rule, most renters cannot afford expensive homes. If they could, they wouldn't be renting a house. Instead, they would be buying one. As with anything, there are exceptions, of course, such as a family relocating from another area and renting temporarily until the construction of their new home is completed. Since the average renter cannot afford more expensive housing, you must concentrate on finding rental units that they can afford. Less expensive housing is a benefit to you as well. The less a house costs, the less investment capital is required, and the less investment capital that is required, the more houses you can buy. Furthermore, if you have a limited amount of investment capital to work with, financing will be easier to obtain on less expensive homes. Smaller rental houses also generate higher returns for your investment dollar because they rent for a higher rate per square foot than do their larger counterparts. For example, you may be able to rent out a 1000-square-foot house for $1000 per month, or $1 per square foot per month. On the other hand, a 2000-square-foot house in the same neighborhood probably would rent for only about $1500 per month, or 75 cents per square foot.

Smart investors know that in order to maximize profits, they have to concentrate on finding rental houses that are priced below the median selling price. I recommend that you look for smaller and more affordable houses that can be rented easily. Doing so will minimize your risk in the rental house business while at the same time maximize your chances for success.

To select great rental houses for your real estate investment portfolio, start by looking for a location in which the neighborhood is established, not too old, and in a desirable part of town. Houses should be the smaller traditional types with two to three bedrooms, two or more bathrooms, and a one- or two-car garage. In addition, you should carefully inspect each house to alleviate unforeseen maintenance costs. Finally, shop for houses that are affordable and that are priced at or less than the median selling price for your specific market.

All who have meditated on the art of governing mankind are convinced that the fate of empires depends on the education of youth.
*—*ARISTOTLE

3

Eight Ways to Locate Rental Houses for the Smart Investor

Taking the time to locate the right rental house for your real estate portfolio is vital to your success. Regardless of where you may live, there is always an abundance of investment opportunities available, many of which can be found right in your own backyard. By using a systematic and all-encompassing approach, you will be able to locate more rental houses than you have time or money to invest in. You must be willing, however, to exercise patience in your search for the right property. This is especially true for beginning investors because they are most often excited and anxious to get started. While enthusiasm is certainly important, it can get you into trouble if you are not careful. To be successful, you must be able to remain impartial and objective in your analysis. Govern your investment activities with prudence, take your time, be thorough, and most of all, be patient.

Included in the following box are eight different methods you can begin using right now to locate great rental houses. You can choose to use as few as one or two of the suggested methods or as many as all eight. I recommend experimenting with several of the methods with which you are most familiar. As you gain more experience and eventually are able to devote yourself full time to the real estate business, I suggest using all eight methods. The more rental properties you have at your disposal to review and analyze, the better and more profitable your chances will become.

Eight Sure-Fire Methods for Locating Rental Houses

1. Classified advertisements
2. Real estate magazines
3. Internet searches
4. Billboards and signs
5. Real estate agents
6. Scouts
7. Professional affiliations
8. For sale by owners (FSBOs)

Classified Advertisements

Most local newspapers carry a section in the classified advertising for single-family houses that are available for sale. Many of these ads are placed by real estate agents and are designed to prompt you to call their offices. Look for ads that use such key words as *investment opportunity, great rental property,* or *starter home.* This kind of descriptive language is usually indicative of older houses in established neighborhoods, which are exactly what you are looking for. This type of classified advertisement is worth taking the time to call on. Even if it turns out that the house is no longer available or does not meet your investment objectives, it still provides you with an opportunity to create a dialogue with a sales agent who might be able to find the right kind of rental house that would better fit your needs. If the agent's listing does not turn out to be what you are looking for, she may refer you to someone in her office who specializes in investment-type properties.

Many of the ads listed in the classified section are for sale by owners (FSBOs). Once again, you want to look for key words that may indicate the owner is anxious to sell, can offer flexible terms, or has a house that may be offered at a price below retail. As you become more familiar with prices in your local market, you will increase your ability to recognize a good deal when you see one. Many owners don't have a clue what their houses are really worth. If, for example, an owner has lived in the same house for 20 or 30 years, he may not realize that home prices have increased to the extent that they have and may very well be offering the house at a well below market price. Some of you may feel that this is taking advantage of such people. My feeling is that sellers have a duty and an obligation to educate themselves with respect to home prices in their area. The way I look at it, they are the ones who set the price, not me. If I'm able to ascertain that the price is very good relative to other houses in that neighborhood, I don't ask the seller, "Why is your price so low?" I operate under the assumption that the owner knows what he is doing and has his own reasons for selling below fair market value.

Finally, you can use the classifieds to place your own ad in the real estate wanted section. You don't need to spend much money on these ads. A well-written and concise ad can be just as effective as a larger and more expensive ad. Your goal is to get people who are motivated and want to sell their houses to call you. Your ad should be designed to solicit the specific type of call for the kind of rental house you are looking for so that you are not bothered by individuals who are not likely to have the type of house for sale for which you are looking. If you are looking for a particular type of house, for example, a three-bedroom, two-bath ranch, in a certain price range, and with any special terms, then be specific and say that in your classified ad.

Real Estate Magazines

Almost all areas publish books or magazines periodically that are specifically designed for residential real estate sales. Usually you can find several different magazines, some for one area and some for another. Real estate magazines can be found in many places, including racks or newsstands located outside real estate offices, drug stores, and grocery stores. Real estate magazines can be a great source for locating single-family houses. You also will find many real estate–related advertisers that can be helpful in these publications, such as real estate agents, mortgage companies, appraisal services, surveying companies, title companies, real estate legal services, and insurance companies.

Most ads in these magazines are placed by real estate agents; often they will advertise all their listings on one page. The ads usually feature a photo of the agent along with some compelling reason why you should contact that agent for your real estate needs. Although most of the ads in real estate magazines are placed by agents and brokers, some magazines do offer an FSBO section. While most of the sales agents with listings in these publications focus on the traditional retail housing segment, there are often several agents or firms that specialize in different niches within the real estate market. For example, some companies concentrate primarily on commercial real estate, whereas others focus on vacant or undeveloped land. Still others specialize in the wholesale market, such as dealers. Be sure to look for these easy-to-find real estate magazines in your area. They can provide a wealth of information, including resources directly applicable to your real estate investment needs.

Internet Searches

There are numerous Web sites that offer all kinds of information about houses for sale. You can do a search in your area, or in any other area, just by keying in a phrase such as "Homes for sale Goodrich, MI," for example. Such a search usually will generate results of 20 to 30 or even more Web sites with listings in your area. Probably the best know site among all real estate sites featuring houses for sale is hosted by the National Association of Realtors. You can find this site on the Web at *www.realtor.com*. This site has over 2 million listings for various types of properties, including single-family homes, condominiums, townhouses, multifamily apartments, mobile homes, vacant land, farms, and rentals. The data derived for these listings come from the Multiple Listing Service, so it will not include any FSBO properties. The site is available to the general public, so you don't have to be a real estate agent to access the listings on it. It is very much like a public multiple-listing service for properties made available to the general population or anyone with a computer and access to the Web. You also can search by property type, state, city, zip code, price range, minimum and maximum square feet, age of home, number of floors, and several other criteria. Most listings provide a descriptive overview of the property, photos, and contact information.

Other good Internet sources include your local newspapers. Almost all major newspapers now list their entire classified section on Web sites. The information is often updated daily. This is usually determined by how often the paper is published. For example, if it is a daily paper, it is most likely updated daily. A weekly paper would be updated weekly. An advantage the newspaper Web sites offer over a site such as Realtor.com is that in addition to providing ads placed by real estate agents, there are also many ads placed by individuals, such as FSBO homes. Newspaper classified ads found on the Web are not nearly as complete as those on a site such as Realtor.com, but they do provide you with a good mix of properties for sale by both real estate agents and individual homeowners.

These are only two of many of locate investment opportunities available on the Internet. The best way for you to properties in your own area is to use a search engine such as Yahoo, Google, or MSN to do a search specific to your area.

Billboards and Signs

As your company grows and you have more available in your advertising budget, you may want to consider using billboards to advertise that you buy houses. These signs can be very effective, especially in areas of town where the traffic count is known to be high. One primary benefit to using billboard advertising is the frequency with which your message is seen. People who take the same route to work day after day will pass by your sign. They may not be interested in selling now, but at some point they may very well be, and even if they don't call you, they may tell a friend, relative, or coworker about you. Another benefit of using billboards is that, believe it or not, they are very cost-efficient when compared with other forms of advertising, such as display ads in newspapers. For example, if the average daily traffic count is 50,000 at a particular location, this is the equivalent of 1½ million people each month who will see your sign. The lower cost per thousand means reaching more people for less money. One good thing to keep in mind when using billboards is to keep your message simple by not putting too much information on the sign. Motorists usually have just a brief moment to read your message as they pass by, so keep it simple and direct, such as "I buy houses! Call (800) 555-5555."

You also may consider using smaller signs that are less expensive than large, full-sized billboards. Smaller signs, such as those measuring approximately 18 by 24 inches, typically are made out of corrugated plastic and are fairly inexpensive to buy. You can buy them with wire frame stands that make them easy to place in high-traffic locations. Just like the billboards, you don't want to put too much information on such signs. Just stick to the basics, such as "I buy houses," your company name, and a telephone number. I've seen some real estate signs that are so overloaded with information that it's difficult to make anything out on them, especially when you are driving by and may only have a few seconds to glance at the sign. Fill the sign with large letters, and keep it simple. I also would suggest using a color that works well both in the winter and in the summer. For example, white signs with blue lettering look great in the summer, but in the winter the white sign will blend in with the snow and will be barely visible. Likewise, a green sign with white lettering looks great in the winter because the colors are sharply contrasting. Once again, though, in the summer the green sign blends in with grassy roadsides and surrounding foliage. I suggest using colors that work well year around, such as a red or blue sign with white letters.

Real Estate Agents

In *The Complete Guide to Buying and Selling Apartment Buildings*, I describe in great detail two techniques that literally can save you thousands of dollars on each and every real estate transaction in which you participate. A comprehensive understanding of these two principles saved me $345,000 on one transaction alone. Ignoring these two vitally important principles can bring your real estate career to an abrupt halt. The following story, as related in my apartment book, is a great example of how important these two laws of success are. See if you can discern them while reading the story.

I acquired a midsized class C apartment complex that met all of my criteria for a value play opportunity. I made a number of improvements to the buildings within the first six months, bringing it up to a class C+ to B– range. The rents were subsequently raised and the property was fairly stabilized by the ninth month. The complex was averaging 97 to 98 percent occupancy with minimal turnover. By the tenth month, it was time to begin implementing my exit strategy. I would do one of two things—either sell the property outright or refinance it to pull as much of my equity out of it as possible. I already had a broker in mind whom I knew from a previous transaction. He happened to work for one of the nation's largest commercial real estate brokerage firms. He was a respected and active broker who knew the apartment market well, or so I thought.

My own analysis of the financial statements for my apartment complex suggested a value of about $2,000,000 to $2,100,000. For what I had into it, I thought I would probably list it at a price of $2,050,000 and would be willing to settle for $1,900,000 to $1,950,000. To my utter dismay, the broker I was about to engage to represent me suggested a value of only $1,800,000 on the high side and said I would be lucky to get $1,650,000. I must admit that I was temporarily devastated by his analysis. This was a broker I trusted and felt certain was competent. A sales price of $1,650,000 was not at all what I had in mind. I began to question myself and wondered where I had gone wrong. After all, I spent a great deal of time and energy, not to mention money, on this project. Was all of this for naught? My feelings of despair lasted for all of about ten minutes.

I've been knocked down enough times to know that I have two choices—I can either stay down, or I can get back up. I chose the latter. It was time for a second opinion, and while I was at it, I may as well get a third opinion, too. I quickly contacted two other brokers who I knew were active in that market and faxed my financials to them. I was careful not to prejudice their opinions with my own as related to the value. The first broker came back with a value of $2,000,000 to $2,100,000, while the second broker estimated the value to be between $2,000,000 and $2,200,000. Bingo! Aahhh, life was good again. My analysis had proven to be right on target and was corroborated by two other brokers. This story, by the way, has a happy ending. The property was subsequently sold for a price of $1,995,000. With new financing being secured, a full-blown appraisal was required. The appraisal report indicated a value of $2,150,000, which further served to validate my original analysis.

Just in case you weren't able to ascertain the two vital principles from this real-life example, allow me to share them with you now. The first principle is that you must have a complete understanding of the concept of value as it relates to your investment property. In the example cited here, not having a working knowledge of this essential real estate tenet potentially could have cost me $345,000. The concept of establishing true market value and measuring the performance of an investment property is fully explored in Chapter 4.

The first principle of understanding value is directly related to the second principle. Although I understood the true value of my apartment building, the real estate agent I was about to hire did not. The second principle states that the real estate agent or agents you choose to work with must be capable and competent in the real estate industry. This second principle is discussed more appropriately in this section about real estate agents.

Before you take time to develop a solid working relationship with an agent, you should assess his level of competency. Many agents work part time and are not really that passionate about what they do. They're usually just looking to make an extra buck. If they sell a house, great. It they don't, oh well. I suggest that you avoid the part-timer and look for someone who loves what he does and can do it well. You want agents who are in the real estate loop each and every day and can bring you fresh opportunities as soon as they hit the market. Your agents always should be on the lookout for potential deals to present to you. Before they do, however, you must review your investment criteria with them so that they know exactly what you are looking for. Real estate agents work for commissions, so I assure you that when they find a rental house that they think you may be interested in, they'll let you know. Don't worry about rejecting some of the opportunities they bring to you. Just explain to the agent what you didn't like about it or why it didn't meet your predetermined investment criteria and send him off to find another for you. Eventually, he'll bring you just the deal you're looking for.

I cannot overemphasize how important it is for you to work with competent real estate agents. I have worked with many brokers and agents whose ranges of expertise have varied greatly. Whether you are buying or selling, the sales agent working for you has a fiduciary obligation to represent your best interests and therefore should do everything possible to help you make sound investment decisions. This includes furnishing you with important market data specific to the area in which you are buying. For example, your agent should be able to easily generate reams of comparable sales data that will help to support your analysis of the property. Almost all agents are members of the Multiple Listing Service (MLS), where sales comp information can be accessed easily. You should ask your sales agent for a list of all active listings, as well as all recent sales, that are related to your transaction. By examining recent sales, you know where the market has been and what similar houses in your area have sold for. By examining active listings, you know where the market is priced currently and what houses comparable to yours are selling for. This vital market information is fundamental to your success in the real estate business. Without it, you have no basis to make sound financial decisions and easily can overpay for a rental house that you have no business owning in the first place.

In addition to employing a competent agent, having several real estate agents scouring the market for rental houses for you as opposed to only one or two is one of the best ways to locate potential investment properties. I recommend establishing a relationship with several residential real estate agents in your area. All people function within their own circles of influence, including real estate agents. While there may be some overlap, no two agents have the same group of friends or business contacts. Using more than one agent will enlarge your exposure to different and unique opportunities. I'm sure you've heard the old adage that "two heads are better than one." Smart investors know that when it comes to finding good deals, this saying holds true every time in this business.

Scouts

Another great way to locate potential investment opportunities is by using a scout. A scout does exactly what the name suggests—he scouts for rental houses that meet your investment criteria. Scouts who served in the U.S. Army years ago provided an invaluable service to their captains. They were sent out in advance of the troops to gather information about the enemy's position, its military strength, and possible areas of vulnerability. The scouts would then report back to their captain to provide key information about the enemy. Important decisions were then made based on the information gathered by the scouts. While military commanders relied heavily on scouts 200 years ago, they now use a much more advanced type of scout. Today's military leaders rely on sophisticated technology such as radar and satellite imagery to report vital information such as the enemy's position, how many tanks the enemy has on the ground, and how many troops the enemy has in place. The process itself is much the same, though, with important information being provided to those authorized to make decisions.

Just as the scouts in the military report vital intelligence to those who have the power to act on it, so do scouts in a real estate capacity report key information regarding potential investment opportunities to you. A good scout should gather as much information as possible so that you can make prudent decisions. Scouts provide such material information as that listed in the following box.

Duties of a Scout Include Providing the Following Information

- The general condition of the rental house
- The property location
- A neighborhood assessment
- The seller's asking price, terms, and timing needs
- The seller's reason for selling and degree of urgency
- Comparable sales data related to the specific area

If the idea of using scouts is new to you, you may be wondering how to go about finding one who can bring opportunities to you. Practically anyone can work as a scout because there are no licenses to obtain, such as there are for real estate agents. Furthermore, no specialized training is required other than the instructions you give them regarding the types of rental houses you are looking for, the price range, and information such as that listed above. For example, you can offer to pay a referral fee of $500 to college students, friends, neighbors, or relatives for every deal they bring you that results in a purchase. I might caution you that before sending anyone on a wild goose chase looking for rental properties, make sure that you are serious about wanting to purchase a house and that you'll be prepared to do so on their bringing you an acceptable investment opportunity. Their time is just as valuable to them as your time is to you. Once the purchase is completed, be sure to honor your commitment by paying whatever referral fee you agreed on.

In summary, a scout's role is similar to that of a real estate agent in that she is constantly on the lookout for rental houses that meet your preestablished investment criteria. When the scout identifies what she believes to be a potential deal, she then passes that information along to you to make a final determination. Just like a real estate agent, the scout is only compensated when you actually go through with the purchase. While in many states you are prohibited from paying a commission to anyone who is not a licensed agent, you can legally pay a referral fee. Using the services of a good scout is another way for investors to efficiently locate good investment opportunities. The more deals you have to look at, the more selective you can be.

Professional Affiliations

Your affiliation with or membership in a professional organization is another great way to find rental houses. Professional organizations include local groups such as the chamber of commerce and national groups such as the National Association of Home Builders. Many areas also have real estate investment–related associations and clubs. Your membership in a professional organization provides you with an excellent opportunity to network with others who share similar interests. Members often include investors like yourself, real estate brokers, tax and real estate attorneys, surveyors, appraisers, and myriad other professionals.

Professional organizations typically have periodic meetings in which information is shared that may be of value to you. Many groups meet monthly, for example, at a local restaurant for breakfast. Guest speakers frequently are featured at the meetings and provide their expertise as it relates to a given topic. You can find real estate associations in your area by looking in the Yellow Pages or by doing an Internet search using a phrase such as "real estate investment clubs." One site that I have used is called Real Estate Promo.com and is located at *www.realestatepromo.com*. Click on the link entitled "Investment Clubs" to locate a club near you. The site lists clubs in almost all 50 states, so you should be able to find something near you. Another similar site is offered by a company called Creative

Real Estate Online. This company's Web site is located at *www.real-estate-online.com*. Go to the home page and click on "Real Estate Clubs" to find an investment association in your area. Once you have identified a club in your area, it is simply a matter of calling the number listed, introducing yourself, and finding out when and where the meetings are held.

I encourage you to join at least one or two professional organizations and to become an active participant in them. Your goal is to meet people and to establish relationships with them. You want to broaden your sphere of influence by getting to know as many people as you can, especially those with whom you share similar interests. Be sure to let others know what it is you do as a real estate investor and what types of houses you are looking for. Although relationships take time to develop, you never know when this type of networking will pay off for you. It may just be that the individual you are talking to happens to be thinking about selling his house and would love to work out a deal with you. One of the chamber of commerces I belong to as a representative of Symphony Homes, for example, distributes a monthly newsletter to its 500-plus membership. For a nominal fee of only $50, the chamber inserts my four-color circulars into the newsletters, which gives me superb exposure to over 500 professionals in my market. The circulars have resulted in an increase of traffic to the communities covered by Symphony Homes and have helped to establish a strong brand identity. One such visitor was the local chief of police and his wife. Although they didn't purchase a new home from me, they did at least take the time to come out and learn about my company and the many fine homes it builds. Furthermore, think of how many people a chief of police knows. Through the course of natural conversations, he potentially could mention my company to many of his own affiliates, who could, in turn, purchase a new home from me.

FSBOs

People who prefer to sell their own house often are referred to as FSBOs. Sellers who fall into this group typically market their houses in one or two ways. The first thing they do is go to the local hardware store and buy a "For Sale By Owner" sign, a black magic marker, and a stand. Next, they write their telephone number on the sign and then proudly place it in the front yard for all to see. Some FSBOs go so far as to purchase two signs and place the second one down the street at the intersection. After the signs have been placed, the seller often will call the local newspaper to run a classified ad for a week or two. After 30 to 60 days with little to no success, the majority of FSBOs become frustrated and eventually enlist the services of a professional, that is, a licensed real estate agent.

Although the FSBOs' purpose, to save money by avoiding paying a real estate commission, is certainly understandable, what they fail to realize is that there is much more to selling a house than just sticking a sign out in the front yard. Whether you're selling used cars or houses, selling is all about marketing and exposure. A sign in the front yard results in putting all the neighbors on notice that the house is for sale but not much more. How many neighbors are going to be interested in buying the house? Probably not many. Signs are useful, however, to help buyers driving from another area to more easily identify the house's location. Advertising in the local newspaper will help some, but in small to midsized towns, the seller is still limiting himself to the immediate community.

The advantages of using a real estate agent are many. The agent's ability to increase market exposure for the seller's house is significant. One of the first things agents do on signing a listing agreement to represent a seller is to put the house in the MLS. Making the house available for sale in the MLS gives the seller access to buyers from all across the nation, many of whom may be relocating from another state. Agents also interact with many other agents on a daily basis and are constantly sharing information about listings. In addition, agents often advertise across a much broader range of media devices, including the Internet, real estate magazines, and other specialized publications. More experienced real estate agents also understand the finesse that is required in negotiating price and terms, as well as many other important aspects of the sales process.

Please do not misinterpret my favorable comments toward agents as being biased or as putting in a plug for them. My remarks are statements of fact and not statements of opinion. I'm all for a person wanting to save money, especially if he isn't in any hurry to sell. Unfortunately, however, what FSBOs fail to realize is that although they may save money on the commission, they may lose even more money on the overall transaction than if they had listed with an agent. This results from their lack of experience, lack of knowledge of market prices, and inability to negotiate with buyers. FSBOs all have an idea of how much they think their house is worth, but in reality, their houses are usually priced too high or too low. For example, some owners have lived in their homes for 20 years or more and have no idea that they have appreciated as much as they have. Other homeowners, on the other hand, have heard that a neighbor down the street sold her house for a certain amount, and therefore, their houses must be worth a greater amount. In truth, none of the sellers really knows what the true market value of their homes are.

The fact that the FSBO doesn't understand property values the way you do is to your advantage. Since you have taken the time to study the area and familiarize yourself with market values in the neighborhoods in which you will be prospecting, you'll know immediately from your initial telephone conversation with the FSBO whether or not the price of the house fits your investment criteria. If you find a seller who is willing to sell his home at a price 10 or 15 percent below market, then all the time and energy you have expended researching the area will have paid off. For those of you who may think this is taking advantage of the seller, let me point out that you have no moral obligation to tell a seller that his house may be worth more than he is asking. The FSBO has set the asking price at a value he believes to be fair for any number of reasons. As a buyer willing to meet his terms, you are an important part of a relationship that is amenable to both parties. Finally, FSBOs are often flexible on terms, so they may be able to provide you with a more favorable and creative deal structure, one that permits you to minimize your cash outlay for the purchase.

So there you have it—eight terrific ways to locate potential investment opportunities. Whether you hire a scout or a real estate agent or whether you shop on the Internet or in a real estate magazine, you are certain to find more excellent rental properties than you know what to do with. To be successful, you must remain impartial and objective throughout the selection process. Don't allow yourself to become emotionally attached to a property by falling in love with it. Doing so will distort your ability to analyze it properly. You will find yourself embarking down the road of rationalization in an effort to justify your decision to purchase. It's kind of like buying a new pair of shoes. You know that you don't really need them, but they sure would go nice with the suit you just bought. One thing leads to another, and before you know it, you need a new brief-case, belt, or tie. Remember to temper your buying decision with caution, take your time, and most of all, be patient. You eventually will find just the right rental house that meets your needs—and probably sooner than you think.

Posterity—you will never know how much it has cost my generation to preserve your freedom. I hope you will make good use of it.

—John Quincy Adams

4

Financial Analysis of Rental Properties

Let me begin this chapter by stating emphatically that I thoroughly enjoy the subject of finance, particularly as it applies to real estate. Finance and real estate are the two greatest passions of my professional life. For as long as I can remember, I have always been fascinated with money. This fascination eventually helped to shape my course in life as I later majored in finance in both my undergraduate and graduate studies. After graduating, I had the opportunity to work as a financial analyst at one of the largest banks in Texas. As part of the mergers and acquisitions group, my work there centered on analyzing potential acquisition targets for the bank. One way companies grow is by acquiring smaller companies that do the same thing they do. This is especially true of banks. Big banks merge with other big banks, and they buy, or acquire, other banks that are usually, but not always, smaller than they are. I believe our bank was at the time about $11 billion strong in total assets. It was my job to analyze banks that typically ranged in size from about $25 million up to as much as about $2 billion in assets. I used a fairly complex and sophisticated model to assess the value of these banks. This experience provided me with a comprehensive understanding of cash-flow analysis that I later applied to real estate. I might point out that to the best of my knowledge, you won't find a chapter like this one in any other real estate book by any other author. What you will find, however, and what I have the good fortune of writing, is an entire book devoted to the subject of finance as it applies to all types of real estate investing, including single-family rental houses, multifamily apartment complexes, rehab properties, condominium projects, and commercial buildings. The book, due out in late 2004, is entitled *The Complete Guide to Real Estate Finance for Investment Properties: How to Analyze Any Single-Family, Multifamily, or Commercial Property*.

The smart investor knows that perhaps more important than any other part of the investment process is having a thorough understanding of the concept of real estate values. I like to compare the process of purchasing rental houses to that of shopping for a new car. If you're anything at all like most people, before you buy a new car, you're likely to look at all the newspaper ads related to the type of car you want. Then you'll probably call several of the local dealers to gather some general information and determine which models they have in stock. After that, you'll begin comparison shopping by going around to several dealerships to see which one is offering the best deal. Somewhere along the way you will have narrowed your selection of cars down to one or two models. Finally, you'll begin the arduous task of negotiating price and terms with the salesperson. Since you've shopped around quite a bit already, you are already familiar with the car's price and what represents a good value. A good value in this case means that the price is equal to or less than fair market value relative to all other cars that are similar in design and features. If you can't reach an agreement with the salesperson, then it's on to the next dealer to try again until finally you've found just the right car at just the right price.

Since purchasing a rental house for investment purposes costs anywhere from 5 to 10 times more than a new car, don't you think that it would be in your best interests to spend at least as much time shopping for a house as you do for a car? Yes, of course it would. The more houses you look at in a particular market, the greater you will understand their relative values. The fact that a 1200-square-foot house with three bedrooms, two baths, and a two-car garage is priced at $125,000 in a particular neighborhood means absolutely nothing by itself. It is only when you compare the price of that house with the price of all other similar houses in the same area that its price becomes meaningful.

To analyze rental property properly for investment purposes requires that each and every property that goes into your real estate portfolio meets two vitally important criteria. First, the house should be purchased only at or below fair market value. Fair market value is determined by examining comparable properties that have sold at some point in the past and applying those values to the house you are considering. Although this is what appraisers are paid to do, you should have a keen sense of value based on your research of the area. The appraisal process is not an exact science and is fairly subjective in nature. This means that appraisers can select certain comparable sales to help them derive a value that is close to the contract price. Although this is an unintended consequence of the appraisal process, it nevertheless happens all the time. The second criterion is equally important as the first. Your investment must cash flow properly, which means that you must be able to charge high enough rents to pay all the expenses, service the debt, and still have some left over. After all, what good does it do you if you are able to buy a house for, let's say, $40,000 below fair market value if you can't charge enough rent to cover all the related expenses? The answer is absolutely none, unless you are buying the house for a quick flip or resell. Every house you buy for rental income purposes should cash flow positively. Cash is the vehicle that provides businesses with life-sustaining nutrients. I've seen many beginning investors ultimately fail because they thought they could buy a house without properly analyzing its market value and its ability to generate income. Promise me that as a smart investor, you'll do your homework, exercise patience, and not make the same mistake.

Traditional Valuation Methods

Three methods have been used traditionally in determining the value of real estate. First is the replacement-cost method, second is the income-capitalization method, and third is the sales-comparison method (see the following box). Each valuation, or appraisal, method has its place and serves a unique function in determining value. For example, commercial income-producing properties such as retail centers, office buildings, and apartment complexes rely primarily on the income-capitalization method, whereas single-family houses typically rely on the sales-comparison method.

The Three Traditional Valuation Methods

1. Replacement-cost method
2. Income-capitalization method
3. Sales-comparison method

The replacement-cost method is used most commonly for estimating the replacement value of physical assets for insurance purposes. For example, if a house were destroyed in a hurricane, an insurance company would want to know what the actual cost to replace it was. The income-capitalization method and the sales-comparison method are of little or no consequence in estimating replacement costs. The insurance policy you have on your home most likely includes a replacement-cost clause with built-in premium adjustments that increase automatically each year due to rises in labor and material costs.

The income-capitalization method is used primarily to value properties that produce income and are considered to be used for investment purposes. The income-capitalization method is appropriately used to value such buildings as retail strip centers, office buildings, industrial buildings, and multifamily apartment buildings. The value from income-producing real estate is derived directly from the net cash flow or income generated by the asset. Investors compare the rates of return produced from various types of assets against their perceived risks and deploy their capital accordingly. Assuming that risk is held constant, an investor's return on her capital is the same regardless of whether it is derived from real estate, stocks, or bonds.

To understand the income-capitalization method more fully, let's break it down to its most fundamental level by examining a simple financial instrument such as a certificate of deposit (CD). For example, assuming a market interest rate of 6.0 percent, how much would you be willing to pay for an annuity yielding $6000 per year? The answer is found easily by taking a simple ratio of the two values as follows:

$$\text{Present value} = \frac{\text{income}}{\text{rate}} = \frac{\$6000}{0.06} = \$100,000$$

In other words, if you purchased a CD for $100,000 that yielded 6.0 percent annually, you could expect to earn an income stream of $6000 per year. It doesn't matter if the income continues indefinitely or perpetually. The present value remains the same and will continue to produce an income stream of $6000 as long as you continue to hold the $100,000 CD. If at some point in your real estate career you decide to invest in income-producing properties such as apartments, strip centers, or office buildings, I encourage you to thoroughly acquaint yourself with the income-capitalization approach and to become proficient in its application. In *The Complete Guide to Buying and Selling Apartment Buildings*, I explain these principles in depth and provide many examples of this particular valuation method.

The third traditional valuation method is the sales-comparison method and is the approach deemed most appropriate to use for the proper determination of value for single-family houses, including rental houses. This method is based on the premise of substitution and maintains that a buyer would not pay any more for real property than the cost of purchasing an equally desirable substitute in that property's respective market. The sales-comparison method examines two or more like properties and adjusts their value based on similarities and differences between them. The best way to understand this more fully is to look at an actual example. Exhibit 4-1 is an actual appraisal report for a single-family house I purchased that later was converted from residential to commercial. Although the property's use was changed to commercial, the original appraisal was done as a single-family dwelling because that was deemed to reflect the most accurate measure of its value. Take a moment now to study Exhibit 4-1.

Note that the appraisal report is organized into several sections beginning with the appraiser's opinion of the estimated market value of the property. Next is a description of the property on the second page, followed by a description of its location, the property site, and the type of house along with improvements. On the third page of the report at the top is a smaller section devoted to determining the replacement cost of the house.

Financial Analysis of Rental Properties

Exhibit 4-1 Uniform residential appraisal report

Complete Appraisal Analysis
UNIFORM RESIDENTIAL APPRAISAL REPORT
File No. 0312778

Property Description

Property Address 410 S State Street	City Davison	State MI Zip Code 48423
Legal Description See Attached...		County Genesee
Assessor's Parcel No. 52-09-576-012	Tax Year —— R.E. Taxes $ ——	Special Assessments $ ——
Borrower Stephen Berges	Current Owner	Occupant: ☐ Owner ☐ Tenant ☒ Vacant
Property rights appraised ☒ Fee Simple ☐ Leasehold	Project Type ☐ PUD ☐ Condominium (HUD/VA only)	HOA$ —— /Mo.
Neighborhood or Project Name City of Davison	Map Reference GeoCode System	Census Tract 0117.11
Sale Price $ 188,000 Date of Sale pending	Description and $ amount of loan charges/concessions to be paid by seller N/A	
Lender/Client	Address	
Appraiser	Address	

Location	☒ Urban	☐ Suburban	☐ Rural	Predominant occupancy	Single family housing	Present land use %	Land use change
Built up	☐ Over 75%	☒ 25-75%	☐ Under 25%		PRICE $(000) AGE (yrs)	One family 60%	☒ Not likely ☐ Likely
Growth rate	☐ Rapid	☒ Stable	☐ Slow	☒ Owner	70 Low new	2-4 family	☐ In process
Property values	☐ Increasing	☒ Stable	☐ Declining	☐ Tenant	200 High 100	Multi-family 20%	To: ___
Demand/supply	☐ Shortage	☒ In balance	☐ Over supply	☒ Vacant (0-5%)	Predominant	Commercial 20%	
Marketing time	☐ Under 3 mos.	☒ 3-6 mos.	☐ Over 6 mos.	☐ Vacant (over 5%)	130	Vacant ( )	

Note: Race and the racial composition of the neighborhood are not appraisal factors.

Neighborhood boundaries and characteristics: The neighborhood consists of the City of Davison.

Factors that affect the marketability of the properties in the neighborhood (proximity to employment and amenities, employment stability, appeal to market, etc.): This is a neighborhood of single family dwellings, multi-family dwellings, and commercial properties located in the City of Davison. Schools and all typical amenities are provided in Davison. The employment stability appears to be average.

Market conditions in the subject neighborhood (including support for the above conclusions related to the trend of property values, demand/supply, and marketing time - - such as data on competitive properties for sale in the neighborhood, description of the prevalence of sales and financing concessions, etc.): Sales prices indicate that values are stable to slightly increasing. Typical marketing time is 3-6 months and few financing concessions are required. Financing is readily available from a variety of sources.

Project Information for PUDs (if applicable) - - Is the developer/builder in control of the Home Owners' Association (HOA)? ☐ YES ☐ NO
Approximate total number of units in the subject project ___   Approximate total number of units for sale in the subject project ___
Describe common elements and recreational facilities:

		Topography	nearly level
Dimensions 66' x 297'			
Site area .45 Acre +/-	Corner Lot ☐ Yes ☒ No	Size	typical
Specific zoning classification and description B-1 Residential Multiple Family District		Shape	irregular
Zoning compliance ☒ Legal ☐ Legal nonconforming (Grandfathered use) ☐ Illegal ☐ No zoning		Drainage	appears adequate
Highest & best use as improved: ☒ Present use ☐ Other use (explain)		View	neighborhood

Utilities	Public	Other	Off-site Improvements	Type	Public	Private		
Electricity	☒		Street	paved	☒		Landscaping	average
Gas	☒		Curb/gutter	yes	☒		Driveway Surface	paved
Water	☒		Sidewalk	yes	☒		Apparent easements	public utilities
Sanitary sewer	☒		Street lights	yes	☒		FEMA Special Flood Hazard Area ☐ Yes ☒ No	
Storm sewer	☒		Alley	none			FEMA Zone Zone C Map Date 9/28/78	
							FEMA Map No. 260074 0005 B	

Comments (apparent adverse easements, encroachments, special assessments, slide areas, illegal or legal nonconforming zoning, use, etc.): No easements, encroachments, or other adverse conditions were apparent other that those for public utilities.

GENERAL DESCRIPTION		EXTERIOR DESCRIPTION		FOUNDATION		BASEMENT		INSULATION	
No. of Units	1	Foundation	conc block	Slab		Area Sq.Ft. 728		Roof	☐
No. of Stories	2	Exterior Walls	brick/wood	Crawl Space	43%	% Finished 0%		Ceiling	☐
Type (Det./Att.)	detached	Roof Surface	asph shingles	Basement	57%	Ceiling		Walls	☐
Design (Style)	2 story	Gutters & Dwnspts.	yes	Sump Pump no		Walls		Floor	☐
Existing/Proposed	existing	Window Type	wood	Dampness	not apparent	Floor		None	☐
Age (Yrs.)	97	Storm/Screens	wood/ yes	Settlement	not apparent	Outside Entry no		Unknown	☐
Effective Age (Yrs.)	35	Manufactured House no		Infestation	not apparent				

ROOMS	Foyer	Living	Dining	Kitchen	Den	Family Rm.	Rec. Rm.	Bedrooms	# Baths	Laundry	Other	Area Sq.Ft.
Basement												728
Level 1	1	1	1	1	1			1	.75		2	1,279
Level 2		1		1				3	2			1,115

Finished area above grade contains:	10 Rooms;	4 Bedroom(s);	2.75 Bath(s);	2,394 Square Feet of Gross Living Area
INTERIOR Materials/Condition	HEATING	KITCHEN EQUIP.	ATTIC	AMENITIES CAR STORAGE:
Floors carpet/avg	Type FA	Refrigerator ☐	None ☐	Fireplace(s) #0 ☐ None ☐

The remainder of the report is used to determine the property value by applying the sales-comparison method, as discussed previously. Notice how this section is organized. The property is listed in the first column, and this is followed by three comparable sales in the next three columns. There are

Exhibit 4-1 Uniform residential appraisal report (*Continued*)

Complete Appraisal Analysis

UNIFORM RESIDENTIAL APPRAISAL REPORT

File No. 0312778

Valuation Section

COST APPROACH				
ESTIMATED SITE VALUE........................... = $		30,000	Comments on Cost Approach (such as, source of cost estimate, site value, square foot calculation and for HUD, VA and FmHA, the estimated remaining economic life of the property):	
ESTIMATED REPRODUCTION COST-NEW OF IMPROVEMENTS:				
Dwelling 2,394 Sq. Ft. @ $ 85.88 = $		205,597	The cost approach is based on the Marshall Valuation	
Basement 728 Sq. Ft. @ $ 12.76 =		9,289	Service and is adapted to local conditions. The contributory	
Patio/Screened Porch =		3,500	value of the paved drive and fence is included in the site	
Garage/Carport 304 Sq. Ft. @ $ 7.90 =		2,402	improvements value of the cost approach. The ceramic	
Total Estimated Cost New .... = $		220,788	floors are included in the per square foot value on the cost	
Less 70 Physical / Functional / External Est. Remaining Econ. Life: 35			approach.	
Depreciation $60,518 = $		60,518		
Depreciated Value of Improvements .... = $		160,270		
"As-is" Value of Site Improvements.......... = $		2,500		
INDICATED VALUE BY COST APPROACH .... = $		192,800		

SALES COMPARISON ANALYSIS

ITEM	SUBJECT	COMPARABLE NO. 1		COMPARABLE NO. 2		COMPARABLE NO. 3	
	410 S State Street	706 W Nepessing St		106 Law Street		1025 Oda Street	
Address	Davison	Lapeer, MI 48446		Lapeer, MI 48446		Davison	
Proximity to Subject		10.3 MI E		10.7 MI E		1.0 MI NW	
Sales Price	$ 188,000	$	199,000	$	200,000	$	202,000
Price/Gross Liv. Area	$ 78.53 ☑	$ 70.77 ☑		$ 66.18 ☑		$ 82.21 ☑	
Data and/or Verification Sources	Interior/Exterior Inspection	MLS/Realtor Exterior Inspection		MLS/ Interior/Exterior Inspection		MLS/ Exterior Inspection	
VALUE ADJUSTMENTS	DESCRIPTION	DESCRIPTION	-( )$ Adjustment	DESCRIPTION	-( )$ Adjustment	DESCRIPTION	-( )$ Adjustment
Sales or Financing Concessions	N/A	Cash	0	Conv	0	Cash	0
Date of Sale/Time	pending	04/06/2002	0	08/06/2001	0	5/10/02	0
Location	City	City	0	City	0	City	0
Leasehold/Fee Simple	Fee Simple	Fee Simple	0	Fee Simple	0	Fee Simple	0
Site	.45 Acre +/-	.12 Acre	5,000	.22 Acre +/-	2,500	Similar Lot	0
View	Neighborhood	Neighborhood	0	Neighborhood	0	Neighborhood	0
Design and Appeal	2 Story/Avg	2 Story/Avg	0	2 Story/Avg	0	2 Story/Avg	0
Quality of Construction	Average	Average	0	Average	0	Average	0
Age	1906/Updated	1917/Updated	0	1850/Updated	0	1961	-4,000
Condition	Average	Average	0	Average	0	Average	0
Above Grade Room Count	Total 15 / Bdrms 10 / Baths 4 2.75	Total 9 / Bdrms 4 / Baths 2.00	1,500	Total 7 / Bdrms 4 / Baths 2.50	500	Total 7 / Bdrms 4 / Baths 2.50	500
Gross Living Area	2,394 Sq.Ft.	2,812 Sq.Ft.	-6,270	3,022 Sq.Ft.	-9,420	2,457 Sq.Ft.	-945
Basement & Finished Rooms Below Grade	Partial Bsmt 0% Finished	Partial Bsmnt 0% Finished	0	Partial Bsmnt 0% Finished	0	Full Bsmnt 0% Finished	-2,500
Functional Utility	Average	Average	0	Average	0	Average	0
Heating/Cooling	NGFA/None	NGHW/None	0	HWBB/None	0	HWBB/None	0
Energy Efficient Items	None	None	0	None	0	None	0
Garage/Carport	Carport	2 Detached	-6,000	2 Detached	-6,000	2 Attached	-6,000
Porch, Patio, Deck, Fireplace(s), etc.	Screened Porch Patio	Enclosed Porch Fireplace	-1,000	Breezeway Fireplace	-2,000	Enclosed Porch Deck	0 -500
Fence, Pool, etc.	Fence	None	500	Fence	0	None	500
Amenities	Cer Flrs/Pvd Dr	None	2,500	Hardwood Floors	0	Small Pole Shed	-1,000
Net Adj. (total)		☐ + ☒ - $ 3,770		☐ + ☒ - $ 14,420		☐ + ☒ - $ 13,945	
Adjusted Sales Price of Comparable		Gross: 11.4% Net: -1.9% $ 195,000		Gross: 10.2% Net: -7.2% $ 185,500		Gross: 7.9% Net: -6.9% $ 188,000	

Comments on Sales Comparison (including the subject property's compatibility to the neighborhood, etc.): All images in this report are digital photos. These images are true representations and have not been changed, altered, or digitally enhanced.All comparable sales are closes to the best of the appraiser's knowledge. Verification is with buyer, seller, realtor, agent or MLS. Comparable sales numbers 1, 2, 4 & 5 are located more than 1 mile from the subject property. The sales chosen are the most similar available.The site adjustments are based on the size, location, and topography of each parcel of land compared to the subject. Comparable sales numbers 1, 2 ,3, 4, & 5 occurred over six months prior to the appraisal date. The sales chosen are the most similar available. See Attached...

ITEM	SUBJECT	COMPARABLE NO. 1	COMPARABLE NO. 2	COMPARABLE NO. 3
Date, Price and Data Source for prior sales within year of appraisal	see below*	see below*	see below*	see below*

Analysis of any current agreement of sale, option, or listing of the subject property and analysis of any prior sales of subject and comparables within one year of the date of appraisal: *There is a purchase agreement on the subject for $188,000 ; the only sales of the comparables that were discovered in the last 3 years are the ones used in this report. The subject property is currently listed for $189,000.

INDICATED VALUE BY SALES COMPARISON APPROACH .... $	188,000
INDICATED VALUE BY INCOME APPROACH (If Applicable) Estimated Market Rent $ /Mo. x Gross Rent Multiplier = $	N/A

This appraisal is made ☒ "as is" ☐ subject to the repairs, alterations, inspections or conditions listed below ☐ subject to completion per plans and specifications.

an additional two comparable sales on page four of the report, for a total of five comparable sales, or *comps* as they are also referred to.

Since each house differs in age, size, equipment, and features, the values of all the comparable sales are adjusted by adding and subtracting val-

Financial Analysis of Rental Properties

Exhibit 4-1   Uniform residential appraisal report (*Continued*)

Complete Appraisal Analysis

UNIFORM RESIDENTIAL APPRAISAL REPORT

Supplemental Valuation Section

File No. 0312778

ITEM	SUBJECT	COMPARABLE NO. 4		COMPARABLE NO. 5		COMPARABLE NO. 6	
Address	410 S State Street Davison	3179 Atlas Road Davison		11152 E Carpenter Davison			
Proximity to Subject		2.7 MI SSW		3.7 MI NNE			
Sales Price	$ 188,000	$ 184,000		$ 225,800		$	
Price/Gross Liv. Area	$ 78.53 ⌀	$ 94.36 ⌀		$ 77.86 ⌀		$ ⌀	
Data and/or Verification Sources	Interior/Exterior Inspection	MLS/Exterior Inspection		MLS/Exterior Inspection			
VALUE ADJUSTMENTS	DESCRIPTION	DESCRIPTION	+ (-) $ Adjustment	DESCRIPTION	+ (-) $ Adjustment	DESCRIPTION	+ (-) $ Adjustment
Sales or Financing Concessions	N/A	Conv	0	Conv	0		
Date of Sale/Time	pending	7/25/02	0	8/14/02	0		
Location	City	Suburban	0	Suburban	0		
Leasehold/Fee Simple	Fee Simple	Fee Simple	0	Fee Simple	0		
Site	.45 Acre +/-	1 Acre	10,000	5 Acres	-7,000		
View	Neighborhood	Neighborhood	0	Neighborhood	0		
Design and Appeal	2 Story/Avg	1 Story/avg	0	2 Story/avg	0		
Quality of Construction	Average	Average	0	Average	0		
Age	1906/Updated	1963	-4,000	1875/Updated	0		
Condition	Average	Average	0	Average	0		
Above Grade	Total 10 : Bdrms 4 : Baths 2.75	Total 6 : Bdrms 3 : Baths 2.50	500	Total 8 : Bdrms 4 : Baths 2.00	1,500	Total : Bdrms : Baths	
Room Count							
Gross Living Area	2,394 Sq.Ft.	1,950 Sq.Ft.	6,660	2,900 Sq.Ft.	-7,590	Sq.Ft.	
Basement & Finished Rooms Below Grade	Partial Bsmt 0% Finished	50% Bsmnt 100% Finished	0 -2,500	Full Basement Partial Finish	-2,500 -2,500		
Functional Utility	Average	Average	0	Average	0		
Heating/Cooling	NGFA/None	GFA/Cntrl	-1,500	GFA/Cntrl	-1,500		
Energy Efficient Items	None	None	0	None	0		
Garage/Carport	Carport	2 Attached	-6,000	None	2,000		
Porch, Patio, Deck, Fireplace(s), etc.	Screened Porch Patio	Patio Fireplace	1,500 -1,000	Deck/Cvd Porch None	0 500		
Fence, Pool, etc.	Fence	None	500	Superior Fence	-4,500		
Amenities	Cer Flrs/Pvd Dr	Shed	0	Barn/Stalls	-15,000		
Net Adj. (total)		☒ + ☐ - : $	4,160	☐ + ☒ - : $	36,590	☒ + ☐ - : $	0
Adjusted Sales Price of Comparable		Gross: 18.6% Net: 2.3% $	188,160	Gross: 19.7% Net: -16.2% $	189,210	Gross: 0.0% Net: 0.0% $	0

Comments on Sales Comparison (including the subject property's compatibility to the neighborhood, etc.):

ITEM	SUBJECT	COMPARABLE NO. 4	COMPARABLE NO. 5	COMPARABLE NO. 6
Date, Price and Data Source for prior sales within year of appraisal	see below*	see below*	see below*	

Analysis of any current agreement of sale, option, or listing of the subject property and analysis of any prior sales of subject and comparables within one year of the date of appraisal:
The subject property is currently listed for $189,000. There is currently a purchase agreement on the subject property for $188,000; the only sales of the comparables that were discovered in the last year are the ones used in this report.

ues in order to reconcile their respective differences. For example, on page three of the report you'll notice that the property does not have a garage, although it does have a carport. Since comparable sales 1, 2, and 3 all have garages, an amount of $6000 is subtracted from their values. Your initial reaction may be to think the values should be added rather than subtracted. The values of the garages, however, are already reflected in the original sales prices of the houses. Since the subject property does not have a garage, you must adjust downward to account for the difference in value.

As you do your own market research, you will become very familiar with property values and how they relate to the rental house you are considering for purchase. By comparing and contrasting like properties, you will gain the necessary experience needed to recognize a good deal when you see one. Remember that the process is very similar to that of buying a new car. You take the necessary time to shop around and learn who is offering what. Your decision on which rental house represents a value that is equal to or less than fair market value is predicated on a broad and encompassing base of knowledge and information gathered over time. Once you have all the facts before you, and only then, are you prepared to make an informed decision.

How Much Rent to Charge Your Tenants

Determining how much rent to charge for your house is not nearly as difficult as you may think. There are several ways to determine what the proper rent level in your market is. The best way is to find out what other property owners are charging for a rental house similar to yours. You should start by looking in the local classified section of your newspaper. See what other houses are being rented for, and compare the amenities of those houses and neighborhoods with the one you are considering. If you are buying a three-bedroom, two-bath house with a two-car garage, call the listings in the newspaper to learn more about those houses. You won't need to call for the price because it is almost always listed in the ad, but you will want to call and learn more specifically what that house has to offer. For example, does it have air conditioning? How large is the house in terms of square feet? How big is the yard? Is there a park or a swimming pool in the community to which residents have access? After calling on no fewer than 8 to 10 houses, you will then want to get in your car and drive around to look at them. You don't necessarily need to go into the houses, but just drive around the neighborhood to see what the area is like. How does it compare with the area your

Financial Analysis of Rental Properties

house is in? Take a minute to reflect on this process. What I am suggesting you do is no more than what a tenant looking to rent a house will do. If you were looking for a house to rent, you would follow the procedure I just outlined. You would look in the classified section of the newspaper, call around, shop and compare, and make your decision. This process will help to familiarize you with the market.

On one particular apartment building I purchased, I personally called 14 different apartment complexes within a three-mile radius to determine what exactly each one was offering and how much each charged. I drove by every one of them and walked the grounds of many of the buildings. I wanted to know what exactly my competitors were doing and what I would need to do to compete with them. This market analysis was done during what is referred to as the *due-diligence period*. The process of due diligence provides an investor with a 30- or 45-day free-look period, as it is often called. It gives you time to complete the physical inspection of the property, do a market analysis, and begin preparing your financing. If at any time during the free-look period you change your mind, you can simply walk away from the deal with earnest money in tact. My analysis on this project determined that the rents being charged at the building I had under contract were below market, therefore giving me some upside in the deal and the opportunity to create value in it. In *The Complete Guide to Buying and Selling Apartments*, I describe this process in much greater detail using a concept I call the *value play*.

After gathering such information as rental rates, amenities, and square footage, you should be able to calculate a fairly accurate estimate for the rent you can charge. If, for example, you gathered information on 10 different houses, you could easily add up the rents on all the houses, divided by 10, and find the average. You could then do the same with the square footage. Take the total square footage of all 10 houses and divide by 10 to calculate the average size of the houses. Then divide the average square footage by the average rent to calculate the rent per square foot. Finally, multiply the square footage of your house by the average rent per square foot to calculate the rent you can charge. This probably sounds more difficult than it actually is, but trust me, the process is really very simple. Take a minute to study Exhibit 4-2 to more fully understand these calculations.

How to Buy Rental Properties the Smart Way

By examining Exhibit 4-2, you can see that the average square footage is divided into the average price per house to calculate the average rent per square foot, which in this example is 70 cents. This number is then multiplied by the number of square feet the house that you are purchasing has to derive the estimated amount of rent you should charge. This simple table assumes that all other things are equal and does not take into account adjustments for such things as air conditioning, property condition, and community amenities such as a swimming pool. If, for example, you know that all the comparable houses have air conditioning and the one that you will rent out does not, then you will need to adjust the average rent per square foot downward. I should mention also that you don't necessarily have to have 10 comparable houses to determine the average rent per square foot. You may only be able to find five or six comparable properties. The more data you have, however, and the more houses you look at, the better you will be able to gauge the true market price of rents in your area.

Exhibit 4-2   Calculating your rent based on comparable averages

Comparable House	Rent Charged	Size in Sq Ft	Rent per Sq Ft
House 1	750.00	1,150.00	0.65
House 2	895.00	1,220.00	0.73
House 3	950.00	1,300.00	0.73
House 4	1,000.00	1,440.00	0.69
House 5	675.00	995.00	0.68
House 6	925.00	1,215.00	0.76
House 7	995.00	1,365.00	0.73
House 8	1,000.00	1,400.00	0.71
House 9	625.00	975.00	0.64
House 10	700.00	1,000.00	0.70
Average	851.50	1,206.00	0.70
Your House	Sq Ft Actual Size	Average Rent Per Sq Ft	Rent You Should Charge
123 Main St.	1,200.00	0.70	840.00

Another good way to determine the average rent per square foot is by contacting a local property management company. These companies are in the business of renting and managing real estate, including rental houses and small multifamily properties such as duplexes or triplexes. Property management firms have their finger on the pulse of the rental market every single day and likely can tell you what the average rent per square foot is provided that they are familiar with your area. There are many such companies, and it doesn't hurt to talk with representatives from several of them. In fact, they *want* you to talk to them because they are interested in procuring your business. Furthermore, on larger projects that you may be considering acquiring, management companies often will provide you with reams of data to help support your decision. This service is often provided free of charge because such companies want the opportunity to earn your business. Property managers know that if they help you to make the best decision for your investment portfolio that you are likely to remember them when the time comes to hire a professional manager.

Smart investors know they must invest the time and energy needed to determine average rental rates in their respective markets. If an investor charges too much, his vacancy rate is likely to increase, and if he doesn't charge enough, he is leaving money on the table in the form of lost rents that rightfully belong to him. This vital market information can be gathered by directly contacting owners of similar properties, as well as by working with professional property management companies. Establishing the proper rate is crucial to your success in the rental house business.

How to Analyze Your Rental House Investment

Locating a rental property that is priced at or below fair market value is only the first part of your real estate investment analysis. The second part is making sure that the property cash flows properly. After having determined the most appropriate rental rate to charge, you must then examine only those expenses that affect the property's cash flow. Since you are not concerned about the impact on your tax liability at this juncture, you do not need to include noncash items such as depreciation. For investors acquiring larger commercial projects, tax implications should be taken into consideration, but for smaller single-family houses, we'll keep it simple.

How to Buy Rental Properties the Smart Way

The best way to understand how to analyze cash flows from a rental property is to look at an example. The property in this example happens to be an actual investment opportunity that I'm working on right now. The seller, who is selling the property without the aid of a real estate agent, is what is referred to as a *for sale by owner* (FSBO). His house is located directly across the street from a beautiful all-sports lake called Lake Orion. The property is not considered to be lakefront but rather lake view. Over the last couple of weeks I've looked at no fewer than 15 houses for sale that sit right on the lake, and every one of them sells for $200 per square foot and up. Houses located across the street that are not lakefront but are lake view sell for between $120 and $140 per square foot. The subject property falls into the second category with a couple of exceptions, which is the reason I'm interested in it to begin with.

Let's back up for a minute, and I'll start from the beginning. It all started just about a month ago on a warm summer day when my wife, Nancy, and I went to pick up our seven-year-old son, Philip, from a boating activity with his friends. We arrived a few minutes early, and while we waited by the edge of the water, we looked out across the glistening lake for any sign of our son. It wasn't long before we saw him and his two little friends come racing across the water on a large raft that was being pulled by a speedboat. What an exhilarating experience for those young boys. They were having so much fun and laughing so hard that it was easy for us to get caught up in their excitement too. Our family doesn't own a boat, nor have we ever owned a boat, but after watching those boys having all that fun, Nancy and I started thinking aloud, "Hmmm. It sure would be nice to have a boat."

One thing led to another, and the next thing you know, we were at the local marina looking at boats. Of course, if you have a boat, you also have to have a place to put it. The going rate for boat slips at the marina is $2000 per season—from ice on to ice off, as they say, since the lakes in this area are frozen solid several months of the year. Since neither Nancy nor I wanted to spend $2000 on a boat slip, we began exploring other alternatives, such as buying a lakefront cottage where we would have our very own boat slip. The only problem with that idea is that home prices on the lake start at $200,000, and that's for nothing more than a run-down shack in most cases. A decent cottage or house on the lake easily costs $300,000, and many are priced in the $550,000 to $800,000 range. I began thinking, "Okay, this whole boat idea is starting to get out of hand." Since my brain is in the habit of thinking creatively, I began exploring ideas on how to get either a free boat slip, a free house or condominium, or both. As a principal of Symphony Homes (*www.symphony-homes.com*), much of my real estate investment activity centers on the construction of new homes. I decided to shift my focus toward properties on which I could somehow create value by building a house or condominium, make money on the transaction, and get a boat slip out of the deal as an added bonus.

It wasn't long after I redirected my search efforts that I came across the property in this example. The house sits directly across the street from the lake on a little over three-quarters of an acre and happens to be the only parcel of land uniquely situated with buildable lot space and zoned RM, which stands for "residential, multiple." This means that it is not a single-family parcel but rather a multifamily parcel that will accommodate more than one house or condominium unit. The real beauty of this deal is that along with the land and the house comes—Guess what? Yes, you're absolutely right! Not one, but two boat slips! The seller happens to own 28 feet of lake frontage right across the street from his house that is currently home to two boat slips and a motorized hoist or lift. This small parcel of land also happens to be deeded separately from the property across the street, so if I decide to buy the house, I will own the boat slips free and clear immediately upon closing. The main house and property will be purchased under one contract for the agreed-on price, and the boat slip will be purchased on anther contract for only $1. See what happens when you let your seven-year-old son go boating with his friends!

Take a few minutes to review Exhibit 4-3 by carefully studying the property's income as it flows through the model. The worksheet you see is a proprietary model I developed that I use to analyze potential rental house investment opportunities quickly and easily. I call it the *value play rental house analyzer.* Once I have gathered the necessary data, I can input the information into the model and, in less than just a few minutes, know with a high degree of accuracy whether or not a deal makes sense based on my investment criteria. All I have to do is key in the variables, and the model makes all the calculations automatically. Although at first glance the model may appear complex, it is actually quite easy to use.

We'll start by analyzing this property as if it were going to be used as a rental house only. The ultimate goal in this particular example is to rent

Exhibit 4-3   Property analysis worksheet: the value play rental house analyzer

Property Value Analysis

Comp #1		Comp #2		Comp #3	
Address:	1492 Columbus Way	Address:	1776 Independence Dr.	Address:	1830 Restoration Ln.
Sales Price	365,500.00	Sales Price	289,900.00	Sales Price	294,000.00
Adjustments to Price	1,600.00	Adjustments to Price	(2,400.00)	Adjustments to Price	3,200.00
Adjusted Price	367,100.00	Adjusted Price	287,500.00	Adjusted Price	297,200.00
Square Feet	2,645.00	Square Footage	2,096.00	Square Feet	2,200.00
Price Per Square Foot	138.79	Price Per Square Foot	137.17	Price Per Square Foot	135.09

Comp Averages		Subject Property 421 Moroni Blvd.		Property Values		Adjustment to Comps		2.50
						2.50	0.00	(2.50)
Sales Price	316,466.67	Purchase Price	370,000	Fair Market Value	390,956	383,956	376,956
Adjustments to Price	800.00	Square Feet	2,800.00	Actual Price	370,000	370,000	370,000
Adjusted Price	317,266.67	Price/Sq Ft	132.14	Difference	20,956	13,956	6,956
Square Feet	2,313.67	Turn Comps Off/On	ON				
Price Per Square Foot	137.13	Est Price/Sq Ft If Turned OFF	135.00				

Financing and Income Analysis

Cost and Revenue Assumptions		Financing Assumptions			Key Rent Ratios	
Purchase Price	370,000	Total Purchase	100.00%	373,500	Total Square Feet	2,800.00
Improvements	0	Owner's Equity	10.00%	37,350	Total Price/Sq Ft	133.39
Closing Costs	3,500	Balance to Finc	90.00%	336,150	Fair Market Value/Sq Ft	137.13
Total	373,500				Rental Income/Sq Ft	0.63
			Annual	Monthly	Total Income/Sq Ft	0.71
Estimated Monthly Rent Income	1,750	Interest Rate	6.000%	0.500%	Capitalization Rate	4.10%
Other Income	250	Amort Period	30	360	Gross Rent Multiplier	17.79
Total Income	2,000	Payment	24,185	2,015	Operating Efficiency Ratio	2.72

Rental Increase Projections			0.00%	4.00%	3.50%	3.50%	3.50%
Average Monthly Rent			1,750	1,820	1,884	1,950	2,018
Operating Expense Projections			0.00%	2.00%	2.00%	1.50%	1.50%

		Actual		Projected			
		Monthly	Year 1	Year 2	Year 3	Year 4	Year 5
Operating Revenues							
Gross Scheduled Rental Income		1,750	21,000	21,840	22,604	23,396	24,214
Vacancy Rate	5.0%	88	1,050	1,092	1,130	1,170	1,211
Net Rental Income		1,663	19,950	20,748	21,474	22,226	23,004
Other Income		250	3,000	3,120	3,229	3,342	3,459
Gross Income	100.0%	1,913	22,950	23,868	24,703	25,568	26,463
Operating Expenses							
Repairs and Maintenance	5.2%	100	1,200	1,224	1,248	1,267	1,286
Property Management Fees	5.5%	105	1,260	1,285	1,311	1,331	1,351
Taxes	18.3%	350	4,200	4,284	4,370	4,435	4,502
Insurance	2.9%	55	660	673	687	697	707
Salaries and Wages	0.0%	0	0	0	0	0	0
Utilities	0.0%	0	0	0	0	0	0
Professional Fees	1.3%	25	300	306	312	317	322
Advertising	0.0%	0	0	0	0	0	0
Other	0.0%	0	0	0	0	0	0
Other	0.0%	0	0	0	0	0	0
Other	0.0%	0	0	0	0	0	0
Total Operating Expenses	33.2%	635	7,620	7,772	7,928	8,047	8,167
Net Operating Income	66.8%	1,278	15,330	16,096	16,776	17,521	18,295
Cash Flow From Operations							
Total Cash Available for Loan Servicing		1,278	15,330	16,096	16,776	17,521	18,295
Debt Service		2,015	24,185	24,185	24,185	24,185	24,185
Remaining CF From Ops		(738)	(8,855)	(8,089)	(7,409)	(6,663)	(5,889)
Plus Principal Reduction		335	4,128	4,383	4,653	4,940	5,245
Total Return		(403)	(4,727)	(3,707)	(2,756)	(1,724)	(645)
CF/Debt Servicing Ratio		63.39%	63.39%	66.55%	69.36%	72.45%	75.65%
Net Operating Income ROI			41.04%	43.09%	44.91%	46.91%	48.98%
Cash ROI			-23.71%	-21.66%	-19.84%	-17.84%	-15.77%
Total ROI			-12.66%	-9.92%	-7.38%	-4.61%	-1.73%

the house out while I am getting the necessary approvals from the local planning commission. Once I receive the approvals, I can continue to rent the house out while the first of potentially four condominium units is being constructed. The rent from the house in this situation is a bonus because most of the time new construction does not include income-producing property such as this. The income from the rents will help off-set the carrying costs of the construction project.

Test 1: Comparable Sales Analysis

The first section of the model allows you to enter information for comparable home sales. This information is needed to help make accurate projections of the estimated resale value of your investment property. Any sales agent can provide you with comparable sales data for your area. In fact, if you ask them, real estate agents can send the comps online to your e-mail address, which you can then access via the Internet. In fact, just a few minutes ago I received an e-mail with links to listings for vacant land in an area where one of my clients wants to build a new home. Next in this section is a provision that allows you to make adjustments to the sales price of the comps. This provision permits you to compare "apples to apples" just like an appraiser would do. For example, if the home you are buying has a two-car garage and the comparable home has a three-car garage, you will need to revise the price downward in the "Adjustments to Price" cell. This is exactly how real estate agents and appraisers derive the market value of a house. They start with an average price per square foot of several similar houses that have sold recently and make adjustments to compensate for differences in value.

The "Comp Averages" section simply takes an average of the three comparable sales prices to come up with an average sales price. This number is then divided by the average price per square foot. The result is a weighted average price per square foot. The "Comp Averages" section also has a provision that allows you to turn the comps section off or on. As you become familiar with a specific market or neighborhood, you are likely to already know what the average sales price per square foot is, so you really don't need to key in comparable sales data. Instead, you can turn the comps section off and plug in your own estimate. In this example, I used three comparable sales of properties similar in characteristics and close in size. My goal was to use houses that were in desirable locations and also having lake views. All three of the comparable sales were on much smaller lots; however, I did not adjust for that because if I decide to purchase the property, I want to be able to separate the house from the additional land and either rent the house out on a temporary basis or resell it immediately on a standard-sized lot. I want to determine if the subject property will comp out without the additional land included.

In the "Subject Property" section, simply enter in the purchase price of the house you want to buy. In this example, the owner is asking $370,000. The asking price is a good place to begin your analysis, but you also can experiment easily with the values merely by changing this one variable, which is exactly what I do in Exhibit 4-4. After entering the purchase price, next enter the square footage of the property, which in this example is 2800. The average sales price per square foot from the comps section is then fed into the "Subject Property" section. The purchase price per square foot is calculated automatically and then multiplied by the square footage of the subject property under the "Property Values" and "Adjustment to Comps" sections.

The "Adjustment to Comps" section is used to create an estimated fair market value using a range of property values for three different scenarios—best case, most likely, and worst case. In this example, $2.50 per square foot is used; however, the number can be changed to anything you want it to be. For the best-case estimated fair market value, the model adds $2.50 to the "Price per Square Foot" cell in the "Comp Averages" section and then multiplies the sum of the two by the square footage of the subject property. The positive value of $2.50 is visible under the "Adjustment to Comps" heading. Here's how the calculation works:

Best-Case Estimate of Fair Market Value

(Average price per square foot + adjustment to comps) × subject property square feet

= best-case estimate of fair market value

($137.127 + $2.500) × 2800 = $390,956

The most-likely estimate of fair market value in the model neither adds nor subtracts the value of $2.50 to the "Price per Square Foot" cell in the "Comp Averages" section. As you can see in Exhibit 4-3, it is set to zero. This calculation is merely the product of the average price per square foot and the square feet. Take a moment to examine the calculation.

Most-Likely Estimate of Fair Market Value

Average price per square foot × subject property square feet

= most-likely estimate of fair market value

$137.127 × 2800 = $383,956

For the worst-case estimate of fair market value, the model subtracts $2.50 from the "Price per Square Foot" cell in the "Comp Averages" section and then multiplies the difference of the two by the square footage of the subject property. Take a minute to review the calculations.

Worst-Case Estimate of Fair Market Value

(Average price per square foot – adjustment to comps) × subject property square feet

= worst-case estimate of fair market value

($137.127 – $2.500) × 2800 = $376,956

The purpose of creating three different scenarios in the model is to provide us with a range of estimated fair market values. This allows you to evaluate the very minimum fair market value that you might expect on the low end of the price range and the very highest fair market value that you might expect on the high end of the price range. In this example, using $2.50 provides us with a total range of $5.00 per square foot— from +$2.50 to –$2.50.

Now let's interpret the output. What is the model telling us? The three different values provide us with a minimum estimate for fair market value and a range of values up to a maximum estimate for fair market value. In order for the subject property to pass the first of the two tests, which is the comps test, it must meet a minimum threshold of any value greater than zero by taking the difference of the fair market value and the actual purchase price. In this example, the subject property passes the test under all three price values reflected in the model, with positive values of $20,956 for the best-case estimate, $13,956 for the most-likely estimate, and $6956 for the worst-case estimate. If everything else looks good in the rest of the model, it is acceptable to have a negative value under the worst-case estimate. The most-likely and best-case estimates, however, must have positive values. The difference in values shown in each of these three scenarios represents a discount of the actual purchase price to the market. So far, so good. Our subject property has passed the first test.

Test 2: Cash-Flow Analysis

The second test involves analyzing all income and expenses that affect the cash flow of the property. Under the "Cost and Revenue Assumptions" heading, the purchase price, cost of improvements, and closing costs are entered, and their values are summed to provide the total cost of the investment. Below the cost assumptions are the revenue assumptions. In this example, I did not call other property owners for an estimate of the appropriate rent to charge. Instead, I contacted a professional property management company that recommended charging approximately $1750 per month in rent. Under "Other Income," I included $250 per month, which represents the rent I could charge for the two boat slips that come with the property. Although the marina charges $2000 per season, I am using $1500 per season for each of the two boat slips, which averages out to $250 per month. Total income estimated for the subject property is $2000 per month.

Under "Financing Assumptions," I entered a value of 10.00 percent, which will represent my investment in this property. Below that I entered in a value of 6.000 percent for the interest rate and 30 for the amortization period in the "Annual" column. The model automatically calculates both the annual and the monthly payment. The owner's equity, interest

Financial Analysis of Rental Properties

rate, and amortization period are all variables that can be changed easily. Experimenting with these variables allows you to see how changes affect the output of the model.

The "Key Rent Ratios" section is especially important and captures data vital to the overall analysis of your investment property. All these calculations are made automatically and change only when the variables that affect them are changed. The rental income per square foot, for example, provides you with a gauge with which to measure the rental income relative to the market as a whole. This measurement is taken on a monthly basis but also could be calculated annually. In this example, the value is $0.63 per square foot, which is low when compared with smaller rental houses. This is so because the rent per square foot is usually higher for smaller houses and drops as houses get bigger. The same relationship also holds true for purchasing houses. Generally speaking, the price per square foot goes down the larger the home is because with each house built there are certain fixed costs that must be overcome, such as land, heating, ventilation, and air conditioning (HVAC) equipment, and so on.

Also under the "Key Rent Ratios" heading is a measure referred to as the "Capitalization Rate," or *cap rate* as it is also known. The cap rate is the ratio between the net operating income and the purchase price. As you can see, this ratio is really a very simple calculation used to measure the relationship between the income generated by the property and the price for which it is being sold. This ratio measures the same relationship as that of the CD we discussed at the beginning of this chapter. The *price* we are willing to pay for the CD is a function of its *yield* or, rather, the *income* the instrument generates. This is precisely consistent with the relationship between the *price* of an income-producing property, the *yield* an investor expects to receive on her investment, and the property's ability to generate *income*.

$$\frac{\text{Net operating income}}{\text{Purchase price}} = \text{capitalization rate}$$

$$\text{Cap rate} = \frac{\$15,330}{\$373,500} = 4.104\%$$

The capitalization rate, or yield on an income-producing property, will vary within a given range, generally about 7 to 12 percent depending on a variety of market conditions, including supply and demand for real estate, the current interest-rate environment, the type and condition of the property, its location, and tax implications imposed by local, state, and federal authorities. Under the "Key Rent Ratios" section in this example, notice the cap rate of 4.10 percent. This number represents the yield of the property as a whole because it is based on its total purchase price, not the equity. It is the return on investment (ROI) that measures this relationship. A cap rate of only 4.10 percent for an experienced investor immediately should raise a red flag. This rate is anemic at best. As you gain more experience in analyzing rental houses, you will begin to appreciate more fully the importance of a thorough understanding of capitalization rates. As you will see, this low cap rate corresponds directly with the property's ability to generate enough income to satisfy all its related expenses and to service its debt obligation. Without even looking at the rest of the output, I know that this property will not cash flow positively because of the low cap rate.

The gross rent multiplier (GRM) measures the relationship between the scheduled gross income and the total purchase price. The high GRM in this example should raise another red flag for an experienced investor. The lower the GRM, the better. This is true because the ratio will decrease the lower the purchase price is relative to income. It also will decrease the higher the income is relative to the purchase price.

$$\frac{\text{Purchase price}}{\text{Gross scheduled rental income}} = \text{gross rent multiplier (GRM)}$$

$$\text{GRM} = \frac{\$373,500}{\$21,000} = 17.786\%$$

Finally, in the "Key Rent Ratios" section is also a computation that measures the operating expenses of the property relative to its size. It is calculated as the ratio of total operating expenses to square feet. The result provides a measure of how efficiently the property can be operated. The lower the number, the less it costs to manage and operate the property. The calculation is made as follows:

$$\frac{\text{Total operating expenses}}{\text{Square feet}} = \text{operating efficiency ratio (OER)}$$

$$\text{OER} = \frac{\$7620}{2800} = \$2.72$$

The next section of the model allows the user to key in rental increases and changes in operating expenses to forecast the profitability of the rental house over a five-year time horizon. In this example I entered in 0 percent for the first year for both "Rental Increase Projections" and "Operating Expense Projections" because this best represents my expectations for the property. In years two through five I have allowed for modest increases in both income and expenses. Using a five-year time horizon gives you a better idea of how your investment will perform over a longer period of time, as opposed to analyzing it as it is operating today only.

The next section of the model is "Operating Revenues." The model determines the gross scheduled rental income based on the estimated monthly rental income entered under the "Cost and Revenue Assumptions" section. In this example I used a vacancy rate of 5.0 percent, which represents about 2½ weeks of the year. The value for "Other Income" is the rental income from the two boat slips, which is again derived from the "Cost and Revenue Assumptions" section.

Under the "Operating Expenses" section, expenses are estimated based on what you know to be true about the property, as well as on information that is assumed or estimated. In this example, the repairs and maintenance expense is relatively low, representing only 5.2 percent of the property's gross income. Repairs and maintenance expenses often run as high as 10 to 15 percent and sometimes even higher. Since the subject property is fairly new and in immaculate condition, I have assumed a lower rate of only $100 per month. Property management fees typically range from about 3.5 percent up to 10.0 percent depending on the size and type of rental unit. The information entered in for taxes is based on what the seller told me but has not been confirmed. Since I will not be using any employees for this property, salaries and wages are assumed to be zero. The tenants are responsible for their own utilities, so this value, too, has been set to zero. I used $25 per month for professional fees in the event I need my attorney to review any of the documents. Advertising expenses are assumed to be zero because the property management company is responsible for that. There are also three "Other" variables that can be set to anything that is needed, but in this case they are all assumed to be zero. Finally, all operating expenses are summed to provide the total operating expenses.

Net operating income is calculated simply by taking the difference of gross income and total operating expenses. This number then flows down to the "Cash Flow from Operations" section and becomes the "Total Cash Available for Loan Servicing." In the monthly column, the value of $2015 for debt service is derived from the model's calculations under the "Financing Assumptions" section. Remember the anemic cap rate of 4.10 percent that we discussed earlier? We concluded that there is a direct correlation between this ratio and the ability of the investment property to generate enough income to satisfy all its obligations, including the debt. In this example we have a negative value of $738 per month. What this means is that based on all the information we know about the subject property and given the assumptions that we have used, an investor who purchases this property under these terms and conditions will have to shell out an extra $738 per month just to break even. Sounds like a great deal, doesn't it? Of course not. The "Principal Reduction" value of $335 in the monthly column does help somewhat, but this amount goes to pay down the property's debt and therefore still represents cash that is being paid out. It is used here only to help measure the overall return and profitability of the project.

Thus, while our subject property passed the first test under the "Comparable Sales" section, it failed the second test miserably. This is why it is absolutely critical for your success as an investor in rental houses to understand how to analyze potential opportunities properly. You must understand the value of the property relative to its surrounding community, and you must then ensure that it can generate enough income to meet all its obligations, including any debt that is incurred.

Financial Analysis of Rental Properties

Before we move on, let's take a moment to examine the last few ratios. The first ratio measures the ability of available cash to service the debt. A value of 1.0 percent means that there is exactly enough cash to make the loan payment. Anything less than 1.0 percent means that there is not enough cash to make the loan payment, and anything greater than 1.0 percent means not only that is there enough to make the required loan payments but also that there will be some left over. It is the portion that is left over that we are most interested in. It is this portion that represents the cash return on your investment, or cash ROI. Lenders usually require a debt service ratio of greater than a minimum of 1.10 percent, but sometimes they will accept less. Other determining factors include the strength of the borrower and the amount of down payment. The ratio is calculated as follows:

$$\frac{\text{Total cash available for loan servicing}}{\text{Debt service}} = \frac{\text{cash flow (CF)}}{\text{debt servicing ratio (DSR)}}$$

$$\text{DSR} = \frac{\$1278}{\$2015} = 63.39\%$$

The cash ROI is the central focus of your investment objective and is the reason you have elected to invest in real estate. This ratio measures the cash portion of the return against the total dollar amount of cash you have invested into the property. In this example, the ratio is negative, meaning that you have a negative ROI, because the cash flow is not sufficient to meet all the obligations. The cash flow is itself negative. The ratio is calculated as follows:

$$\frac{\text{Remaining CF from operations}}{\text{Owner's equity}} = \text{cash ROI}$$

$$\text{Cash ROI} = \frac{(\$8855)}{\$37,350} = (23.71\%)$$

The primary purpose of analyzing the subject property in Exhibit 4-3 was to determine its value relative to other comparable sales and to determine its ability to generate enough income to satisfy all its obligations using the seller's asking price. According to our analysis, we have thus far concluded that while the investment property meets the comparable-sales test, it does not meet the cash-flow test. The next step in the analysis is to begin experimenting with the variables. For example, we want to answer the following question: At what price can we purchase the property using the existing total monthly income of $2000 so that we achieve a breakeven cash flow? Using the model, we can quickly solve for the correct purchase price simply by adjusting the price downward until the remaining cash flow from operations is exactly zero. Now take a minute to review Exhibit 4-4.

In order to achieve a breakeven point of zero in the cash-flow analysis, the purchase price must be adjusted to a surprisingly low $233,250. Remember that the seller's asking price is $370,000. This is a difference of $136,750. Do you think that the seller is prepared to accept that much less for his property? The answer is probably no. Now take a minute to review Exhibit 4-5.

In this example the question is asked, "How much rent do I have to charge to exactly cover all expenses associated with the property?" Solving for the answer is done simply by increasing the rental income just enough to break even while leaving the purchase price at the original asking price of $370,000. You can see that the rental income has to be increased by $777 per month to achieve our objective of breaking even. According to the property management company I spoke with, this is highly unlikely.

By now I think you'll agree with me that having a tool like the model used in these examples can mean the difference between success and failure in the investment rental house business. The kind of objective information dispensed by the model can be used very effectively to your advantage merely by sharing your analysis with the seller. For example, I have already had a follow-up discussion with the seller explaining to him that my initial assessment of his property has determined that the price he is asking is too high and will not support the debt. I explained to him that

Financial Analysis of Rental Properties

Exhibit 4-4   Property analysis worksheet: the value play rental house analyzer

Property Value Analysis

Comp #1		Comp #2		Comp #3	
Address:	1492 Columbus Way	Address:	1776 Independence Dr.	Address:	1830 Restoration Ln.
Sales Price	365,500.00	Sales Price	289,900.00	Sales Price	294,000.00
Adjustments to Price	1,600.00	Adjustments to Price	(2,400.00)	Adjustments to Price	3,200.00
Adjusted Price	367,100.00	Adjusted Price	287,500.00	Adjusted Price	297,200.00
Square Feet	2,645.00	Square Footage	2,096.00	Square Feet	2,200.00
Price Per Square Foot	138.79	Price Per Square Foot	137.17	Price Per Square Foot	135.09

Comp Averages		Subject Property 421 Moroni Blvd.	Property Values	Adjustment to Comps	2.50	2.50		(2.50)
				2.50	0.00			
Sales Price	316,466.67	Purchase Price	233,250	Fair Market Value	390,956	383,956		376,956
Adjustments to Price	800.00	Square Feet	2,800.00	Actual Price	233,250	233,250		233,250
Adjusted Price	317,266.67	Price/Sq Ft	83.30	Difference	157,706	150,706		143,706
Square Feet	2,313.67	Turn Comps Off/On	ON					
Price Per Square Foot	137.13	Est Price/Sq Ft If Turned OFF	135.00					

Financing and Income Analysis

Cost and Revenue Assumptions		Financing Assumptions			Key Rent Ratios	
Purchase Price	233,250	Total Purchase	100.00%	236,750	Total Square Feet	2,800.00
Improvements	0	Owner's Equity	10.00%	23,675	Total Price/Sq Ft	84.55
Closing Costs	3,500	Balance to Finc	90.00%	213,075	Fair Market Value/Sq Ft	137.13
Total	236,750				Rental Income/Sq Ft	0.63
			Annual	Monthly	Total Income/Sq Ft	0.71
Estimated Monthly Rent Income	1,750	Interest Rate	6.000%	0.500%	Capitalization Rate	6.48%
Other Income	250	Amort Period	30	360	Gross Rent Multiplier	11.27
Total Income	2,000	Payment	15,330	1,277	Operating Efficiency Ratio	2.72

Rental Increase Projections			0.00%	4.00%	3.50%	3.50%	3.50%
Average Monthly Rent			1,750	1,820	1,884	1,950	2,018
Operating Expense Projections			0.00%	2.00%	2.00%	1.50%	1.50%

	Actual Monthly	Year 1	Year 2	Projected Year 3	Year 4	Year 5
Operating Revenues						
Gross Scheduled Rental Income	1,750	21,000	21,840	22,604	23,396	24,214
Vacancy Rate	5.0%	88	1,050	1,092	1,130	1,170	1,211
Net Rental Income		1,663	19,950	20,748	21,474	22,226	23,004
Other Income		250	3,000	3,120	3,229	3,342	3,459
Gross Income	100.0%	1,913	22,950	23,868	24,703	25,568	26,463
Operating Expenses						
Repairs and Maintenance	5.2%	100	1,200	1,224	1,248	1,267	1,286
Property Management Fees	5.5%	105	1,260	1,285	1,311	1,331	1,351
Taxes	18.3%	350	4,200	4,284	4,370	4,435	4,502
Insurance	2.9%	55	660	673	687	697	707
Salaries and Wages	0.0%	0	0	0	0	0	0
Utilities	0.0%	0	0	0	0	0	0
Professional Fees	1.3%	25	300	306	312	317	322
Advertising	0.0%	0	0	0	0	0	0
Other	0.0%	0	0	0	0	0	0
Other	0.0%	0	0	0	0	0	0
Other	0.0%	0	0	0	0	0	0
Total Operating Expenses	33.2%	635	7,620	7,772	7,928	8,047	8,167
Net Operating Income	66.8%	1,278	15,330	16,096	16,776	17,521	18,295
Cash Flow From Operations						
Total Cash Available for Loan Servicing		1,278	15,330	16,096	16,776	17,521	18,295
Debt Service		1,277	15,330	15,330	15,330	15,330	15,330
Remaining CF From Ops		0	0	766	1,446	2,191	2,966
Plus Principal Reduction		212	2,617	2,778	2,949	3,131	3,324
Total Return		212	2,617	3,544	4,395	5,323	6,290
CF/Debt Servicing Ratio	100.00%	100.00%	104.99%	109.43%	114.29%	119.34%
Net Operating Income ROI		64.75%	67.99%	70.86%	74.01%	77.28%
Cash ROI		0.00%	3.23%	6.11%	9.26%	12.53%
Total ROI		11.05%	14.97%	18.56%	22.48%	26.57%

WWW.THEVALUEPLAY.COM - COPYRIGHT PROTECTED 1998

I have relationships with several lenders and that obtaining financing to buy his house would be no problem provided that it would cash flow properly. I also told him that since the property is to be used for investment purposes, the lender will want to make sure that there is adequate rental

Exhibit 4-5   Property analysis worksheet: the value play rental house analyzer

Property Value Analysis

Comp #1		Comp #2		Comp #3	
Address:	1492 Columbus Way	Address:	1776 Independence Dr.	Address:	1830 Restoration Ln.
Sales Price	365,500.00	Sales Price	289,900.00	Sales Price	294,000.00
Adjustments to Price	1,600.00	Adjustments to Price	(2,400.00)	Adjustments to Price	3,200.00
Adjusted Price	367,100.00	Adjusted Price	287,500.00	Adjusted Price	297,200.00
Square Feet	2,645.00	Square Footage	2,096.00	Square Feet	2,200.00
Price Per Square Foot	138.79	Price Per Square Foot	137.17	Price Per Square Foot	135.09

Comp Averages		Subject Property 421 Moroni Blvd.		Property Values		Adjustment to Comps	2.50		2.50
						2.50	0.00	(2.50)	
Sales Price	316,466.67	Purchase Price	370,000	Fair Market Value		390,956	383,956	376,956	
Adjustments to Price	800.00	Square Feet	2,800.00	Actual Price		370,000	370,000	370,000	
Adjusted Price	317,266.67	Price/Sq Ft	132.14	Difference		20,956	13,956	6,956	
Square Feet	2,313.67	Turn Comps Off/On		ON					
Price Per Square Foot	137.13	Est Price/Sq Ft if Turned OFF		135.00					

Financing and Income Analysis

Cost and Revenue Assumptions		Financing Assumptions				Key Rent Ratios	
Purchase Price	370,000	Total Purchase	100.00%	373,500		Total Square Feet	2,800.00
Improvements	0	Owner's Equity	10.00%	37,350		Total Price/Sq Ft	133.39
Closing Costs	3,500	Balance to Finc	90.00%	336,150		Fair Market Value/Sq Ft	137.13
Total	373,500					Rental Income/Sq Ft	0.90
			Annual	Monthly		Total Income/Sq Ft	0.99
Estimated Monthly Rent Income	2,527	Interest Rate	6.000%	0.500%		Capitalization Rate	6.48%
Other Income	250	Amort Period	30	360		Gross Rent Multiplier	12.32
Total Income	2,777	Payment	24,185	2,015		Operating Efficiency Ratio	2.72

Rental Increase Projections			0.00%	4.00%	3.50%	3.50%	3.50%
Average Monthly Rent			2,527	2,628	2,720	2,815	2,914
Operating Expense Projections			0.00%	2.00%	2.00%	1.50%	1.50%

		Actual			Projected		
Operating Revenues		Monthly	Year 1	Year 2	Year 3	Year 4	Year 5
Gross Scheduled Rental Income		2,527	30,324	31,537	32,641	33,783	34,966
Vacancy Rate	5.0%	126	1,516	1,577	1,632	1,689	1,748
Net Rental Income		2,401	28,808	29,960	31,009	32,094	33,217
Other Income		250	3,000	3,120	3,229	3,342	3,459
Gross Income	100.0%	2,651	31,808	33,080	34,238	35,436	36,677
Operating Expenses							
Repairs and Maintenance	3.8%	100	1,200	1,224	1,248	1,267	1,286
Property Management Fees	4.0%	105	1,260	1,285	1,311	1,331	1,351
Taxes	13.2%	350	4,200	4,284	4,370	4,435	4,502
Insurance	2.1%	55	660	673	687	697	707
Salaries and Wages	0.0%	0	0	0	0	0	0
Utilities	0.0%	0	0	0	0	0	0
Professional Fees	0.9%	25	300	306	312	317	322
Advertising	0.0%	0	0	0	0	0	0
Other	0.0%	0	0	0	0	0	0
Other	0.0%	0	0	0	0	0	0
Other	0.0%	0	0	0	0	0	0
Total Operating Expenses	24.0%	635	7,620	7,772	7,928	8,047	8,167
Net Operating Income	76.0%	2,016	24,188	25,308	26,310	27,389	28,509
Cash Flow From Operations							
Total Cash Available for Loan Servicing		2,016	24,188	25,308	26,310	27,389	28,509
Debt Service		2,015	24,185	24,185	24,185	24,185	24,185
Remaining CF From Ops		0	3	1,123	2,125	3,205	4,324
Plus Principal Reduction		335	4,128	4,383	4,653	4,940	5,245
Total Return		335	4,131	5,506	6,778	8,145	9,569
CF/Debt Servicing Ratio		100.01%	100.01%	104.64%	108.79%	113.25%	117.88%
Net Operating Income ROI			64.76%	67.76%	70.44%	73.33%	76.33%
Cash ROI			0.01%	3.01%	5.69%	8.58%	11.58%
Total ROI			11.06%	14.74%	18.15%	21.81%	25.62%

Financial Analysis of Rental Properties

income to cover all the expenses and, in particular, the note to the bank. After having listened intently to my explanation as to why it would be difficult to buy his house at full asking price, the seller agreed that maybe there was some room to negotiate. I threw out a number of $330,000, and this didn't seem to scare him off. We both agreed to think about it over the next few days and then get back together. I intend to further test the waters by throwing out a comment such as, "$300,000 cash and close in 30 days." We'll see if he bites. I do know that the seller is anxious and wants to return to Colorado. He also told me that his grandmother gave him the house about six years ago. My guess is that he doesn't owe very much on it and that $300,000 may sound very good to him. You may be wondering why I would be willing to pay more than the cash flows from the property will support. My purpose for purchasing this property from the very beginning has been twofold. First, I want the boat slips that come with the deal, and second, I want the three-quarters of an acre of land that the house is sitting on to build condominiums on for Symphony Homes. The house in question is a bonus and just happens to be on the land I want. Although the rental income from the house is not sufficient to pay all the expenses, it certainly will help to offset them while I spend the next several months getting the project approved through the local planning commission. (Be sure to read Chapter 13 to learn how this story ends.)

In summary, analyzing rental houses properly requires that each property considered for your real estate investment portfolio meet two vitally important criteria. First, the house should be purchased at or below fair market value, and second, the investment must at a minimum cash flow properly by generating sufficient income to satisfy all its related obligations, including the debt. The smart investor knows that if the property being considered for purchase does not meet these two criteria, then it's time to keep looking for other opportunities.

What we obtain too cheaply, we esteem too lightly; it is dearness only that gives everything its value. Heaven knows how to put a price upon its goods, and it would be strange indeed if so celestial an article as freedom should not be highly rated.

—Thomas Paine

5

Financing Your Rental Property

Your success in the rental property business will depend largely on your ability to obtain financing for your investment properties. To become proficient in using the various options available to you, it is essential that you first have a complete understanding of the basic components that have a direct impact on the property's ability to generate income. Since the terms and conditions set forth by lenders are different for almost every loan, it is important to understand how those differences will affect you. In this chapter we'll first examine the intricacies of the various components that affect the financing of your investment property, then we'll review the documentation required by most lenders, and finally, we'll explore some of the many financing techniques available so that you can take full advantage of the other people's money (OPM) principle discussed in Chapter 1.

Financing Terms and Conditions

Three primary variables affect real estate loan payments. They are the interest rate, the amortization period, and the loan amount. It is essential for you to understand how each of these variables affects the profitability of your investment property. A material change in any one of the three variables will alter the net cash flow from the property and easily could make the difference in its viability as an investment opportunity.

The *interest rate* is the first of the three variables that affects real estate loan payments. *Interest* on a loan refers to the cost to borrow funds and represents the additional portion paid over and above the balance due, or principal. Interest rates vary widely among the many choices available for financing rental properties. Both banks and mortgage companies tend to be fairly competitive. Bank loans typically have shorter terms, and banks usually use the prime lending rate as the benchmark to price their loans. Mortgage company loans, on the other hand, often have a longer duration and are priced based on an index such as Treasury bills or the London International Bank Offered Rate (LIBOR) index. Since the interest paid on borrowed money represents the cost of funds, the higher the rate, the greater will be the amount paid. On a small loan of $100,000, for example, a difference of 0.5 percent in the interest rate will have only a minimal impact on the viability of an investment property. On a larger loan of $1 million, however, a difference of 0.5 percent will be much more significant. When applying for financing, smart investors know to take every precaution to negotiate for the best possible rate, especially on larger loans.

To help you to better understand and analyze the impact of various differences in changes in the interest rate, take a moment to review Exhibit 5-1. Using a real estate loan calculator developed for Symphony Homes and The Value Play, we can examine the effect of changes in interest rates on a base loan of $250,000. The loan-spread matrix illustrates how changes in the rate affect changes in the monthly payments. With a loan amount of $250,000 and a rate of 6.0 percent, the monthly payment would be $1498.88. By reducing the rate 0.5 percent, the payment is reduced to $1419.47, which represents a direct savings of $79.41 to the investor. The matrix allows you to quickly and easily examine the effect of changes in rate applied to different loan amounts.

The second variable that affects real estate loan payments is the *amortization period*. While the interest paid on a loan is the cost of borrowing funds, the amortization period is the length of time used to cal-

Exhibit 5-1   Chart of monthly payments

Loan Amount: $250,000.00   Total Interest Paid: $289,695.47
Interest Rate: 6%   Total Amount Paid: $539,595.47
Term: 360 months

Loan / Rate	Loan Amounts incremented by $2500			Interest Rates incremented by 1/2%			
	4.5%	5%	5.5%	6%	6.5%	7%	7.5%
$237,500	$1,203.38	$1,274.95	$1,348.50	$1,423.93	$1,501.16	$1,580.09	$1,660.63
$240,000	$1,216.04	$1,288.37	$1,362.69	$1,438.92	$1,516.96	$1,596.73	$1,678.11
$242,500	$1,228.71	$1,301.79	$1,376.89	$1,453.91	$1,532.76	$1,613.36	$1,695.60
$245,000	$1,241.38	$1,315.21	$1,391.08	$1,468.90	$1,548.57	$1,629.99	$1,713.08
$247,500	$1,254.05	$1,328.63	$1,405.28	$1,483.89	$1,564.37	$1646.62	$1,730.56
$250,000	$1,266.71	$1,342.05	$1,419.47	$1,498.88	$1,580.17	$1,663.26	$1,748.04
$252,500	$1,279.38	$1,355.47	$1,433.67	$1,513.87	$1,595.97	$1,679.89	$1,765.52
$255,000	$1,292.05	$1,368.90	$1,447.86	$1,528.85	$1,611.77	$1,696.52	$1,783.00
$257,500	$1,304.71	$1,382.32	$1,462.06	$1,543.84	$1,627.58	$1,713.15	$1,800.48
$260,000	$1,317.38	$1,395.74	$1,476.25	$1,558.83	$1,643.38	$1,729.79	$1,817.96
$262,500	$1,330.05	$1,409.16	$1,490.45	$1,573.82	$1,659.18	$1,746.42	$1,835.44

culate loan payments if the loan were fully amortized, or repaid, over the stated period. An amortization schedule provides owners with a list or schedule of the payments to be made over the life of the loan that shows the portion of the payment applied to principal and the portion applied to interest. This information is useful because it allows investors to see at a glance how much of the payment is being applied to reduce the balance of the loan at any give point over the period the loan is amortized. The shorter the amortization period, the higher is the payment; conversely, the longer the amortization period, the lower is the payment. Let's look at a simple example:

Loan amount = PV = $250,000

Interest rate = i = 6.0%

Amortization period = n = 180; payment = pmt = $2109.64

Amortization period = n = 360; payment = pmt = $1498.88

In this example, the difference between a 15-year loan period and a 30-year loan period is $610.76 per month. The question naturally arises, therefore: It is better to get a 15-year loan with a higher monthly payment or a 30-year loan with a lower monthly payment? I recommend using the 30-year amortization period because it gives you greater flexibility. Cash flow is the name of the game in this business, so you should do everything possible to minimize your monthly cash outflows. I've worked with many clients, however, whose intentions were to buy an investment property and hold it for the long term and who therefore preferred shorter amortization periods. Even then, I recommend building flexibility into the loan by using the longer amortization period. If you want to pay the loan off over a shorter period of time, you have the *option* to pay a little extra each month but are not required to do so.

Take a moment to review Exhibit 5-2, which illustrates a monthly loan amortization schedule using $250,000 as the amount borrowed, an interest rate of 6.0 percent, a 30-year period, and a monthly prepayment of $125. Only the first 39 months are shown for the sake of brevity. Now take a look at Exhibit 5-3, which illustrates the same loan but shows the annual portions applied to both principal and interest rather than the

Exhibit 5-2 Loan amortization schedule—monthly

Loan Amount: $250,000.00	Interest Rate: 6.000%	Number of Payments: 360	Payment Amount: $1,498.88				
PMT	Month	Principal	Interest	Total Principal	Total Interest	Prepayment	BALANCE
1	Jan 2004	$373.88	$1,250.00	$373.88	$1,250.00	$125.00	$249,626.12
2	Feb 2004	$375.75	$1,248.13	$749.63	$2,498.13	$125.00	$249,250.37
3	Mar 2004	$377.63	$1,246.25	$1,127.26	$3,744.38	$125.00	$248,872.74
4	Apr 2004	$379.52	$1,244.36	$1,506.78	$4,988.74	$125.00	$248,493.22
5	May 2004	$381.41	$1,242.47	$1,888.19	$6,231.21	$125.00	$248,111.81
6	Jun 2004	$383.32	$1,240.56	$2,271.51	$7,471.77	$125.00	$247,728.49
7	Jul 2004	$385.24	$1,238.64	$2,656.75	$8,710.41	$125.00	$247,343.25
8	Aug 2004	$387.16	$1,236.72	$3,043.91	$9,947.13	$125.00	$246,956.09
9	Sep 2004	$389.10	$1,234.78	$3,433.01	$11,181.91	$125.00	$246,566.99
10	Oct 2004	$391.05	$1,232.83	$3,824.06	$12,414.74	$12500	$246,175.94
11	Nov 2004	$393.00	$1,230.88	$4,217.06	$13,645.62	$125.00	$245,782.94
12	Dec 2004	$394.97	$1,228.91	$4,612.03	$14,874.53	$125.00	$245,387.97
13	Jan 2005	$396.94	$1,226.94	$5,008.97	$16,101.47	$125.00	$244,991.03
14	Feb 2005	$398.92	$1,224.96	$5,407.89	$17,326.43	$125.00	$244,592.11
15	Mar 2005	$400.92	$1,222.96	$5,808.81	$18,549.39	$125.00	$244,191.19
16	Apr 2005	$402.92	$1,220.96	$6,211.73	$19,770.35	$125.00	$243,788.27
17	May 2005	$404.94	$1,218.94	$6,616.67	$20,989.29	$125.00	$243,383.33
18	Jun 2005	$406.96	$1,216.92	$7,023.63	$22,206.21	$125.00	$242,976.37
19	Jul 2005	$409.00	$1,214.88	$7,432.63	$23,421.09	$125.00	$242,567.37
20	Aug 2005	$411.04	$1,212.84	$7,843.67	$24,633.93	$125.00	$242,156.33

#	Date						
21	Sep 2005	$413.10	$1,210.78	$8,256.77	$25,844.71	$125.00	$241,743.23
22	Oct 2005	$415.16	$1,208.72	$8,671.93	$27,053.43	$125.00	$241,328.07
23	Nov 2005	$417.24	$1,206.64	$9,089.17	$28,260.07	$125.00	$240,910.83
24	Dec 2005	$419.33	$1,204.55	$9,508.50	$29,464.62	$125.00	$240,491.50
25	Jan 2006	$421.42	$1,202.46	$9,929.92	$30,667.08	$125.00	$240,070.08
26	Feb 2006	$423.53	$1,200.35	$10,353.45	$31,867.43	$125.00	$239,646.55
27	Mar 2006	$425.65	$1,198.23	$10,779.10	$33,065.66	$125.00	$239,220.90
28	Apr 2006	$427.78	$1,196.10	$11,206.88	$34,261.76	$125.00	$238,793.12
29	May 2006	$429.91	$1,193.97	$11,636.79	$35,455.73	$125.00	$238,363.21
30	Jun 2006	$432.06	$1,191.82	$12,068.85	$36,647.55	$125.00	$237,931.15
31	Jul 2006	$434.22	$1,189.66	$12,503.07	$37,837.21	$125.00	$237,496.93
32	Aug 2006	$436.40	$1,187.48	$12,939.47	$39,024.69	$125.00	$237,060.53
33	Sep 2006	$438.58	$1,185.30	$13,378.05	$40,209.99	$125.00	$236,621.95
34	Oct 2006	$440.77	$1,183.11	$13,818.82	$41,393.10	$125.00	$236,181.18
35	Nov 2006	$442.97	$1,180.91	$14,261.79	$42,574.01	$125.00	$235,738.21
36	Dec 2006	$445.19	$1,178.69	$14,706.98	$43,752.70	$12500	$235,293.02
37	Jan 2007	$447.41	$1,176.47	$15,154.39	$44,929.17	$125.00	$234,845.61
38	Feb 2007	$449.65	$1,174.23	$15,604.04	$46,103.40	$125.00	$234,395.96
39	Mar 2007	$451.90	$1,171.98	$16,055.94	$47,275.38	$125.00	$233,944.06

Exhibit 5-3   Loan amortization schedule—annual

		Loan Amount: $250,000.00 Interest Rate: 6.000% Number of Payments: 360 Payment Amount: $1,498.88		
Year	Period	Principal Paid during Period	Interest Paid during Period	Total Paid during Period
Year	Period	Total Annual Principal	Total Annual Interest	Total Annual Payment
1	Jan - Dec 2004	$4,612.03	$14,874.53	$19,486.56
2	Jan - Dec 2005	$4,896.47	$14,590.09	$19,486.56
3	Jan - Dec 2006	$5,198.48	$14,288.08	$19,486.56
4	Jan - Dec 2007	$5,519.12	$13,967.44	$19,486.56
5	Jan - Dec 2008	$5,859.53	$13,627.03	$19,486.56
6	Jan - Dec 2009	$6,220.93	$13,265.63	$19,486.56
7	Jan - Dec 2010	$6,604.61	$12,881.95	$19,486.56
8	Jan - Dec 2011	$7,011.98	$12,474.58	$19,486.56
9	Jan - Dec 2012	$7,444.46	$12,042.10	$19,486.56
10	Jan - Dec 2013	$7,903.61	$11,582.95	$19,486.56
11	Jan - Dec 2014	$8,391.10	$11,095.46	$19,486.56
12	Jan - Dec 2015	$8,908.63	$10,577.93	$19,486.56
13	Jan - Dec 2016	$9,458.12	$10,028.44	$19,486.56
14	Jan - Dec 2017	$10,041.47	$9,445.09	$19,486.56
15	Jan - Dec 2018	$10,660.80	$8,825.76	$19,486.56
16	Jan - Dec 2019	$11,318.35	$8,168.21	$19,486.56

17	Jan - Dec 2020	$12,016.43	$7,470.13	$19,486.56
18	Jan - Dec 2021	$12,757.58	$6,728.98	$19,486.56
19	Jan - Dec 2022	$13,544.42	$5,942.14	$19,486.56
20	Jan - Dec 2023	$14,379.82	$5,106.74	$19,486.56
21	Jan - Dec 2024	$15,266.75	$4,219.81	$19,486.56
22	Jan - Dec 2025	$16,208.35	$3,278.21	$19,486.56
23	Jan - Dec 2026	$17,208.06	$2,278.50	$19,486.56
24	Jan - Dec 2027	$18,269.41	$1,217.15	$19,486.56
25	Jan - Jul 2027	$10,299.49	$193.99	$10,493.48

monthly payments. Note how paying an additional $125 per month reduced the repayment period from 30 years to about 24½ years. As stated previously, there is a tradeoff when prepaying the loan because the monthly cash flow from the investment is reduced directly by the amount of additional principal paid each month.

Finally, the third variable that affects real estate loan payments is the *loan amount.* The loan amount is simply the amount of money being borrowed. The relationship between the loan amount and the down payment is an inverse relationship, meaning that as the amount of money being borrowed for a particular rental property increases, the amount applied toward the down payment will decrease and, conversely, as the loan amount decreases, the down payment must increase. It is logical to assume that the more money borrowed, the greater will be the monthly payment, and the less money borrowed, the smaller will be the monthly payment. Although an investor could conclude from this logic that it makes sense to put down as much money as possible to decrease the monthly payment and hence increase the property's cash flow, it would be wrong to do so. Remember the section in Chapter 1 pertaining to the OPM principle? According to this principle, the more money borrowed, the greater will be the return on invested capital. Thus, even though the monthly payment will increase by borrowing more, since the returns are measured as a ratio of the income generated by the property to the amount actually invested in it, the rate of return is greater as a result of the increase in leverage.

Let's look at two different scenarios to see more clearly how this works. In Exhibit 5-4, an investor has used the rental house analyzer to evaluate a potential investment opportunity. Under this scenario, the property has met both the tests illustrated in Chapter 4 according to the criteria established by the investor. It passes the comparable-sales test, indicating a positive fair market value (FMV) of $3898 with an adjustment of zero. Using a total down payment of $25,640, or 20 percent, the investor will realize a cash return on investment (ROI) of 12.43 percent in year 1 on his or her invested capital. This is not bad, but it is nothing to get excited about either.

Now take a look at Exhibit 5-5. In this example all variables within the model are held constant and are exactly the same as in Exhibit 5-4, with the

Financing Your Rental Property

Exhibit 5-4   Scenario 1

Property Value Analysis

Comp #1		Comp #2		Comp #3	
Address: 1492 Columbus Way		Address: 1776 Independence Dr.		Address: 1830 Restoration Ln.	
Sales Price	124,000.00	Sales Price	127,000.00	Sales Price	132,300.00
Adjustments to Price	3,700.00	Adjustments to Price	2,200.00	Adjustments to Price	1,400.00
Adjusted Price	127,700.00	Adjusted Price	129,200.00	Adjusted Price	133,700.00
Square Feet	1,600.00	Square Footage	1,650.00	Square Feet	1,750.00
Price Per Square Foot	79.81	Price Per Square Foot	78.30	Price Per Square Foot	76.40

Comp Averages		Subject Property 421 Moroni Blvd.		Property Values		Adjustment to Comps		2.50
						2.50	0.00	(2.50)
Sales Price	127,766.67	Purchase Price	125,000	Fair Market Value	133,023	128,898	124,773
Adjustments to Price	2,433.33	Square Feet	1,650.00	Actual Price	125,000	125,000	125,000
Adjusted Price	130,200.00	Price/Sq Ft	75.76	Difference	8,023	3,898	(227)
Square Feet	1,666.67	Turn Comps Off/On	ON				
Price Per Square Foot	78.12	Est Price/Sq Ft If Turned OFF	75.00				

Financing and Income Analysis

Cost and Revenue Assumptions		Financing Assumptions			Key Rent Ratios	
Purchase Price	125,000	Total Purchase	100.00%	128,200	Total Square Feet	1,650.00
Improvements	0	Owner's Equity	20.00%	25,640	Total Price/Sq Ft	77.70
Closing Costs	3,200	Balance to Finc	80.00%	102,560	Fair Market Value/Sq Ft	78.12
Total	128,200				Rental Income/Sq Ft	0.88
			Annual	Monthly	Total Income/Sq Ft	0.88
Estimated Monthly Rent Income	1,450	Interest Rate	6.000%	0.500%	Capitalization Rate	8.24%
Other Income	0	Amort Period	30	360	Gross Rent Multiplier	7.37
Total Income	1,450	Payment	7,379	615	Operating Efficiency Ratio	3.61

Rental Increase Projections			0.00%	4.00%	3.50%	3.50%	3.50%
Average Monthly Rent			1,450	1,508	1,561	1,615	1,672
Operating Expense Projections			0.00%	2.00%	2.00%	1.50%	1.50%

		Actual Monthly	Year 1	Year 2	Projected Year 3	Year 4	Year 5
Operating Revenues							
Gross Scheduled Rental Income		1,450	17,400	18,096	18,729	19,385	20,063
Vacancy Rate	5.0%	73	870	905	936	969	1,003
Net Rental Income		1,378	16,530	17,191	17,793	18,416	19,060
Other Income		0	0	0	0	0	0
Gross Income	100.0%	1,378	16,530	17,191	17,793	18,416	19,060
Operating Expenses							
Repairs and Maintenance	13.4%	185	2,220	2,264	2,310	2,344	2,379
Property Management Fees	5.6%	77	924	942	961	976	990
Taxes	10.5%	145	1,740	1,775	1,810	1,837	1,865
Insurance	3.3%	45	540	551	562	570	579
Salaries and Wages	0.0%	0	0	0	0	0	0
Utilities	0.0%	0	0	0	0	0	0
Professional Fees	1.5%	20	240	245	250	253	257
Advertising	1.8%	25	300	306	312	317	322
Other	0.0%	0	0	0	0	0	0
Other	0.0%	0	0	0	0	0	0
Other	0.0%	0	0	0	0	0	0
Total Operating Expenses	36.1%	497	5,964	6,083	6,205	6,298	6,392
Net Operating Income	63.9%	881	10,566	11,108	11,588	12,118	12,668
Cash Flow From Operations							
Total Cash Available for Loan Servicing		881	10,566	11,108	11,588	12,118	12,668
Debt Service		615	7,379	7,379	7,379	7,379	7,379
Remaining CF From Ops		266	3,187	3,729	4,209	4,739	5,289
Plus Principal Reduction		102	1,259	1,337	1,420	1,507	1,600
Total Return		368	4,447	5,066	5,629	6,246	6,889
CF/Debt Servicing Ratio		143.19%	143.19%	150.54%	157.04%	164.22%	171.68%
Net Operating Income ROI			41.21%	43.32%	45.19%	47.26%	49.41%
Cash ROI			12.43%	14.54%	16.42%	18.48%	20.63%
Total ROI			17.34%	19.76%	21.95%	24.36%	26.87%

WWW.THEVALUEPLAY.COM - COPYRIGHT PROTECTED 1998

exception of the down payment, or owner's equity. In this example, the down payment has been decreased to $6410, representing a 5 percent investment. Since the down payment was decreased, the loan amount must be increased. The monthly payment of $730 in this example compares

89

Exhibit 5-5   Scenario 2

Property Value Analysis

Comp #1		Comp #2		Comp #3	
Address:	1492 Columbus Way	Address:	1776 Independence Dr.	Address:	1830 Restoration Ln.
Sales Price	124,000.00	Sales Price	127,000.00	Sales Price	132,300.00
Adjustments to Price	3,700.00	Adjustments to Price	2,200.00	Adjustments to Price	1,400.00
Adjusted Price	127,700.00	Adjusted Price	129,200.00	Adjusted Price	133,700.00
Square Feet	1,600.00	Square Footage	1,650.00	Square Feet	1,750.00
Price Per Square Foot	79.81	Price Per Square Foot	78.30	Price Per Square Foot	76.40

Comp Averages		Subject Property 421 Moroni Blvd.		Property Values		Adjustment to Comps		2.50
						2.50	0.00	(2.50)
Sales Price	127,766.67	Purchase Price	125,000	Fair Market Value	133,023	128,898	124,773
Adjustments to Price	2,433.33	Square Feet	1,650.00	Actual Price	125,000	125,000	125,000
Adjusted Price	130,200.00	Price/Sq Ft	75.76	Difference	8,023	3,898	(227)
Square Feet	1,666.67	Turn Comps Off/On	ON				
Price Per Square Foot	78.12	Est Price/Sq Ft If Turned OFF	75.00				

Financing and Income Analysis

Cost and Revenue Assumptions		Financing Assumptions			Key Rent Ratios	
Purchase Price	125,000	Total Purchase	100.00%	128,200	Total Square Feet	1,650.00
Improvements	0	Owner's Equity	5.00%	6,410	Total Price/Sq Ft	77.70
Closing Costs	3,200	Balance to Finc	95.00%	121,790	Fair Market Value/Sq Ft	78.12
Total	128,200				Rental Income/Sq Ft	0.88
			Annual	Monthly	Total Income/Sq Ft	0.88
Estimated Monthly Rent Income	1,450	Interest Rate	6.000%	0.500%	Capitalization Rate	8.24%
Other Income	0	Amort Period	30	360	Gross Rent Multiplier	7.37
Total Income	1,450	Payment	8,762	730	Operating Efficiency Ratio	3.61

Rental Increase Projections			0.00%	4.00%	3.50%	3.50%	3.50%
Average Monthly Rent			1,450	1,508	1,561	1,615	1,672
Operating Expense Projections			0.00%	2.00%	2.00%	1.50%	1.50%

		Actual Monthly	Year 1	Year 2	Projected Year 3	Year 4	Year 5
Operating Revenues							
Gross Scheduled Rental Income		1,450	17,400	18,096	18,729	19,385	20,063
Vacancy Rate	5.0%	73	870	905	936	969	1,003
Net Rental Income		1,378	16,530	17,191	17,793	18,416	19,060
Other Income		0	0	0	0	0	0
Gross Income	100.0%	1,378	16,530	17,191	17,793	18,416	19,060
Operating Expenses							
Repairs and Maintenance	13.4%	185	2,220	2,264	2,310	2,344	2,379
Property Management Fees	5.6%	77	924	942	961	976	990
Taxes	10.5%	145	1,740	1,775	1,810	1,837	1,865
Insurance	3.3%	45	540	551	562	570	579
Salaries and Wages	0.0%	0	0	0	0	0	0
Utilities	0.0%	0	0	0	0	0	0
Professional Fees	1.5%	20	240	245	250	253	257
Advertising	1.8%	25	300	306	312	317	322
Other	0.0%	0	0	0	0	0	0
Other	0.0%	0	0	0	0	0	0
Other	0.0%	0	0	0	0	0	0
Total Operating Expenses	36.1%	497	5,964	6,083	6,205	6,298	6,392
Net Operating Income	63.9%	881	10,566	11,108	11,588	12,118	12,668
Cash Flow From Operations							
Total Cash Available for Loan Servicing		881	10,566	11,108	11,588	12,118	12,668
Debt Service		730	8,762	8,762	8,762	8,762	8,762
Remaining CF From Ops		150	1,804	2,346	2,826	3,355	3,905
Plus Principal Reduction		121	1,496	1,588	1,686	1,790	1,900
Total Return		272	3,299	3,933	4,511	5,145	5,806
CF/Debt Servicing Ratio	120.58%	120.58%	126.77%	132.25%	138.29%	144.57%	
Net Operating Income ROI			164.84%	173.29%	180.78%	189.04%	197.62%
Cash ROI			28.14%	36.59%	44.08%	52.34%	60.93%
Total ROI			51.47%	61.36%	70.38%	80.27%	90.57%

WWW.THEVALUEPLAY.COM - COPYRIGHT PROTECTED 1998

unfavorably with the monthly payment of $615 in the preceding example, resulting in a net decrease in available free cash flow of $115. Surely the investor in scenario 1 would fare better than the investor in scenario 2, right? Not so. The investor in this example would realize a cash ROI of

28.14 percent, which is over twice as much as the investor in scenario 1. This is our trusted friend, the OPM principle, at work for us. By investing less of your own money, you actually earn a higher rate of return than you otherwise would despite the fact that the remaining cash has decreased.

After reviewing the interest rate, amortization period, and loan amount, you can see how changing just one of these three key variables can make a significant difference in the viability of an investment property. The better you understand the interplay among the variables and their relationship with one another, the greater will be your chances for success in the rental property business.

Additional Financing Considerations

Three important additional factors that have an impact on real estate financing are the term of the loan, the fees assessed by the lender to originate the loan, and prepayment penalties. The term must be considered prior to procuring a mortgage so that its life doesn't expire prematurely. It is equally important to understand how the many different types of fees charged by the lender affect the total cost of the investment as well. Finally, it is important to be aware of prepayment penalties, if any, that may be associated with the loan.

The *term* of a loan refers to its duration, or life. A loan with a 3-year term, for example, means that the loan will expire in 3 years and must either be renewed or paid in full at the end of the 3-year period. Don't confuse the term of a loan with its amortization period. They are not the same. A mortgage with a 5-year term can have a 15-, 20-, or 30-year amortization period. Regardless of the type of financing secured for the investment property, you must know what the term is and how it will affect your investment objectives. Using the most appropriate term is a function of the life of the project. In other words, before purchasing the rental property, you already should have defined your investment objectives. For example, if you intend to hold the property for 10 or more years, then you most likely will want to procure a fixed-rate loan with a term that matches the full amortization period, which is typically 30 years. Financing the property with a shorter term, say, 5 years, would force you to refinance the property at the end of the term, or in 5 years.

Depending on the current interest-rate environment, you may prefer to lock in a lower rate now because you don't know what the future holds. If you intend to hold the property for 10 or more years, then you will need a term that matches your objectives. If interest rates happen to be more favorable at some point in the future, you can always refinance to take advantage of the lower rates. On the other hand, an increase in interest rates will not affect the mortgage because a measure of protection has been built in to insulate the investment from a higher rate environment by choosing the most appropriate financing term to begin with.

Using a loan with a longer term is not always the better choice. If, for example, you have determined that your investment objective is to purchase a rental property, make some minor improvements to it over the next one or two years while renting it out, and then selling it, it probably will be to your advantage to use a short-term financing instrument. Loans with shorter terms often have lower rates. This is so because lenders can predict interest rates more accurately over a shorter period of time than they can over, say, 30 years. A 3-year adjustable-rate mortgage (ARM) is almost certain to have an interest rate ranging from 0.5 to 1 percent lower than a loan with a 30-year term. A 3-year ARM typically has a fixed rate for the first three years and then adjusts either annually or semiannually thereafter. A comparable loan from a bank may carry a rate to match a 3-year ARM but have a 3-year term, meaning that instead of adjusting, the loan will expire and have be renewed altogether.

In order to choose the most appropriate term for the financing of a rental property, you must first define your investment objectives. You need to determine how long you intend to hold the property in your portfolio. Do you plan to purchase the property, add it to your portfolio of other rental properties, and hold it for many years, or will this particular investment property be held for only a short time to capture a gain created by making improvements to it? Determine your investment objectives prior to making a commitment to the lender, and choose the term best suited to the project.

One of the biggest expenses related to financing your rental property can be the many different types of *loan fees* that are assessed. These include application fees, underwriting fees, loan origination fees, mortgage broker fees, and points charged at closing. Since some lenders are overly aggressive and assess a fee or charge for just about everything you can think of, I recommend asking for a list of all costs that will be charged by both the lender and the mortgage broker (if there is one). Although by law they are required to disclose all costs, these are issues that should be addressed up front. Even after receiving the schedule of costs, it pays to be careful because some charges may not show up until the loan closes. This is especially true with mortgage brokers. Although the broker is legally obligated to disclose all reasonable and customary fees under the Truth in Lending Act, the broker doesn't always know what fees the lender will charge. The broker and the lender are not the same parties. The broker acts as a third party to assist the purchaser in procuring the most appropriate type of financing. If the broker uses a lender she has not used before, she may not be aware of the lender's complete fee structure. I myself have been surprised on more than one occasion by unexpected charges that show up at the time of closing.

The *loan application fee* is a charge that some lenders assess at the time formal application is made. Fees range anywhere from no charge at all to about $500. The fee is charged to offset costs incurred by the lender or broker for personnel costs and credit reports. Justification for the charges results from a need to recover costs, as well as the inability of some applicants to qualify for loans. Charging an application fee serves to filter out individuals who may not be capable of qualifying for a loan by acting as a deterrent. If, for example, the applicant believes that he may not be able to qualify for a loan and knows that an application fee of $250 will be charged regardless of whether or not he qualifies, chances are that he will not bother with the application. Application fees frequently are negotiable. If you know that you have a good credit rating and will have no problem qualifying for a loan, be sure to tell this to the lender or broker and ask him or her to waive the application fee. Often the answer will be yes.

Underwriting fees have come about in recent years as yet another way to tack on an additional charge. The supposed justification for this fee is similar to that of the application fee in that like the personnel who must get paid for processing the loan application, so must the underwriting department get paid for its job of underwriting the loan. Using this logic, it seems reasonable to expect that at some point in the future we may begin to see other types of fees show up, such as maybe a loan committee fee for reviewing the loan or perhaps a human resources fee to cover the cost of hiring all the other departments that are charging us fees.

Loan origination fees, yet another way of charging the borrower, are usually equivalent to 1 point, or 1 percent, of the total amount of the loan. On a $100,000 loan, for example, the fee would be $1000. Justification for this fee is supposedly based on the costs incurred by the lender to actually make the loan once it has been approved. Legal documents must be drawn up and processed, the loan must be funded, and everything must be recorded properly. Some lenders will waive the loan origination fee altogether or roll it into the interest rate on the loan by increasing the rate by 25 basis points, which is the equivalent of 0.25 percent.

Mortgage brokers earn most of their income from the fees generated by placing loans. Since they are not direct lenders, brokers do not earn anything from the interest being charged. Interest is paid to the lender, not to the broker. A mortgage broker is similar to a real estate broker in that they are both compensated only when they sell something. Both types of brokers are paid on a percentage basis. While the real estate agent is paid a *commission,* the mortgage broker is paid *points.* Brokers typically charge between 1 and 2 percent of the loan amount but sometimes more and sometimes less. Factors that may affect the fees they charge are items such as the borrower's creditworthiness, the size of the loan, and their ability to receive back-end fees from the lender. Don't be fooled by the broker who charges 1 percent on a $100,000 loan amount and tells you that he is only making $1000 on the transaction. Brokers are almost always compensated by the lender for differences in the spread of the rate charged. For example, if the base rate a lender charges is 6.00 percent with 0 points to the borrower, the broker likely will be paid a back-end fee of 1 percent by the lender. If the broker is able to sell the same loan to you at, let's say, 6.25 percent, the broker can double his income on the loan and receive 2 percent from the lender. If you're a solid borrower with good credit, mortgage brokers are less likely to play these games with you, but if you're not, watch out! Although broker's fees are sometimes negotiable, you still need to be prepared for these added costs when purchasing a rental property.

Points are often made available to borrowers to buy down the interest rate applied to a loan. Since 1 point is equivalent to 1 percent, an investor paying 1 point on a $100,000 loan would pay $1000 in additional upfront fees. For every point paid, the interest rate on the loan is decreased by approximately one-eighth to one-quarter of a percent. This is only a general guideline because rate spreads vary widely among lenders, but the lender you are working with usually can provide an exact quote by looking at its rate sheets. Since rate spreads are dynamic and change with minor fluctuations in the market, the rate quoted may be good for just that particular moment, or it may be good for the remainder of the day.

Now take a minute to look at Exhibit 5-6. In this example, six different rate scenarios are compared. The loan amount of $250,000 and the term of 360 months are held constant, whereas the interest rate and the points are changed. We are assuming a base interest rate of 6.50 percent with 0 points applied on the first line and then buying the rate down in ¼-point increments while simultaneously increasing the amount of discount points paid. In the first example, if an investor borrowed $250,000, paid 0 points, and held the loan for its full 30-year life, she would pay a total of $568,861.22 with a monthly payment of $1580.17. In the last example, if the investor borrowed the same $250,000 for a 30-year period but instead elected to pay 5 discount points to buy the rate down from 6.50 to 5.25 percent, she would pay a total of $509,483.33 (includes $12,500 for points paid) with a monthly payment of $1380.51. Buying down the rate in this example would save the investor $200 per month and $59,378 over the life of the loan. What this example assumes, however, is that the investor will hold the rental property for a full 30-year period, which may or may not be the case. This is why I continue to emphasize the need to identify your objectives before investing. If you determine ahead of time that a rental property is going to be held in your portfolio for the long term, then it makes sense to pay the additional points up front. On the other hand, if you know you're only going to hold the property for, let's say, 3 years, then you're better off paying the higher interest rate with no points. You would, in fact, need to hold the property for 5 years and 3 months to realize any benefit from paying the additional points. The breakeven point can be calculated by dividing the cost of points over the savings per month. Thus, in this example, the breakeven point would be as follows:

$$\text{Breakeven} = \frac{\text{cost of points}}{\text{monthly savings}} = \frac{\$12,500}{(\$1580.17 - \$1380.51)} =$$

$$62.61 \text{ months}$$

Prepayment penalties sometimes are charged for paying off a loan too soon. Although many commercial lenders impose penalties for prepaying a loan before the expiration of its term, it is not common on single-family residential loans. If an investor obtained a loan with a 5-year term that had a prepayment penalty provision, for example, but decided to sell the property after just 12 months, the lender would charge a fee, or penalty, for prepaying the loan. Prepayment penalty fees are structured in numerous ways and sometimes can be substantial. A loan with a 5-year term, for example, may have a declining prepayment penalty fee structure as follows:

Prepay Loan in Year 1	Prepayment Penalty Fee
1	5%
2	4%
3	3%
4	2%
5	1%
6	0%

If an investor's intentions are to acquire a rental property, to create value in it by making improvements to it, and subsequently to turn around and sell the property within 1 to 2 years, then he will need to take into consideration the prepayment penalty structure of the loan. It is best to minimize your exposure by procuring a loan that doesn't have a prepayment penalty to begin with. Then you don't have to worry about it.

In summary, three additional financing considerations investors need to be cognizant of are the term of a loan, any ancillary fees that may be assessed by the lender or mortgage broker on origination of the loan, and any penalties that may be imposed as a result of paying off the loan early. Smart investors can procure financing with a shorter term to take advantage of investment opportunities with a quicker life cycle and also use points to buy

Exhibit 5-6   Loan comparisons

Loan Amount	Interest Rate	Payments	Points	Payment	Total Paid	Cost of Loan	Cost of Points
$250,000.00	0.065%	360	0%	$1,580.17	$568,861.22	$318,861.22	$0.00
$250,000.00	0.0625%	360	1%	$1,539.29	$556,645.48	$304,145.48	$2,500.00
$250,000.00	0.06%	360	2%	$1,498.88	$544,595.47	$289,595.47	$5,000.00
$250,000.00	0.0575%	360	3%	$1,458.93	$532,715.57	$275,215.57	$7,500.00
$250,000.00	0.055%	360	4%	$1,419.47	$521,010.10	$261,010.10	$10,000.00
$250,000.00	0.0525%	360	5%	$1,380.51	$509,483.33	$246,983.33	$12,500.00

down the interest rate applied to a loan for investment opportunities that may have longer life cycles. Finally, it is easy enough to obtain single-family residential mortgages that carry no prepayment penalties at all.

Loan Documentation Checklist

The documentation required to apply for a mortgage will vary from lender to lender. Some banks or mortgage companies require what is in my opinion overly excessive documentation before approving a loan, whereas others are much more lenient. For example, I recently purchased a piece of investment property using a lender I have never used before. This particular mortgage company called for more documentation than any other lender I've worked with. I jumped through their hoops once, but never again. I literally spent several hours going through files over two years old looking for both a bank statement and its corresponding canceled check that showed evidence that a personal loan had been created by me to another entity. The loan eventually was approved, and I purchased the property, but not without a great deal of distress on my part. By comparison, two days ago I applied for a loan on another piece of investment property. This time all it took was just a few recent bank statements to verify the cash available for the down payment and my credit report, which the lender pulled. Working with this lender was relatively painless compared with the first lender. Guess who I'll go back to the next time I need this type of financing? You're exactly right if you guessed the second lender.

The kind of excess documentation required by the first lender occurs more often when you are working with large mortgage companies than with a smaller local lender. The larger mortgage companies have an entire department of underwriters whose job it is to make people like me miserable. Small local banks, on the other hand, are careful about whom they loan to but tend not to be nearly as aggressive on the paperwork.

Before submitting a formal application, lenders often will prequalify an applicant to determine how much he can borrow based on certain criteria previously established by them. Exhibit 5-7 illustrates an example of a typical mortgage prequalification schedule. Based on this couple's combined monthly income of $7250, monthly debt obligations of $1075, and a down payment of $10,000, they will qualify for a mortgage ranging from $208,442.75 to $219,747.95 given the rates and terms listed in the schedule. This example is for an owner-occupied home only and does not take into consideration income that would be earned from a rental property.

Once a borrower has been prequalified, the lender will then require verification of certain documents. The following box presents a checklist of items that may be required by a bank or mortgage company. As stated previously, some lenders will require more than the items addressed in this list, and some will require fewer.

Loan Documentation Checklist

___ Lender's loan application forms

___ Copy of executed agreements between buyer and seller, including the purchase agreement and related addenda

___ Financial statement showing personal assets, including other real estate owned

___ Income and balance statements for your business, if applicable

___ Income tax returns for a minimum of the preceding two years, both personal and business

___ Verification of cash required for down payment and reserves— bank statements, savings and retirement account information, other applicable assets

___ Credit references along with full FICO reports

___ Historical operating statements for the subject property if it is currently being operated as a rental unit

___ Leases used for the subject property, if applicable

___ Verification of property taxes for the subject property

___ Insurance binder for rental property

___ Third-party reports, including property survey and appraisal

---

Exhibit 5-7   Mortgage prequalification schedule

Your Personal Financial Variables

	Monthly Income	Other Monthly Income	Monthly Minimum Due on Credit Cards	Monthly Auto Payment(s)	Monthly Student Loans/Other Notes Due
Borrower	$5,400.00	$250.00	$325.00	$410.00	$125.00
Co-Borrower	$1,200.00	$400.00	$100.00	$115.00	$0.00

Estimated Monthly Property Taxes: $320.00
Estimated Monthly Homeowners Insurance: $50.00
Cash Available for Down Payment: $10,000.00

Based on your personal financial variables and the mortgage variables you have entered, you may meet the criteria to qualify for monthly payments and/or loan amounts as indicated below.

	Housing	Debt
Qualifying Ratios:	38	33
Your Ratios	23	33

Interest Rate	Term in Years	Monthly Payment	Loan Amount	Purchase Price
6.5%	30	$1,317.50	$208,442.75	$218,442.75
6.25%	30	$1,317.50	$213,978.11	$223,978.11
6%	30	$1,317.50	$219,747.95	$229,747.95

Six Smart Ways to Finance Your Rental Property

In order to apply the OPM principle described in Chapter 1, you have to have access to other people's money (OPM). Borrowing as much money as possible and using as little of your own money as possible will enable you to leverage up the returns on your investment capital. More traditional lenders will require anywhere from a 5 percent down payment to as much as a 20 percent down payment. For beginning investors, this may be more than some of you have. We'll examine ways to raise cash for the down payment in just a minute, but first, what about all those late-night TV real estate gurus who talk about the nothing-down deals? While nothing-down deals do exist, my experience has been that it's much easier to find a solid investment opportunity requiring 5 to 10 percent down than it is to hold out for the nothing-down deal. In other words, the pool of available rental properties requiring a little bit down is much larger than the pool of nothing-down deals. It's like comparing an Olympic-sized swimming pool to my one-year-olds' baby pool that we bought at a local discount store. There's a lot more water in the Olympic pool. If you absolutely can't come up with any money for a down payment, then you may want to hold out for a nothing-down deal, but if you have at least a little bit of money to work with, I recommend broadening your investment scope by looking at properties that may require a down payment. It's not my intention to discourage you, especially if you are just getting started investing in real estate. However, I prefer to tell it like it is based on my more than 25 years of experience. I think the more experienced investors reading this book will agree with me that you're better off having a little bit of money to work with than trying to conquer the world buying nothing-down deals.

The following box lists six smart ways to finance your rental property. This is not by any means an exhaustive list of the many ways there are to raise money, nor is it intended to be. The focus of this section is on providing you with several of the more common methods of raising money primarily through debt instruments, with the exception of option agreements. There are just as many creative ways to raise money through equity financing as well. Take a moment to review this list.

Six Smart Ways to Finance
Your Rental Property

1. Credit lines
2. Small local banks
3. Conventional mortgages
4. Mortgage brokers
5. Option agreements
6. Owner-finance arrangements

Credit Lines

A variety of credit lines are available to almost anyone. Some of the more common ones are home equity lines of credit and national credit cards such as Discover, MasterCard, and VISA. The terms and conditions vary widely with these types of credit lines. The most favorable interest rates and the longest terms typically are found with home equity lines of credit, whereas national credit cards and store credit cards tend to offer higher rates and shorter repayment terms.

Many of you are likely to own your own home. For those of you who do, you are probably already familiar with home equity lines of credit (HELOC) loans. A HELOC is a second mortgage secured by the borrower's primary residence that allows the homeowner to borrow against the equity in her home, often up to 100 percent of the value of the home and sometimes even more. Since this type of loan is secured by the residence, the interest rate usually is lower than with other types of credit such as credit cards. HELOC loans provide borrowers with the flexibility of borrowing against a home simply by writing a check. The funds can be used for just about anything and represent a good source of funds to be used as a down payment. You should verify with the lender, however, that it will allow you to borrow funds for the down payment. Some lenders have absolutely no problem doing this, whereas others require that the money for the down payment comes from cash already on hand. One way to circumvent this requirement is to draw against your credit line and deposit the funds in a bank account in anticipation of purchasing an investment property. This is perfectly legal as long as you act according to the terms and conditions set forth in the HELOC loan. You are simply borrowing money against an already approved line of credit and placing those funds into your bank account. One potentially adverse implication of using money from a line of credit is that it will increase your personal debt ratios. Since most lenders have predetermined debt ratios that must be adhered to, you have to be careful that the borrowed funds don't exceed the limit and end up disqualifying you.

For investors who insist on that nothing-down deal, borrowing money using a home equity line of credit and using it for a down payment on a rental property provides a way to accomplish this. Since those funds are borrowed funds, they do not represent cash equity. If you purchased a house, for example, for $100,000 and borrow $90,000 from the mortgage company and the remaining $10,000 from a home equity line of credit, you have created a true nothing-down transaction because 100 percent of the funds used to purchase the rental property are borrowed funds.

National credit cards such as MasterCard and VISA also represent a good source of funds. Credit cards are available to almost anyone and can be used for just about anything. Most credit cards offer you the ability to get a cash advance against your credit line up to some predetermined limit. You also can write checks that can be used for most anything, including your investment property. National credit cards tend to carry higher interest rates than do other forms of borrowing, so you should use them wisely.

While lines of credit can be a great source of borrowing power and will allow investors the ability to leverage up, I caution you to use them wisely. Remember that you are using these funds for investment purposes, so be sensible and responsible in the way they are used. Don't go out and "max out" all your cards thinking that you can conquer the world. This is a sure way to get into trouble. If you're not careful, you can create a negative-cash-flow black hole that will be difficult at best to get out of. Just remember that the money has to be repaid at some point in time. Since your objective is to earn a predetermined rate of return on all funds borrowed for investment purposes, including the many types of credit lines available to you, be certain that the cash flow generated from the investment is great enough to cover all sources of debt and still meet your return requirements.

Small Local Banks

Conventional bank financing is often available through small local banks. These types of banks may operate with just one or two branches and have a small deposit base of only $15 to $20 million, or they may be somewhat larger with as many as five to ten branches and $200 million in deposits. One primary advantage to using local banks is that they often can provide borrowers with more flexibility than more conventional sources such as a mortgage company. Local banks may, for example, loan money to purchase a rental property as well as to make improvements to it.

Small local banks are also much more likely to be familiar with the local area and therefore would have a greater degree of confidence in the specific market than a larger regional or national lender would. A personal relationship with a local banker also is much easier to establish than with other types of lenders, such as conventional mortgage companies. In a local bank where decisions are made in part based on these relationships, an investor can go in, introduce himself, and speak directly with the lender. This affords investors an opportunity to sell themselves as well as their project. Once a relationship has been established and the banker gets to know you and is comfortable with you, future loan requests will be much easier and likely will require less documentation, possibly as little as updating your personal financial statement.

Another thing you might consider is to establish a line of credit with a small local bank, much like a home equity line of credit. The credit line could be either secured or unsecured. If you have equity built up in another rental property, for example, it is usually quite easy to use the equity as collateral to secure the credit line. Some lenders also will provide investors with an unsecured line of credit, often starting with a smaller limit and increasing the limit over time as the lender's trust and confidence in you grow. A line of credit will enable you to borrow money up to the lender's predetermined credit limit. For example, with a $1 million line of credit, an investor could purchase several properties at one time. An investor could purchase up to 10 houses with an average selling price of $100,000 assuming a down payment requirement of 10 percent.

Conventional Mortgages

Conventional mortgages represent an excellent source for financing real estate investment property. There are many loan programs available at any given time that offer a wide range of terms and conditions available to investors such as yourself. Depending on the interest-rate environment, conventional mortgage rates can be some of the most competitive of all the types of financing. Unlike bank loans, which usually are priced based on the prime lending rate, mortgage loans often are priced based on 10-year Treasury bills or Treasury notes plus an additional spread or margin. The result is that conventional mortgage loans generally carry a more favorable interest rate than do other types of financing instruments. This is especially true for borrowers who have maintained a good credit rating.

Conventional mortgages usually are available with 30-year amortization periods. This longer amortization period allows borrowers to minimize their monthly cash-flow-out obligation to the lender by reducing the amount that must be paid back each month. By way of comparison, a loan through a local bank may offer only a 15- or 20-year amortization period. This is not always the case, however, because sometimes interest-only loans are available from a bank. An interest-only loan requires that only the interest be paid each month or quarter as opposed to both interest and principal. Since no principal payments are being made, the monthly cash flow out can be reduced even further. Interest-only loans are useful to investors who intend to hold a property for only a short while, perhaps long enough to make some needed improvements and then flip, or sell, the property.

Another advantage of using a conventional mortgage company to finance a rental property is that there are many companies that will loan up to 90 percent of the purchase price on investment properties. This means that the borrower only has to come up with 10 percent for the down payment. For investors who are accustomed to reading the nothing-down types of books, keep in mind that the selection of available investment opportunities is much smaller. I prefer to work with a lender that will loan as much as 90 percent on a rental property, leaving me to come up with only 10 percent and thereby giving me a much broader selection of properties to choose from, than to spend time looking for that proverbial needle in a haystack.

Although conventional mortgage companies provide a good source of financing, there are some drawbacks to using them. The primary drawback is the documentation required by the lender on each and every transaction. Mortgage companies are notorious for demanding excessive documentation. For example, if a large deposit has been made into your bank account recently, some lenders will want documentation to determine its source. They may even ask for a copy of the canceled check, depending on where the funds came from. Another disadvantage to using a conventional mortgage company is the fees charged for the loan. Depending on the lender, these may or may not include a loan application fee, an underwriting fee, a loan origination fee, and whatever other creative fees the lender can come up with.

Mortgage Brokers

Just as real estate brokers play an important role in matching up buyers and sellers, so do mortgage brokers play an important role in matching up borrowers and lenders. Mortgage brokers usually have many contacts in the industry, know which lender is best suited for the type of financing you are seeking, and know who's offering the best deal. Experienced brokers have well-established relationships directly with the lenders and usually have two or three with whom they do a large volume of business. While you generally can expect to pay 1 percent to the broker for his or her services, the fee can be well worth it if you are working with a professional broker who has solid relationships with several lenders.

The broker's service sometimes can make up the difference between whether or not the financing for your deal will be accepted. Furthermore, brokers know how to qualify your particular property before ever sending it to a lender because they know what each lender will accept and what they will not accept. A good mortgage broker usually can tell you if he can place your loan after spending just 10 to 15 minutes with you on the phone. The broker knows what questions to ask to qualify your property and which lender is likely to be the most interested in financing it. Unless you already have a relationship directly with a mortgage company, brokers can save you a great deal of time because they are more likely than you to know who will accept your loan and who will not. You potentially could spend time contacting 5 or 10 different mortgage companies and still come up empty-handed, whereas a good mortgage broker may already know a lender who makes exactly the type of loan you are looking for.

Option and Lease Option Agreements

An *option agreement* is a legal instrument that gives an individual the right to purchase property at a predetermined price. The use of options is very common in the stock market. For example, investors can buy a call option on Dell stock with a strike price of, let's say, $32. As with all options, time t is one of the variables that determines the value of an option using the Black-Scholes model. Investors have the right to exercise options at their discretion within a specified period of time. It is possible that the outcome will be favorable, and it is also possible that the option will expire worthless. For example, if an investor has an option to purchase Dell stock at $32, and the price of the stock rises to $35 before the option expires, the investor is said to be "in the money" and can exercise his right to purchase at $32 and thus lock in an instant gain of $3 per share.

The use of options works fundamentally the same way with real estate as it does with stocks. Some sellers may require the purchaser to meet other obligations, however, such as assuming responsibility for carrying costs such as interest and taxes. When using options with real estate, investors have the legal right to purchase a piece of property at a predetermined price. Then, at some point before the expiration of the option agreement, they may exercise their right to purchase the property at whatever price was established. In addition, since the investor holds a legal interest in the property, the interest is usually transferable, which means that the investor has the right to sell the property without ever taking title to it. Options are a great way to purchase property with very little of your own cash, especially if you find another buyer before having to take title to the property. Options also afford investors the opportunity to limit their risk exposure in a particular project to only the premium paid for the option. If the investor decides not to exercise his right to purchase, the option expires worthless, and all that is lost is the premium paid for the option.

Some of my real estate investment activities for Symphony Homes include the use of options for the development of new residential construction in single-family communities. Options are used to acquire rights to property to build on without ever taking legal title until we are ready to begin construction. We do, however, have a recordable interest in the property. We just don't take title, at least not until the construction of a new home has begun. I recently optioned several lots in a newly developed community consisting of 83 lots. This gave Symphony Homes a legal interest in the property and the right to acquire the lots at a predetermined price. When the company gets a purchase agreement to build a new home for a client on one of our lots, we then exercise the option on that lot and take legal title to it. The advantages of using an option in this case are twofold. The first is that if we have difficulty selling new homes to prospective buyers, we are not stuck with the burden and cost of ownership. The only thing we have at risk is our option money. The second reason is that if we were to actually purchase the lots, the sale would trigger an increase in taxes due to a new and much higher assessed value. As the new owners, we would then be obligated to assume the tax liability.

Lease options are similar to options in that they give investors the right to purchase property at a predetermined price. The primary difference between them, however, is that with a lease option, control of the rental house is given to the lessee/buyer. The lessee then has the right to sublease the rental property if so desired. Under a lease-option agreement, a portion of the monthly lease amount usually is applied toward the purchase price, so it is, in effect, just like getting a loan or mortgage on the house. At some point in the future the buyer can exercise her right to purchase the property and pay off the remaining loan balance with a new loan if desired. If at some time during the option period the purchaser finds another buyer, then she may exercise her right without ever taking legal title to the property by creating a sale that transfers legal interest in the property directly from the original seller to the buyer who is purchasing from the lessee. If, on the other hand, the lessee decides not to exercise her right to purchase, then control reverts back to the original owner, who is then entitled to keep the option money deposit as well as any portion of the monthly lease payments that would have been applied toward the purchase price.

As you can see, the use of options and lease options can be a very effective tool for real estate investors who are interested in tying up a rental property without having to take title to it. Options enable you to gain control of a property with very little money down, thereby allowing you to maximize your use of leverage. I recommend, however, that options and lease options be used with care. Remember that time is one of the variables, and when t expires, so does the agreement. Carefully analyze the market as it applies to your particular investment opportunity before committing any capital to it so as to determine that the probability of a profitable outcome is favorable.

Owner-Finance Arrangements

Owner financing refers to financing provided by the seller, or owner, in one form or another. The seller may provide financing in whole or in part for a property she owns. If the seller owns the property free and clear, for example, then she may be willing to provide the buyer with 100 percent financing. More than likely, though, the seller will want a minimal down payment, even if it is only a thousand dollars. If the seller still has an underlying mortgage on the property, then she may be agreeable to carrying back a second mortgage for a smaller amount, say, 10, 20, or 30 percent of the purchase price. An investor still may have to procure a loan for the property from a more traditional source such as a mortgage company, but having the seller carry back a second mortgage provides an opportunity to purchase the rental property with less money down. One caveat investors should be aware of, however, is that not all lenders will allow secondary financing to be attached. Before proceeding with this option, make sure that your mortgage company does not have a provision in place that would preclude you from attaching a second mortgage to the property.

There are several advantages to using owner financing. One of the main benefits is that the purchaser is not required to conform to all the underwriting guidelines that banks and mortgage companies require. The seller, unlike an underwriter working for a mortgage company, is likely to require very little in the way of documentation. The seller providing the financing doesn't care where the money for the down payment comes from as long as it comes from somewhere. To the seller, cash is cash whether it comes from an advance on a MasterCard, from a HELOC loan, or from a personal savings account. The more traditional lenders, such as banks and mortgage companies, on the other hand, can be very particular about where the money for a down payment comes from. In many cases, the money cannot even come from a family member or friend. Moreover, if this is in fact the case, you must be able to prove that the money is your own and did not come from a relative.

Another advantage of using owner financing is that it allows investors to save money by avoiding the fees and transaction costs commonly charged for new loans. With owner financing, for example, there are no loan application fees, no underwriting fees, no loan origination fees, and no points to be paid. Finally, the time needed to close on a rental property when using an owner-financed note is much less than for traditional financing arrangements because virtually no loan approval process is required.

Another type of owner-financed note is referred to as a *wrap-around mortgage*. Under this arrangement, the seller retains title to the property and continues to make mortgage payments to the original lender. The new owner, in turn, makes mortgage payments directly to the seller. Thus, in effect, there are two sets of payments being made. Let's look at the example illustrated in Exhibit 5-8. Say that you purchased a rental property for $100,000 and put $5000 down. You now owe the seller $95,000, which you agree to pay over 30 years. Meanwhile, the seller has an underlying obligation to her lender, with an original loan balance of $51,000, which she must continue to pay. Thus, while you make a payment to the seller on your $95,000 note, she makes a payment to her lender on the $51,000 note. The difference in monthly payments is $310, and the difference in annual payments is $3725, all of which the seller gets to keep. Furthermore, since the seller's note originated at some point prior to the newly created financing, her note will be paid in full

Financing Your Rental Property

before the new seller-financing note is paid in full. When that happens, the difference in notes will be the full amount of $616 monthly and $7394 annually, all of which the seller will be entitled to.

When using owner financing to purchase a rental property, one provision to be aware of in mortgage documents is a potential due-on-sale clause in the deed of trust that may expressly prohibit this type of financing arrangement. Lenders often will not allow the transfer of ownership interests without their having been notified. One way to circumvent this requirement, however, is to create an option agreement in place of a wrap-around mortgage in which a portion of the monthly option money is applied to the purchase price in the event that the right to purchase is exercised. The same thing also can be done with a lease-option agreement

Exhibit 5-8   Wrap-around mortgage

Seller's Original Note to Lender		
Purchase Price	100.00%	60,000
Owner's Equity	15.00%	9,000
Balance to Finance	85.00%	51,000

	Annual	Monthly
Interest Rate	6.000%	0.500%
Amort Period	30	360
Payment	3,669	306

New Financing Provide by Owner/Seller to Buyer		
Purchase Price	100.00%	100,000
Owner's Equity	5.00%	5,000
Balance to Finance	95.00%	95,000

	Annual	Monthly
Interest Rate	6.750%	0.563%
Amort Period	30	360
Payment	7,394	616

Differences Created by Wrap Around Mortgage	
Total Gain On Sale	40,000
Difference in Loan Balances	44,000
Difference in Monthly Payments	310
Difference in Annual Payments	3,725

that provides for a portion of the monthly rental payments to be applied to the purchase price. Option and lease-option agreements are perfectly legal, and in my experience, I have never personally seen any provisions that would preclude their use.

Although second-lien positions are the most common form of owner-financing arrangements, owners or sellers are not limited to just debt financing. They may be open to an equity agreement, wherein a portion of their ownership interest is retained. Rather than being required to make monthly payments to the seller, the buyer and seller agree to share in the profits of the newly formed entity. Depending on the specifics of the agreement, the original seller also may be entitled to a share of any capital gains when the property is sold at some point in the future.

In summary, success in the rental property business will hinge largely on an investor's ability to raise financing from one of the many sources available to them. As a smart investor, the more you know and understand about debt instruments, the more successful you will be. A working knowledge of financing terms and conditions, including interest rates, amortization periods, and loan amounts, is paramount to your achieving your financial goals. Furthermore, a comprehensive understanding of additional financing considerations, such as the term of a loan, the various fees assessed by lenders, and any prepayment penalties, is essential to accomplishing your objectives. Finally, you should be fully aware of the many different types of financing arrangements that are available to investors for rental properties.

Intelligence, patriotism . . . and a firm reliance on Him who has never forsaken this favored land are still competent to adjust in the best way all our present difficulty.

—ABRAHAM LINCOLN

6

Real Estate Sales Forms and Closing Documents

I n Chapter 5 we discussed several financing alternatives available to investors for the purchase of rental properties. In this chapter we'll examine some of the real estate forms needed to make the purchase legally binding. Once the purchase of a rental property has been formalized through the use of real estate documents, the next step will be to begin preparing to close the transaction, which is typically done at a title company.

Real Estate Sales Forms

Real estate forms are used for many purposes, some of which involve buying and selling, others of which are designed for leasing, and still others of which are used for construction and repair work. This chapter focuses on some of the more common real estate forms used for the purpose of purchasing investment property and is in no way intended to be an exhaustive guide. This chapter includes a discussion of six essential real estate forms, as outlined in the following box. They are the residential contract for sale, also known as the *purchase agreement,* the seller's disclosure of property condition, various financing addenda, and the notice of termination.

Six Essential Real Estate Sales Forms

1. Residential sales contract
2. Property condition disclosure
3. Third-party financing addendum
4. Loan-assumption addendum
5. Seller-financing addendum
6. Notice of termination

Residential Sales Contract

The *residential sales contract,* or *purchase agreement* as it is also known, is used to legally bind two or more parties together in contractual form to specify the terms and conditions under which real property is to be bought or sold. Sales contracts are written with numerous variations to cover the many needs of the parties involved. A residential sales contract can be as short as 1 page or as long as 15 or more pages. Some are written with simplicity in mind, whereas others are drafted more carefully for the purpose of protecting buyers and sellers from almost any unforeseen condition that may arise. Regardless of their length or complexity, most sales agreements have several basic components in common. Let's start by taking a look at the sales agreement and some of its basic components.

1. Parties. In Section 1, the seller and the buyer are identified as the parties to the contract. If there is more than one seller or buyer, they should be listed as well. The sales contract is filled out initially by either the buyer or the buyer's agent. On filling out an agreement that is satisfactory to the buyer, the contract is used as an offering agreement and subsequently is presented to the seller. In other words, it does not become a valid sales contract until after having first been used as an offering agreement to submit to the seller. On receiving the offer, the seller can respond in one of three ways. He can (1) reject the offer, (2) make a counteroffer, or (3) accept the offer as is with no changes. It is only when both parties have come to a mutual agreement that the contract becomes valid.

2. Property. Section 2 of TREC's residential sales contract is used to describe the real property's street address, as well as the property's legal description. It is important to review this section for accuracy, especially the legal description, because it is very easy to transpose the numbers. I once purchased two individual rental properties that closed on the same day. The title company got the legal addresses mixed up, and unfortunately, the problem wasn't discovered until some time later when I sold them. This created additional title and legal work that ended up being at my expense. The property section is also used to identify more specifically items to be included with the purchase, such as appliances, air-conditioning equipment, ceiling fans, garage door openers, and anything else the parties wish to include. Do not make the mistake of assuming that certain items should be included because about the time you do, you may end up discovering the item is missing after the closing. I recently bought a property that had a window air-conditioning unit in an upstairs bedroom. I didn't list it in the property section because I knew I would be completely updating the furnace and installing a new central air system, so I really wasn't that concerned about it. As it turns out, it's a good thing I wasn't because the seller took the window unit with him.

3. Sales Price. Section 3 is self-explanatory. It consists of the cash portion of the purchase price payable by the buyer, the amount of the purchase price to be financed, and the total of the two.

4. Financing. The financing section of the TREC sales contract is fairly comprehensive and provides buyers with several different financing options. This section also sets forth the number of days the buyer has to apply for financing. I recommend 3 to 5 days and no more than 7. The buyer should begin making a concerted effort to apply for financing right away if he has not been prequalified already. As the seller, you don't want to waste time with a buyer who is not qualified to purchase your property by taking it off the market unnecessarily. The third-party financing section provides for mortgage or bank financing, or any other third party, and also outlines the terms and conditions for the loan the buyer is seeking. There is also a provision for seller financing and loan assumptions if needed. Finally, there is a provision to have the buyer deliver satisfactory evidence of credit to the seller if the seller-financing or loan-assumption provisions are used.

5. Earnest Money. The earnest money section is used to describe the deposit the buyer will provide on acceptance of the contract by the seller. *Earnest money* is a form of consideration that must be given in any business contract. While consideration can be anything of value given in exchange that both parties agree on, it is usually given in the form of money. Sometimes a buyer may not have all the required earnest money readily available and so will give a portion on acceptance by the seller and provide the remainder at a later date, usually within 30 days or so. Earnest money also can be given in stages of the buyer's level of commitment. This is especially true in larger transactions involving multifamily and commercial properties. For example, on one particular apartment building I purchased, the seller required a $25,000 earnest money deposit up front and another $25,000 after the contract went "hard." A contract goes hard when the buyer's feasibility period, or inspection period, expires. The incremental earnest money deposits are used to step up the level of commitment by the purchaser.

6. Title Policy and Survey. The title policy is issued by a title company to insure the buyer and, more particularly, the lender that the title is free and clear of any encumbrances that may adversely affect the property. If, for example, work was performed by contractor who was not paid, the contractor may have, unbeknownst to the seller, placed a lien on the property. The title company will do a search on the title, which should reveal any such encumbrances. In the case of a contractor's lien, it will have to be satisfied or resolved as a condition of closing. Otherwise, the new property owner, or buyer, would assume the previous owner's liability.

The survey, also covered in section 6, is an item not to be taken lightly. Some lenders require it, and some do not. The survey identifies the metes and bounds of the subject property. In other words, it identifies the exact physical location of the property. The corners or boundaries typically are set off with temporary wooden stakes and more permanent iron rods usually about one inch in diameter and one foot long or so. The "irons," as they are called, are hammered into the ground to serve as permanent markers for the property's boundaries. Chances are that the house you live in now has irons set in the ground along the perimeter of the property. If the house is even a few years old, the irons may be difficult to find because grass or plants and sometimes landscaping may be covering them. The problem with not getting a survey is that you may not be buying what you think you are buying. Let's look at an example.

Not too long ago, my company began construction of a new house on a lot that was adjacent to another house that had been there for about three years. We had our property physically staked by a surveying company just as we always do. When building a house from the ground up, you can't afford to take a chance on not having the lot lines and the house staked. Otherwise, the house could violate the setback lines required by the city. In this particular instance, the neighbor's grass and irrigation system encroached on our lot by a full 15 feet, which was almost right up against the edge of the house we were building. The neighbor, who was too cheap to get his own survey when he purchased his property, had the irrigation system and grass installed where he thought they should go. Well, guess what? He was wrong. He threatened to sue us, called the city inspector out, and was downright unruly. I suppose in a way I don't blame him, but on the other hand, it wasn't our fault that he didn't have his property surveyed. Being the good neighbors that we are and in an effort to maintain the peace, we agreed to reinstall the irrigation lines along his new property line at our expense. So just a friendly word of advice here: Don't be a cheapskate and try to skimp on the survey. It may cost you a whole lot more in the long run.

7. Property Condition. Section 7 of the sales agreement outlines property inspection obligations for both the buyer and the seller. The buyer has the right to personally inspect the property for acceptable condition, as well as the right to hire a professional company to inspect it for him. As the buyer, if you believe that you can identify the more common problems with a house and already have a good idea of what to look for, you may want to save yourself the money and do the inspection yourself. On the other hand, if your knowledge of maintenance issues is limited, then it is probably a good idea to hire an inspector who can provide you with a detailed analysis of the property's physical condition. At Symphony Homes, we occasionally have buyers who want their brand-new home inspected. As builders, this seems redundant to us because the house has undergone a whole series of inspections from start to finish. We don't mind, however, because the inspectors help to instill greater confidence in the consumer's mind about the quality of the product we offer. The home buyer is essentially paying for a third-party impartial opinion of his own choosing.

Also embodied within section 7 is language that requires the seller to fully disclose any known defects pertaining to the house. The seller's disclosure will be covered more fully later in this chapter. In addition, the seller must disclose any knowledge of the use of lead-based paint if the house was built before 1978. The lender also may require certain repairs if they are deemed necessary before agreeing to provide financing for the house. If the cost of the repairs exceeds 5 percent of the sales price, the buyer has the right to terminate the agreement. Finally, this section states that the seller must complete all required repairs prior to the date of closing unless otherwise agreed on by both parties in writing.

8. Broker's Fees. The section on broker's fees is very brief and to the point and basically states that the fees are provided for in a separate agreement. If there are no agents involved, then this section, of course, is irrelevant.

9. Closing. The date of closing is specified in section 9 of the TREC residential sales agreement. If the closing date is not met, then certain actions may be required. In this particular contract, it states: "If either party fails to close this sale by the Closing Date, the nondefaulting party will be entitled to exercise the remedies contained in paragraph 15." Whatever sales contract you end up using, be sure that the penalties for not closing by the date specified are clearly defined. In the sales agreements for Symphony Homes, we require buyers to pay an additional $100 per day for every day the date of closing is delayed beyond a seven-day grace period. Our contracts did not contain the penalty clause initially, but as a result of buyers who found a myriad of creative ways to delay the closing because they had not yet sold their homes, the language was added as a protective measure. This may sound a bit severe to some readers, but from our perspective, the penalty serves two important functions. First, it signals to the buyer that we are serious about closing on time and that failure to do so will result in a substantial penalty; and secondly, the penalty helps to offset our carrying costs, which include interest, taxes, insurance, and loss of use of the company's capital. In summary, consider your specific needs as they relate to the closing, and make sure that they are included in the sales contract.

10. Possession. Section 10 of the agreement pertains to the date possession is given to the buyer. The date of possession is usually, but not always, the date of the closing. Circumstances may arise that preclude the granting of possession until a later date. For example, our company happens to be closing with a family on their new home next Friday, at which time possession will be given to them. The family buying our house, however, has a closing to sell their house scheduled two days prior to the closing with us. If forced to deliver possession on the day of closing, they would have to move out of their current house for two days before they would be allowed to move into our house. The buyer of their house has agreed not to take possession until Friday, the day of the family's closing with us.

Another situation to be aware of when granting possession is that it should not just be given at the time of closing. In our contracts, we specify that the date of possession is granted "on closing and *funding*." This means that not only does all the paperwork have to be completed with the necessary signatures and such but also that the buyer's loan must fund. In other words, the title company managing the closing for us must be prepared to give us a certified check at the time of closing. If a closing is scheduled for a Friday, be careful that it is not too late in the day. If, for example, it is at 4:00 P.M. and all the documents are not signed until 5:00 P.M. or after, the deal probably will not fund. What happens is that as soon as all the documents are signed and all conditions have been met, the title company's agent, or closer, must call the lender to get a funding number before issuing a check. Without that number, the company will not issue a check. Guess where everybody is, including the lender's mortgage department, at 5:00 P.M. on Friday afternoon? That's right. They're gone for the weekend. This means that the loan will not fund until the following Monday. This puts the seller in a precarious predicament. He must either be prepared to hand over the keys to an anxious buyer who already has a moving service lined up, along with Uncle Bob and Aunt Sue and all the cousins to help with the big move. As the seller, you're stuck. Do you hand over the keys to accommodate them, or do you stand firm until you get your money? The best answer is to schedule the closing early enough on Friday so that you don't put yourself in this position to begin with.

11. Special Provisions. This section allows both parties to write in anything that falls outside the standard provisions already contained within the contract. For example, one common special provision buyers like to include is a clause that states, "This agreement is contingent on the sale of the buyer's house." This is a perfectly legitimate clause and certainly serves the interests of the buyer, but not one that I get very excited about as the seller. The clause allows the buyer to bail out of the contract for just about any reason while hiding behind the excuse that he couldn't sell his house. Unless the real estate market is extremely weak in your area and you haven't been able to get any offers for some time, I recommend striking this particular language from the agreement. I prefer to work only with buyers whom I know are committed to following through with the purchase of a house. Most often I am able to allay the buyer's fears through reassuring him or her by stating something like, "Mrs. Buyer, I understand your concern about selling your

Real Estate Sales Forms and Closing Documents

house. Most buyers we work with share that very same concern. It has been our experience, however, that more often than not, our clients have discovered that their house sold much quicker than expected and ended up needing us to complete the construction of their new home as quickly as possible." Once again, the special provisions section can be used for just about anything you wish to expressly state that is not embodied elsewhere in the agreement.

12. Settlement and Other Expenses. Settlement charges vary from area to area and state to state. What may be considered buyer's settlement charges in one area may be seller's charges in another area. In general, as outlined in the TREC agreement, the buyer pays for an appraisal because it is almost always a condition of the lender, who wants to ensure that the stated property value is in agreement with its market value. The buyer also usually pays for any fees associated with the new mortgage, which include points, recording fees, and other miscellaneous fees such as preparation of the deed. Some states require that a transfer tax be paid at the time of sale. Michigan is one of them. Unless otherwise specified, the seller is required to pay the tax. In our purchase agreements, we always expressly state that the buyer pays this tax. Therefore, in effect, what may be reasonable and customary expenses for buyers and sellers in one area may not be in another area.

13. Prorations. This section simply states that costs or expenses associated with the property shall be prorated, or apportioned, as of the date of the transfer, which is usually the date of closing. Items that typically are prorated include taxes, association fees, maintenance fees, rental income, and any other income related to the property. To *prorate* means to apportion or to assign the expense or income to the party entitled to it based on the date of ownership. Let's look at a simple example.

If the seller prepaid $2400 in taxes for the current year and the closing occurred on March 31, then the seller would be entitled to receive a credit at closing as follows:

$$\left(\frac{\$2400}{365}\right) \times (365 - 90)$$
$$= \$6.5753 \times 275$$
$$= \$1808.22$$

So, in this example, since the seller has prepaid the taxes in advance for the current year, she would be entitled to receive a credit on the day of closing for the remaining balance of the tax that has already been paid at a rate of roughly $6.58 per diem, or per day. The per-diem rate is then multiplied by the number of days prepaid to calculate the credit due her.

14. Casualty Loss. This section provides for unforeseen property damage due to what is referred to as a *casualty loss*. It essentially covers damage to the property resulting from acts of nature such as wind, rain, or ice, as well as damage from fire. In the event the property suffers some type of damage, it becomes incumbent on the seller to repair the damage by the date of closing or a date at some time beyond the date of closing provided that both parties agree. If the seller cannot repair the property in a timely manner that is satisfactory to the buyer, the buyer then has the right to terminate his interest in the contract and is entitled to a refund of his earnest money deposit.

15. Default. Default provisions specify what actions are to be taken in the event either party defaults on the contract. Both parties generally have the right to enforce performance of the defaulting party by seeking legal redress or extending the time or date of the contract to allow for performance. If the buyer is in default and cannot cure, depending on the circumstances, the seller will be entitled to keep the earnest money as liquidated damages. If the seller is in default, the buyer will be entitled to a refund of the earnest money.

16. Dispute Resolution. Rather than attempt to resolve disagreements through the courts, provisions often are established to encourage the use of a more peaceable solution, such as an impartial third-party mediator. Although representation by an attorney may be advised, it will be much quicker and much less costly if a solution can be reached outside the court system.

17. Attorney's Fees. Section 17 simply states that in the event an agreement cannot be reached through arbitration, the prevailing party will be entitled to a reimbursement of all legal and court costs.

18. Escrow. Escrow accounts are used to hold the buyer's earnest money deposit. Buyers and sellers use an escrow agent, often from a title company, to deposit the earnest money into an account. An escrow agent is used to protect the interests of both buyer and seller. Since the buyer putting up the earnest money deposit does not want to give it directly to the seller, the money usually is given to an escrow agent to hold in an escrow account. If a dispute arises, the party not in default is entitled to the earnest money. The escrow agent, however, must have a signature by both parties agreeing to the release of funds to the nondefaulting party. Most of the time, this requirement does not present a problem. If, however, the buyer defaults and does not purchase the house for a reason that he believes is justified and the seller seeks to receive the earnest money as liquidated damages, the buyer may refuse to sign the escrow agent's release. Failure to do so will force the parties into either arbitration or the courts.

19. Representations. Section 19 provides for the seller's representations that "there will be no liens, assessments, or security interests against the property which will not be satisfied out of the sales proceeds." In other words, this section helps to ensure that all debts against the property made by the seller will be satisfied at the time of closing and will not be carried forward to the new property owner, or buyer.

20. Federal Tax Requirement. This section provides for the collection of taxes by the Internal Revenue Service (IRS) for sellers who are deemed to be "foreign persons," as defined by applicable law.

21. Agreement of Parties. Section 21 contains a very brief provision that simply states that the contract embodies the entire agreement and no other contracts will have any effect on this agreement except for any addenda that may be attached.

22. Consult Your Attorney. This section is self-explanatory and states that real estate agents cannot give legal advice and that if the parties to the contract have any questions regarding interpretation of the agreement, they should seek the advice of an attorney *before* signing the document.

Property Condition Disclosure

The *seller's disclosure of property condition form* is intended to have the seller fully disclose to the buyer any and all property defects or conditions that warrant repair. At one time, the Latin term *caveat emptor* was the prevailing rule. The term means "let the buyer beware." In other words, it was up to the buyer to use the process of discovery to detect any repair the property may be in need of, and the seller had little to no obligation to disclose anything. The courts in recent years have begun to lean more toward protecting the buyer and now place a much greater burden on the seller than they have in the past. The prevailing law now requires sellers to disclose known property defects to the buyer. Depending on what is wrong with the property, the seller may claim that she was unaware of a particular condition that the buyer discovered after having closed and taken possession. In a case such as this, the buyer must be able to present compelling evidence that the seller was in fact aware that the defect existed.

The seller's disclosure of property condition is presented in five sections and requires the seller to make the information available to the buyer after having filled out the form in its entirety. Section 1 of the form contains a checklist of items such as appliances; heating, ventilation, and air-conditioning (HVAC) equipment; pools; fences; and other items that are to be included with the sale of the house. The seller required to address each item on the form by writing "Yes," "No," or "Unknown" in the appropriate blank.

It also asks the seller to disclose any known defects with the items listed in this section. Section 2 addresses structural items such as walls, roofs, foundations, and windows and again asks the seller to disclose known defects with any of these components. Section 3 asks the seller to provide information regarding damage from termite infestation, water, toxic waste, radon gas, or other such conditions. Section 4 asks the seller once again to disclose any item that is in need of repair. Finally, section 5 addresses the seller's awareness of known modifications to the house or any of its structural components such as room additions. It also asks the seller to provide information regarding homeowner's association fees, maintenance fees, or lawsuits that may be pending against the seller that may have an adverse effect on the sale of the property.

Third-Party Financing Addendum

The *third-party financing condition addendum* requires that a "buyer shall apply promptly for all financing described . . . and make every reasonable effort to obtain financing approval." The addendum provides a greater level of detail for buyers seeking third-party financing such as a bank loan or mortgage than does the sales contract. The addendum provides for buyers seeking a conventional loan, veteran's housing assistance, Federal Housing Administration (FHA) financing, or a Veterans Administration (VA) guaranteed loan. Finally, the form sets forth the terms and conditions required by the buyer to meet his or her financing needs should a third-party loan be desired.

Loan-Assumption Addendum

The *loan-assumption addendum* as promulgated by TREC provides a greater level of detail to buyers desiring to assume a loan that is held by the seller. The form includes provisions for verification of the buyer's creditworthiness by requesting such information from the buyer as a credit report, verification of employment, and verification of funds available for the down payment. Although this particular addendum grants sole discretion to the seller to determine the buyer's creditworthiness, more often than not it is the mortgage company that has sole discretion. Most lenders incorporate into their mortgage documents a due-on-sale clause that may preclude the transfer of title through a loan assumption. Many years ago when interest rates were much more stable, loan assumptions were very common, and due-on-sale clauses were rarely seen. Today, however, while the ability to assume a loan still exists, it generally requires the lender's review and approval of the new borrower. Moreover, the lender typically charges an origination fee just as if it were a new loan. Many times lenders have the right to adjust the interest rate at their sole discretion if the loan is assumed, so it may be just as easy to get a new loan as it is to assume an existing one. Do not rule out the possibility of assuming loans as a method of financing, though, because there are older mortgages that may still allow the buyer to assume them easily.

Seller-Financing Addendum

The *seller-financing addendum* as promulgated by TREC is similar to the other financing addenda in that it mandates sufficient credit documentation to be furnished by the buyer. The primary difference in this case, however, is that since the seller is the one providing the financing, he or she will have sole discretion in determining the creditworthiness of the buyer. This addendum also contains a provision enabling the parties to outline the terms and conditions of the promissory note that will be created for the seller financing. The note provides for a choice of either a single payment, also known as a *balloon payment,* a standard note amortized over a predetermined period of time, or an interest-only note initially and then changing to interest plus principal continuing until the note is repaid in full. Although the repayment arrangements in this promissory note section offer buyers and sellers a limited number of ways to structure debt payments, they are some of the more common methods preferred. The repayment of debt can be structured in whatever ways the parties choose to agree on and are by no means limited to the methods illustrated here. In the next section, the seller-financing addendum provides for the deed of trust that will be used to secure the note. Furthermore, it may grant the right to the buyer to sell the property without prior consent of the seller, or it may instead require consent. As the seller carrying the note, I recommend adding a provision similar to a due-on-sale clause that would preclude the buyer from selling the property without first paying off the underlying obligation to the seller. This gives the buyer the flexibility he is seeking for the purchase of your house but in addition leaves you in control. Like the bank, you can either grant or deny the assumption of the note to another buyer. If the provision is included, the seller will then have the option of being cashed out in the event the property is sold at a later date. Finally, the seller-financing addendum contains a provision for escrow payments for taxes and insurance that may or may not be required by the seller. If the seller does not require an escrow account to be set up, then proof of annual or semiannual tax and insurance payments must be furnished to the seller as evidence that the payments have been made and do not become delinquent. If you are the seller, I suggest using the same general guidelines as lenders do for escrow requirements. Most mortgage companies will allow the borrower to pay his own taxes and insurance on any loan that has an 80 percent or less loan-to-value (LTV) ratio. The implied logic is that any borrower who has 20 percent or more invested in a property is not likely to default on the note. Conversely, since borrowers with a down payment of 20 percent or less have a higher default rate, lenders typically require that escrow accounts be maintained.

Notice of Termination

The *notice of termination of contract* as promulgated by TREC is self-explanatory in that it provides the buyer with the means to cancel or terminate the sales contract. The buyer can only terminate, however, for legitimate reasons as set forth in the sales agreement. The notice of termination does not grant buyers the right to terminate without just cause.

Closing Documents

The closing is the point in time when everything comes together to finalize the transaction between buyers and sellers. As a real estate investor, you have spent countless hours studying the market and analyzing opportunities, you have successfully negotiated terms and conditions acceptable to both you and the seller, and you have sought out the best financing alternative for this investment. It is now time to bring all requisite parties together to close the sale. Although there are numerous ancillary closing forms and letters that will need your attention, the primary closing documents that necessitate a careful review are the title report, settlement statement, deed, and promissory note, as listed in the following box.

Four Fundamental Closing Documents

1. Title report
2. Settlement statement
3. Deed
4. Promissory note

Title Report

A *title* refers to the rights and usage of ownership and possession of a particular piece of property. In real estate usage, *title* may refer to the instruments or documents by which a right of ownership is established (title documents), or it may refer to the ownership interest one has in the real estate. A title search or examination, which generally occurs at the local courthouse, is performed to check the history of the title records to ensure that the buyer is purchasing a house from the legal owner and also to be certain that there are no liens, overdue special assessments, unpaid taxes, unpaid water and sewer charges, or other claims or outstanding restrictive covenants filed in the record that would adversely affect the marketability or value of the title.

The *title report,* also known as the *abstract of title,* provides information about the property's chain of title. In other words, it gives a history of ownership, judgments, liens, and anything else that may have been recorded against the property over time. The title insurance company issues an insurance policy to the buyer and a separate policy to the lender that ensure that the title is clean and that there are no encumbrances that may adversely affect the new owner. In addition, title insurance protects lenders or homeowners against loss of their interest in property due to legal defects in the title that may remain undiscovered until some time after the closing has occurred. Title insurance may be issued to a mortgagee's title policy. Insurance benefits will be paid only to the "named insured" in the title policy, so it is important that an owner purchase an owner's title policy for protection against loss from any such defects.

Settlement Statement

Settlement statements, also known as *closing statements,* are commonly prepared by the title company handling the closing. They detail by line item all the associated debits and credits assessed to both buyer and seller. The following list provides a sample of a few of the more common items found on a settlement statement but is by no means an exhaustive list.

- Contract sales price
- Earnest money deposit
- Principal amount of new loan(s)
- Existing loan(s)
- Seller financing
- Prorated tax adjustments
- Prorated rental or income adjustments, if applicable
- Lender charges, including underwriting fees, loan origination fees, and points
- Title insurance or title policy charges
- Third-party reports, including inspection, appraisal, and survey charges
- Legal fees
- Recording fees

In *The Complete Guide to Flipping Properties*, I addressed this very important topic of settlement statements. In it, I wrote the following:

You should take the necessary time to review each and every charge on the settlement statement to verify its accuracy. I can't think of a deal yet that I have been involved in where all settlement charges on the closing statement were completely accurate. Errors are inadvertently made for one reason or another. For example, the title company may have the incorrect payoff amount of the seller's loan, or they may prorate the rents or taxes incorrectly, or they may not be aware of a credit you are entitled to because of a specific clause in your purchase agreement negotiated by you and the seller. Don't assume that because the closing officer works at the title company and acts as the facilitator in numerous closings that "she must be right because she is the closer and she should know." Precisely the opposite is true. Because the closer does act as the facilitator in numerous closings is all the more reason she must rely on you to provide accurate information for the settlement statement. . . .

The inherent risk to you by neglecting to review the closing statement can be substantial and potentially cost you hundreds or even thousands of dollars. Here in Michigan, for example, the state and county assess what is referred to as a transfer tax. The transfer tax is calculated as a percentage of the sales price and is collected at closing on all real estate sold. It is just like paying tax on a new car, new furniture, school supplies for the kids, or just about anything else Uncle Sam can get his hands on. The tax rate applied is usually about 1 percent or just a little less, so for every $100,000 in property value sold, approximately $1000 in taxes is assessed. Unless otherwise stated, the seller is responsible for paying this tax. In my purchase agreements, however, I require the buyer to pay the tax. Unless the title company has been made aware of this, the transfer taxes will be placed on my side of the settlement statement, which is the incorrect side. This error, which has been made many times, could easily cost me two to three thousand dollars. Although I thoroughly review all of the charges on the statement, this is one in particular that I am very careful to check for accuracy.

Deed

A *deed* is a formal written instrument by which title to real property is transferred from one owner to another. The deed should contain an accurate description of the property being conveyed, should be signed and witnessed according to the laws of the state where the property is located, and should be delivered to the purchaser on the day of closing. There are two parties to a deed—the grantor and the grantee. The grantor is the seller, and the grantee is the buyer. There are several types of deeds, including a deed of trust, a quitclaim deed, and a special warranty deed.

Like a mortgage, a *deed of trust* is a security instrument whereby real property is given as security for a debt; however, in a deed of trust there are three parties to the instrument—the borrower, the trustee, and the lender (or beneficiary). In such a transaction, the borrower transfers legal title for the property to the trustee, who holds the property in trust as security for payment of the debt to the lender or beneficiary. If the borrower pays the debt as agreed, the deed of trust becomes null and void. On the other hand, if the borrower defaults in the payment of the debt, the trustee may sell the property at a public sale, as set forth under the terms of the deed of trust. In most jurisdictions where the deed of trust is in force, the borrower is subject to having the property sold without benefit of legal proceedings. A few states have begun in recent years to treat the deed of trust like a mortgage.

A *quitclaim deed* is used to transfer whatever interest the maker of the deed may have in a particular parcel of land. A quitclaim deed is often given to clear the title when the grantor's interest in a property is questionable. By accepting such a deed, the buyer assumes all the risks. Such a deed makes no warranties as to the title but simply transfers to the buyer whatever interest the grantor has.

A *special warranty deed* is a deed in which the grantor conveys title to the grantee and agrees to protect the grantee against title defects or claims asserted by the grantor and those persons whose right to assert a claim against the title arose during the period the grantor held title to the property. In a special warranty deed the grantor guarantees to the grantee that he has done nothing during the time that he held title to the property that has or might at some point in the future impair the grantee's title.

Promissory Note

The *promissory note* is a document used to outline the terms and conditions under which a lender has agreed to loan money. Whether the lender is a mortgage company, a bank, or the seller makes no difference. All three will require that a promissory note be fully executed. Notes may be either secured or unsecured. If the note is secured, that means there is something tangible being held as collateral. Most of the time, the collateral given is the property or item against which the note is made. So in the case of real estate, the collateral is most likely the property for which the note is being made. This does not have to be the case, however. It could be anything else the borrower has that may be of some worth or value to the seller. It could be a boat, a car, or another rental property owned by the borrower. If the note is unsecured, this means that there is no collateral being used to secure the note. The seller or lender is accepting on good faith that the borrower will have the ability to repay the loan. Usually, this good faith is supported by the borrower's proven credit history, having demonstrated in the past the ability to repay. The promissory note also contains provisions for the repayment terms that are specified in the note. These include the amount of the loan, the interest rate, the amortization or repayment period, and any prepayment penalties that may be imposed. In addition, the note may contain an acceleration clause that would necessitate the note being repaid immediately should certain conditions arise. Finally, other lender requirements that also may be included in the note are escrow conditions for taxes and insurance, minimum insurance amounts, the standard of care for property condition, a due-on-sale clause, and default provisions.

In summary, by studying and fully understanding all pertinent closing documents, you will be better prepared to ensure that the closing for the rental property you are purchasing will go smoothly. For the most part, you can have confidence in the expertise of the individuals who are preparing all the related forms, but you also must keep in mind that these individuals are human and that the possibility of making errors exists. Protect your interests by carefully reviewing all the closing documents. Doing so potentially could save you thousands of dollars.

That this nation, under God, shall have a new birth of freedom, and that government of the people, by the people, for the people, shall not perish from the earth.

—ABRAHAM LINCOLN

SECTION 2

How to Manage Rental Properties the Smart Way

7

How to Find, Qualify, and Keep Good Tenants

In Section 1 we discussed many of the various methods used to locate, select, and purchase rental property. The process of buying rental property is one that requires a degree of creativity, ingenuity, and objectivity. It challenges one's intellect to find and discover ways to utilize the necessary analytical skills required to determine the viability of an investment property. The process is largely objective in that predetermined investment criteria have been established that the given returns on a property must meet. If the returns meet the investor's criteria, as well as all other conditions having been satisfied with respect to location, property condition, and financing, the property is purchased. On the other hand, if the returns fail to meet the investor's requirements, the opportunity is rejected.

The focus of Section 2 is the management of a rental property once an investor has located and purchased a property that satisfies his needs. Managing rental property is much different from purchasing it. Whereas buying rental property requires an *objective* approach, managing rental property requires a *subjective* approach. That is to say, the business of managing real estate is people-oriented, in which there are no hard and fast rules on which to base decisions. Although numerous general guidelines and tools exist that a manager can use to augment the decision-making process, the element of uncertainty is ever present when you work with people.

Some of you may enjoy working with other people, whereas others of you may prefer to work independently. I personally derive the most pleasure from analyzing, buying, and selling property. This is the nature of my personality. I am more of a goal-oriented and analytical type of person than a people type of person. This is not to say that I do not know how to communicate effectively with people but rather that I derive the most satisfaction from using my creative skills to put profitable deals together. While I may prefer to hire a professional manager to oversee my property, you, on the other hand, may prefer to manage your real estate and leave the analysis to individuals like me. Regardless of what your personal preference may be, the fact remains that someone who is qualified must be able to manage and communicate effectively with your tenants. Remember that your investment property was purchased with the intention of renting it out. The person or persons you lease to are your customers. Since the income from the property depends on the rents paid by your tenants, it is imperative that you learn to become proficient in managing them. To be a successful property manager, you also must be a successful people manager.

Although there are many different classifications of tenants, ranging from younger college students to middle-aged couples with growing families to retired seniors, there are two primary classifications with which you should concern yourself—good tenants and bad tenants. Don't confuse the use of these adjectives with the actual people, but rather apply them to the behavior of the tenants. Generally speaking, a *good* tenant is defined as one who pays the required deposit in advance, pays her rent on time each and every month, never calls to complain, takes excellent care of the premises, and lives in the rental property for 10 or more years. Actually, this description more accurately depicts the *ideal* tenant, not just a good one. Unlike the good tenant, the *bad* tenant can be characterized as one who makes excuses about the deposit, seldom pays her rent on time, complains about almost everything, damages the property, and moves after six months still owing three months of back rent.

As a property manager, there are several steps you can take to ensure that you attract and lease to good tenants. This chapter is devoted to finding, qualifying, and retaining good tenants. A word of caution is warranted to those of you who may be new at managing rental property: It is very easy to get overly excited about the prospect of leasing to the first person who comes along. This isn't to say that the first person who is ready to lease may not be the ideal tenant but rather to say that you must be patient and follow the steps outlined in this chapter so as to increase the probability that you are in fact leasing to a good tenant.

How to Find Good Tenants

Beginning investors who just purchased their first rental property may be wondering, " Okay, now that I own a rental house, whom do I lease it to?" Finding someone to lease your property is not as difficult as you may think. Some of the more cost-effective ways include using signs, advertising in newspaper classified ads and in rental guides, and implementing a referral system. Other methods that are somewhat more expensive but still affordable include using a service such as a tenant locator company. Numerous other marketing strategies can be used that require a larger budget and typically are reserved for property managers with 50 or more rental units in their portfolios. Since this book is directed more toward investors who maintain smaller rental property holdings, such strategies are not included here. The following box lists the strategies that will be addressed here.

How to Find Good Tenants

1. Signage
2. Classified ads
3. Referrals
4. Locator services

Signage

Using signs to advertise your rental property and to direct tenants toward it is literally one of the most cost-effective ways of getting it leased. Probably the least expensive way of doing this is to go to a hardware store and buy several of the generic "For Rent" or "For Lease" signs. Although you may be thinking that using signs such as these is stating the obvious, perhaps it is, but don't underestimate the power of these inexpensive little signs. You'd be surprised at how many inquiries they can produce. Market studies show that, on average, about half of all calls come from signs. I know this to be true from data collected from rental units, as well as in my company's new home communities. When Symphony Homes first began collecting market data from first-time visitors to one of our model homes, I was surprised to learn that over 40 percent of traffic came from our signs. In fact, I was so surprised that I instructed our sales staff to probe deeper when polling visitors. For example, if the client stated that he saw one of our many signs when asked how he heard about us, the staff member would respond by saying something like, "That's wonderful! Where else have you seen our ads?" Often the client would say, "Well, I really can't remember seeing any specific ads, but I did see your signs on my way to the grocery store." The bottom line, therefore, is to use the signs.

I recommend placing a minimum of one sign, and possibly as many as two or three, in the yard of the property, depending on the size of the lot and whether or not the house is situated on a corner. The sign should have a blank space on it large enough to accommodate your contact information. All that is needed to write the information on the sign is a large marker so that the telephone number will be clearly visible from the road. If the sign is in the yard, all it needs to say is "For Rent" and have the telephone number listed on it. Off to the side or at the top you may list the number of bedrooms, but don't try to put any more information on the sign than this. I have seen some professionally made real estate signs that were the standard 18 by 24 inches with more writing on them than a driver passing by could ever hope to read. All this excess writing just creates "noise" on the sign and clutters it up. By providing only the basic information on the sign, you are giving people a reason to call.

I suggest that you also buy a few extra signs and place them at the nearest cross street, especially if your rental property is off the beaten path. Be creative, and look for opportunities to increase the visibility of your rental house. If there are major intersections nearby, these can be especially effective places to locate signs because of the higher traffic counts typically prevalent there. By way of comparison, the traffic count immediately in front of your rental property may not be more than 50 to 100 cars per day, if that. In contrast, the traffic count at a nearby intersection may be anywhere from 10,000 to 100,000 cars per day. It only takes one person out of all those passing by to call the number on your sign and lease your rental property. Finally, signs can be used as directionals to show prospective tenants the way to your property by placing them at various strategic locations. You can either draw arrows on them with a marker or purchase arrow-shaped vinyl stickers or labels.

As your real estate portfolio grows, you may want to consider spending a little more money on signage. Corrugated plastic signs can be professionally designed and printed for a relatively low cost per unit provided that you order a large enough minimum quantity. Usually all it takes to get the cost per unit low enough to make it worthwhile is 40 to 50 signs. The signs have to be generic enough to be used across multiple applications, meaning that each sign must contain the same basic information so that it can be used at any of your rental properties. If your real estate investment company has grown to the point where you have given it a name and perhaps formed a legal entity such as a limited-liability corporation (LLC), I suggest listing the company name, "For Rent" or "For Lease," and a telephone number, such as illustrated in the following box. Notice also how the reverse print helps the information to jump off the sign.

> # SYMPHONY HOMES
> # FOR LEASE
> # (810) 658-3600

Classified Ads

Classified ads are another terrific way to advertise rental properties. Classifieds are often one of the first places people check when looking for a place to rent. Small local newspapers tend to be more effective than large metropolitan papers. They are usually much less expensive, too. Depending on the size of the paper, the classified section may further be subcategorized by area or region. A large metropolitan area may, for example, have sections such as "South," "Southeast," "Southwest," and so on. Classified ads also should be written in such a way that the message is crisp and concise. Besides reducing excessive verbiage, a succinctly written ad will save you money because newspapers typically charge either by the word or by the line. In addition, every rental property ad should include four primary pieces of information—location, price, size, and a contact number. Although including this information will reduce the number of calls you receive, it will increase the quality of incoming calls by prequalifying the prospective tenants.

The first thing renters want to know is the location of the rental property. If it's not in the right area of town, they usually won't be interested in renting, regardless of the property's price or size. The location must fit the tenant's needs. In large newspapers that categorize their ads by areas using generalized headings such as "Southeast," you may need to describe the location more fully. For example, "Southeast" in the *Houston Chronicle* encompasses several cities, including Clear Lake, Deer Park, La Porte, and Pasadena, to name a few. Since a prospective tenant interested in the Deer Park area likely would not even consider living in Clear Lake, it's essential to include "Deer Park" in the ad. The location can be narrowed further by stating its proximity to anything that is significant to the area, such as a major employer, a beach, or anything else that may enhance the desirability of the neighborhood. In the example using Deer Park, since the area is known to have an excellent public school system, it would be helpful to include a description such as "Only five minutes from Deer Park schools." When preparing your ad, you must take into consideration the target market for your rental property. For example, advertising that the property is close to the schools is great if you have a three-bedroom house for rent because your target market is likely to be a family with children. On the other hand, if you are leasing a small, one-bedroom efficiency unit, the target market is more likely to be a single man or woman or perhaps a couple with no children. Advertising that the schools are nearby is irrelevant in this case. It would be better to include something like "Seven minutes from the Shell Oil Refinery" because the refinery is a major employer in that area. In short, including a location designed with your target market in mind is the first essential component of a well-written classified ad.

The second item to incorporate into your ad is the price of the rental unit. People want to know how much something costs before wasting their time calling or driving across town. If the price is excluded from the ad, readers are likely to skip over it, assuming that the unit must be too expensive, and go right on to the next ad that does include the price. Furthermore, prospective tenants can prequalify themselves quickly and easily by knowing in advance how much the property is renting for. If it is being advertised for $875, for example, and the tenant can only afford $650, he won't even bother to call you because he knows that it's out of his price range. So, by including the price in the ad, you will save time by eliminating calls from prospects who cannot afford to rent your property and at the same time generate more qualified leads from individuals who can afford to rent your property.

The third essential element of a well-written classified ad is size. The size of the rental property will help to define your target market. Size does not necessarily refer to total square feet available, although it can. People are more interested in knowing about size at it relates to the functionality of the property. For example, they primarily want to know how many bedrooms it has. Secondary considerations are the number of bathrooms or perhaps if there is a garage. An ad that includes a description such as "Spacious three-bedroom, two-bath, two-car garage house" is likely to appeal to a different target market than one advertising a one-bedroom efficiency unit, for example. The three-bedroom house is more likely to attract families with children, whereas the one-bedroom is more likely to attract singles or couples or perhaps retired seniors. A one-bedroom efficiency also would be very appealing to college students, especially if it is a close distance to the university, because many of them may walk or bike to school. Thus, by including this third essential element of a classified ad, you are further increasing the quality of calls you receive to just prospective tenants who are truly qualified to lease your rental property.

The fourth essential element of a well-written classified ad is your contact information. I recommend making yourself as accessible as possible. If you have a mobile phone, for example, that you use regularly, it is a good idea to use that number, provided that you can take calls on it throughout the day or that you can at least check the voice-mail messages periodically. When people want information about something, they usually want it now. If a telephone number is provided that you can only check after hours, for example, the prospective tenant may have already leased another property similar to yours in which the owner was readily available. If you don't have a mobile phone or another number, such as an office telephone, to answer throughout the day, then it is best to include information in the ad specifying when to call. For example, the ad might read "Call (888) 555-1234 from 5 to 9 P.M." This additional information helps to clarify for the prospective tenant that you are not available during the day and that it is best to call during the evening hours. Otherwise, the tenant may call during the morning and leave a message and by that afternoon wonder why no one has returned her call. Therefore, remember when including this fourth essential element of a classified ad to make yourself as accessible as possible so as to maximize the opportunity to lease your rental property.

Referrals

Implementing a tenant referral system is yet another way of locating potential renters. Although building a network of referrals takes time, it can pay handsome dividends for investors willing to devote themselves to doing so. The quality of prospective tenants produced by such a system is also likely to be more consistent with the types of renters you are looking for because they will come from people you already know and associate with. We've all done business by referral at one time or another. You may have asked your neighbor, for example, if she could recommend a good pediatrician for your children, or you may have asked a business associate if he knows a reputable painter. The objective now is to get people to recommend you if they know of someone looking for a place to rent. Admittedly, if you only own one or two rent houses and it is fairly easy to keep them rented, building a referral system may not be for you. However, if you're thinking ahead and are planning to build a large portfolio of rental properties, then creating a referral system is an excellent way to generate tenant leads.

When implementing a referral program, people to involve in your network include just about everyone you know. A referral network should include family, friends, neighbors, business associates, coworkers, students, doctors, dentists, and just about anyone else you can think of. It also can include existing tenants and prior tenants. This is especially true if you have a small multiple-unit property, such as a duplex, triplex, or fourplex. If a unit becomes vacant, an existing tenant may very well know someone who is looking for a place to live. Furthermore, if you know that one of the units will become available soon because a tenant is moving, it's best to let the other tenants in the building know as soon as possible so that they can begin looking, too.

To create your network system, simply begin by telling people about your rental business and asking them to refer anyone they know to you who may be looking for a house to rent. You may want to offer to pay a small referral fee of $50 to $100 to individuals who refer a tenant to you to whom in turn you lease a rental property. The referral fee paid will be more than made up by reducing your vacancy loss. The longer a rental property sits empty, the more money it costs you due to lost revenues. At Symphony Homes, we have a generous referral program that offers individuals referring clients to us a $500 cash reward, as illustrated in Exhibit 7-1. The primary qualifying condition is that the client referred to us must purchase a home. Although on the surface this seems self-evident, we've actually had clients referred to us by one of their family members who thought they could turn around and collect $500 from us just for giving us the name and with no real intention of purchasing a new home. Our referral program is promoted widely using various methods. For example, it is mentioned in almost all our display ads in print, it is publicized on our Web site, and we have special brochures that describe the program. In addition, the following short, concise message is included in the footer of all fax memos and letters and is printed directly in the body of checks being sent for payment to our trades and vendors. The message reads

> **$500 Cash Reward for Referrals!!!**
> **Log on to *www.symphony-homes.com* for details!!!**

By sending memos, letters, or payments with a message such as this on it month after month, the idea eventually will take root and begin to bear fruit for you. I encourage you to take advantage of this relatively simple yet cost-effective approach to generating leads for your rental business. It's easy enough to do, costs very little, and can produce great results.

Locator Services

Although more expensive than the advertising methods mentioned thus far, an apartment locator service can be another great way to find tenants. Locator companies provide services for practically any kind of residential rental unit, so just because it may be called an apartment locator company does not mean that the company provides services exclusively for apartment owners. Locator service companies can be found easily by looking in the Yellow Pages of your local telephone directory under such headings as "Real Estate Services" and "Rental Agencies."

Rental agencies work first by representing multiple owners whose properties are vacant or may soon become vacant and then by providing this information to prospective tenants with a consolidated list of available rental units in a given area. The renter specifies the type of dwelling desired, such as a house or apartment, and other particulars, such as the number of bedrooms and bathrooms required. The renter also specifies the location and price range of the unit desired. The rental agency then performs a search in its database of all available properties that meet the tenant's requirements and provides him with the list of available properties from which to choose. The service saves the tenant the hassle of culling through newspaper ads and other publications to find a place to rent.

Exhibit 7-1   The Symphony Homes cash reward for referrals brochure

Since locator services earn their fees from the owners who use them, excluded from the consolidated list of available units are all owners who do not participate with the rental agency. Locator service fees typically are about a half month's rent but can range anywhere from one week's to one

month's rent. Depending on the price range of your rental property, this may represent a good value relative to the cost of other forms of advertising, such as a classified ad, or it may represent a poor value. One primary advantage to using a rental agency, however, is that the fees assessed are based most often on whether or not the company actually provides a tenant to whom you lease. In other words, if the agency does not send a tenant to whom you in turn lease to, then there is no charge. On the other hand, if the agency sends a prospective tenant to whom you end up leasing, then the company assesses the agreed-on fee.

Overall, rental agencies provide tenants with a service that as a property owner you can choose to participate in or not participate in. Using the service provides your rental property with greater market exposure and, in areas where vacancy rates tend to be high, could make the difference between a negative annual cash flow and a positive one. If you only accept a term of one year on your lease agreements, then the cost of using a locator service is low relative to the property's turnover ratio. On the other hand, if you accept month-to-month lease agreements or even six-month lease agreements, then the cost of using a locator service may be too high relative to the property's turnover ratio.

How to Qualify Good Tenants

Once you've put your advertising mechanisms into place, the next step is to be prepared to screen and quality prospective tenants who call and eventually apply to lease your property. In this section we examine several of the most common ways property owners protect themselves against deadbeat tenants. They include requiring the tenant to fill out an application and to provide references, as well as submitting potential tenants' personal information to screening services such as credit bureaus, doing background checks, and searching databases for rental history.

Rental Applications

All the requisite information for tenant screening can be collected on the rental application. Separate applications should be filled for each applicant who is over the age of 18 years because their information will be verified independently of a spouse or roommate. Any prospective tenant who may be interested in leasing from you should be given an application to fill out regardless of whether or not your first impression of them tells you otherwise. Protect yourself against charges based on any type of discrimination by making the application available to anyone who desires to fill one out. This doesn't mean that you have to lease to them, of course. Such decisions can be made after verifying the information they have provided to you. One way to reduce the number of applications received is by charging a nominal application fee of $25 or so. Only tenants who are sincerely interested in leasing will spend the required fee for the application. The money collected also will help to offset expenses related to screening services and background checks. A good rental application will provide sections for applicants to include information about themselves, any additional occupants, their rental and employment histories, sources of income, credit information, and references.

Applicant. This section of the application is used to collect basic information such as the tenant's name and telephone number. In addition, standard identifying data such as a driver's license number and Social Security Number should be required. Other information that may be useful is the make and model of any vehicles the prospective tenant owns, as well as their respective license plate numbers.

Additional Occupants. This section of the application should be used to list anyone else who will be living in the rental property with the primary tenant. It should include husbands, wives, children, roommates, or any other relatives such as aunts, uncles, and in-laws.

Rental History. The prospective tenant's current address and the name of the property owner or manager should be listed in this section of the application. You also will need the manager's phone number to verify the applicant's information. In addition to the current residence, the applicant also should provide a previous address, along with the manager's name and contact information. This section of the form is especially important because it will provide a recent history of the tenant's payment patterns.

Employment. This section is used to ascertain information about the applicant's current employment. The tenant should provide the name, address, and telephone number of her current employer. In addition, she should provide information about how long she has been employed, as well as information about her monthly income. All other sources of income, such as alimony or child support, also should be listed here. It is important to verify this information directly with the employer because you want to be sure that the tenant can afford the monthly rent. If what's reported on the application does not match up with what the employer tells you, chances are that the applicant will not qualify, and you're probably better off rejecting him.

Credit and Bank References. This section is used to collect information about the applicant's creditworthiness. The prospective tenant should list all major credit cards and account information, as well as outstanding balances owed. Other financial data, such as checking and savings accounts, money market accounts, retirement accounts, and investment accounts, also should be listed. This information will provide you with a better picture of the overall financial strength of the applicant. The application also should contain a clause authorizing the property owner to obtain a credit report to verify the information provided in this section. The tenant's name, Social Security number, and address will be needed to obtain his or her credit history. Credit reporting information can be obtained readily through most apartment and rental property associations. Services that provide background checks revealing any criminal history or convictions are also widely available. If you are unable to find these services locally, many companies provide them nationally via the Internet. Try doing a search using key words such as *tenant screening, background checks, landlord services,* or *credit reports.* You'll be surprised at how many companies there are that offer these services over the Internet. Many companies allow you to enter the applicant's personal information over their secure servers to obtain a full credit history. This can all be done in just a few minutes for a very nominal fee, often less than $10.

Personal References. This section is used to list any personal references the applicant may wish to provide. The references should be individuals who know the applicant personally and can vouch for their character. They can include family members or relatives, acquaintances or business associates, bishops or pastors, or anyone else the applicant may wish to use. A minimum of three references should be listed.

Signature and Date. All rental or lease applications should provide a place for the prospective tenant to sign and date the form. In addition, the application should include language that states that by signing and dating the form, the applicant is granting legal permission to the owner to verify all the information contained in it.

How to Keep Good Tenants

Studies show that the cost to keep or retain customers is only about one-fifth the cost of replacing them. Replacing customers as it relates to rental properties means replacing tenants. As tenant turnover rises, operating expenses, of necessity, will rise with them due to increases in advertising, cleaning, and all other costs associated with "make readies." Conversely, revenues will decrease due to increases in vacancies. The result is a net adverse change in profitability. If a property owner can enhance the overall profitability of her rental units by keeping the customers she already has, then one could logically conclude that it makes sense to build customer retention into the framework for developing the very core of a sound business strategy. Positive changes in tenant retention are correlated directly with positive changes in service and value, whether they are real or perceived. The remainder of this chapter is devoted to three actions you can take to improve tenant retention immediately. By implementing the principles outlined in the following box, your real estate investment company is certain to enjoy a higher level of profitability.

How to Keep Good Tenants

1. The Golden Rule
2. Visibility adds value
3. Concentric circles

The Golden Rule

About 2000 years ago, Jesus taught as recorded in the Bible in the book of Matthew, what is now known as "The Golden Rule." This discerning utterance is an expression of love and respect for others. Paraphrasing, the Golden Rule states plainly that we should do unto others as we would have them do unto us. Although simplistic in structure, the Golden Rule is profound in meaning. Adherence to this precept necessitates that we merely think about how we would like to be treated in a given situation and that we, in turn, apply that same course of action to others. If we want to be treated with kindness and respect, then we must first be willing to treat others the same way. In his ministry, Jesus manifested this principle through numerous acts of love and compassion, even healing the sick and infirm and washing his disciples' feet. Jesus led an exemplary life of service devoted to his followers.

Okay, so what does the Golden Rule have to do with managing rental property and does this mean you have to wash your tenants' feet? First, the Golden Rule has everything to do with managing rental property, that is, if you wish to be successful in this business. I have seen all too often investors come and go because they failed to adhere to this simple principle. Perhaps they read a book or bought some tapes about investing in real estate, got excited and purchased their first property, and then failed miserably at managing it because they were ill prepared to deal with the people aspect of the business, that is, the business of managing people. The key to dealing effectively with tenants is simply to treat them just as you would like to be treated. How does it make you feel when another person of authority is impolite and disrespectful to you or has a demeaning air about them? Not very good, I'm sure. Let's say, for example, that you shopped week after week at a particular grocery store that got progressively busier, and with the increase in business, you began to notice a decrease in service. As a regular patron, you could respond in one of three ways: You could approach the store manager and register a complaint, you could continue shopping without saying anything, or you could demonstrate your dissatisfaction by taking your business elsewhere—which is exactly what many people do. No business is immune to the silent majority who vote with their feet, especially a business that ignores the precepts set forth in the Golden Rule. As the owner, manager, or landlord, you are not above your tenants, but rather you are beside them. You are their equal and just happen to be on the other side of the equation. You are the owner, and they are the tenants. More important, they are your customers. If anything, you should be going out of your way to be of service to them. Does this mean you may have to work a little harder? Perhaps. But if it is your intent to reduce turnover and increase profits, then you are likely to be working smarter rather than harder.

Now, for the second question: Does this mean that you have to wash your tenants' feet? The answer is both yes and no. It is yes in a figurative sense and no in a literal sense. Figuratively speaking, as the owner, you have an obligation to provide your tenant with a minimum standard of care and then some. This implies that in addition to providing tenants with the bare minimum of having just a roof over their heads, you should make sure that the roof doesn't leak. Unless you want to be known as a slumlord, then take pride in each and every one of your rental properties by keeping them in good repair and looking nice. Your tenants will appreciate it, and in the long run, you'll come out ahead. Your turnover will be lower, your profits will be higher, and your tenants' feet will be cleaner.

Visibility Adds Value

In their remarkably insightful book entitled *The Resident Retention Revolution,* published by the Institute of Real Estate Management in 1994, authors Laurence and Kathleen Harmon apply traditional customer service strategies to the apartment industry to help owners and property managers to improve their own operations. After recounting some of the more common business practices used in operating apartment buildings, the authors describe the impact of retail service strategies on the multifamily industry as follows:

How to Manage Rental Properties the Smart Way

Apartment properties traditionally have been operated in the same manner as fast-food restaurants, dry cleaners, and tanning booths—the longer a company is in business, the less attention it pays to its customers. The natural propensity of any company engaged in any enterprise is to turn inward and, in introspection, to isolate itself from its clients. Imperceptibly, its operations are arranged to cater to the owners, managers, and employees—its so-called internal customers—at the expense of its external patrons, the people who buy the products and thereby pay the staff's salaries and keep the companies afloat. As a result, the customer relations process becomes impersonal, aloof, and mechanized. Rules and regulations, policies and procedures, standards and forms are prepared, interpreted, and revised so that the company comes first, the customer last. From signs in convenience stores blaring "No Shoes, No Shirt, No Service" to lease provisions that proscribe, prohibit, and punish, companies establish—and then nourish—adversarial, potentially confrontational, and probably unpleasant relationships with their customers. Fortunately, as is the case with conquest marketing, retailers have developed a collection of customer friendly approaches that can be productively transported to the apartment management business.

One of the so-called customer friendly approaches the authors refer to is known as the *element of visibility.* To be visible means to be seen. There are many routine tasks that occur behind the scenes on a daily basis of which tenants often are unaware. What the Harmons propose is to make those tasks more visible to the customers, or tenants, so that they gain a greater appreciation for the level of service they receive. If, for example, the owner or manager is responsible for maintaining the grounds, have that work performed at a time when it is the most visible to the tenants if possible. If the gardener trims the hedges during the day, chances are the tenants won't even notice when they return from work. If, on the other hand, the gardener is seen busily trimming the hedges as the tenants return, they can more fully appreciate the service that is being provided to them.

An important point to note here is that although the *actual* level of service has not changed, the *perceived* level of service is greatly improved and thereby adds value. While visibility refers to *what* can be seen, perception is the *way* something is seen. I often think of my one-year-old son, Benjamin, and the world he lives in. From his perspective, I must look like the giant—Goliath from the story in the Bible. He lives in a world where everything within his reach is only one to two feet above the floor. Little Ben doesn't seem to mind, though, because he is perfectly content to play in the kitchen, bathroom, and living room cabinets. He pulls out pots and pans, shampoo and toilet paper, books and toys and just about anything else he can get his hands on. By the time he's done, it looks like a cyclone has blown through. When I think about Ben in his tiny world, he really doesn't seem to mind being a little guy. In fact, it's a safe bet to say that he's just as content to play with pots and pans as anything else. Although Ben's perception of life is much different from yours or mine, his perception will change with corresponding changes in what becomes visible to him. This concept applies equally to changes in what becomes visible to your tenants. Give them the opportunity to actually see the service they are receiving, and their perception of it is certain to improve. According to the Harmons, visibility is a key element in any service-oriented business. They assert

Making service visible is nearly as important as providing it at all. Consider the array of ethnic restaurants that perform the entire food preparation and cooking procedure at the diner's table—and then charge a premium price for the experience—or expensive car wash operations that allow the patron to see the entire process, from high-powered washing through sudsing and finally waxing. How about bakeries that publicly feature their employees' cake decorating skills? The examples are numerous, and the lesson is clear: Visible service is valuable service. Visibility becomes part of the product "bundle" and thereby is entitled to pricing consideration in addition to—and separate from—the goods themselves.

Apartment managers have a host of opportunities to let their residents know they are being served. For instance, grounds cleaning, lawn mowing, and window washing can be scheduled at times when residents are leaving for or returning home from work. Straightening the mailbox area at the end of the day also makes it apparent that this work is being done. Even though these tasks are ordinary, people generally are not aware that they are being handled until, for some reason, they are not done. The wise property manager will strategize ways to make even routine tasks visible to residents.

Concentric Circles

If you were to stand at the edge of a lake and toss a pebble into the water, it would first make a small "plop" and then sink quickly beneath the surface, hidden from the human eye. What remains clearly visible, however, is a ripple effect that starts where the pebble first made its entry and then quietly disseminates in an outwardly circular pattern. This pattern creates what is known as *concentric circles*. Concentric circles such as these share a common base or point of origination and grow progressively larger as they move outward. In *The Resident Retention Revolution,* authors Laurence and Kathleen Harmon introduce a marketing model based on the principle of concentric circles as taught by Harvard Professor Theodore Levitt. In *The Marketing Imagination,* Professor Levitt describes a marketing model consisting of four levels of qualities that customers expect all products or services to have. He classifies these four levels as generic, expected, augmented, and potential. Each level progresses in the degree of service or amount of quality of the product provided while building on a common base or center, hence the name *concentric circles*.

The first ring of the concentric circles is known as the *generic* product or level and represents the inner circle, the point of origination, on which all others build. It is the product or service in its most basic and elementary form. It is the minimal item or service that a company is providing and that a customer can expect. For a bakery, it is the bread. For a gas station, it is the gas. For a hair salon, it is a haircut. For a rental property company, it is four walls and a roof. The generic level is the minimum level of a product or service required for a company to be in business.

The second ring of the concentric circles is referred to as the *expected* product or service and represents additional products or services bundled with the base product to enhance its perceived value. The Harmons assert:

> This naturally results in a higher price for the improved goods, as well as greater customer satisfaction, product loyalty, and splendid word-of-mouth. The expected product might be termed support because it includes whatever the organization does to make the basic product more reliable, accessible, usable, enjoyable, convenient, dependable, accurate, or useful.

Applying Levitt's marketing model to rental properties, the expected level of service would include more than the generic four walls and a roof. For instance, tenants *expect* to have readily available access to the owner or property manager in the event of an emergency. Such emergencies might include a furnace in disrepair resulting in a total loss of heat in the middle of winter or perhaps a main sewer line becoming obstructed, resulting in the inability to use any of the toilet or bath facilities. If the property is a multifamily complex, tenants also might expect certain other basic services, such as access to a common laundry facility or adequate parking for themselves as well as guests.

The third ring of the concentric circles is known as the *augmented* product or service. The augmented product or service offers yet another level of benefits bundled with the goods and services and typically exceeds what a customer normally would expect. The Harmons affirm:

> The augmented product becomes "aspirational"—what buyers would really prefer among the competition, assuming that real or anticipated impediments (for example, high price or limited availability) could be overcome. Certain automobiles, vacation locales, and brands of jewelry—How about Lexus, Gstaad, Rolex?— are readily identifiable as leaders among augmented products. They are presumed to be peerless, supreme, incomparable. Whether or not they are the most expensive—and some augmented products are not—prospective customers consider them to be the *ultimate* acquisition of their type; their proud owners believe they enjoy a *relationship* with such products and the people who sold them.

Once again, if Levitt's model is applied to the rental property business, the augmented level of service would include more than both the generic and the expected levels of service. For instance, the augmented level of service for tenants might include a guaranteed call-back time of, let's say, 10 minutes, for any problems that might arise and not just for emergency situations. This higher level of service can be used as a selling point to prospective tenants to assure them that their comfort and well-being are priorities. For tenants living in multifamily properties, augmented services might include access not only to a laundry facility but also to a staff who provides the cleaning service for them or perhaps not only ample parking but also a valet service that parks the cars for them. It is important to note that this additional element of service can provide a tremendous return on the owner's invested capital. The cost of such services is minimal relative to the perceived higher value by tenants who enjoy the personal benefits and the prestige of having an augmented service level.

The fourth ring of the concentric circles is the outer ring and is referred to as the *potential* product or service. The potential product differs from the augmented product in that it represents everything that is not yet being done that could be. The Harmons suggest using the Levitt paradigm to engage in an activity referred to as *outer-circle thinking,* also known as *brainstorming.* The intent is to generate ideas among the staff or work associates to determine creative ways in which an elevated level of service can be offered to absolutely *delight* the customer and far surpass their expectations. Potential services often cost very little and are designed more to provide a personal level of service that contains a human element.

To illustrate the point, as a builder of new residential homes, I know that on the day they move in, our families are very busy unloading and unpacking. In many instances, they may not have a refrigerator yet and are likely to have only a little food on hand. Even if they do have plenty of food, on the day of the move, since they are likely to be too busy to cook a meal, one of our staff members personally delivers fresh, hot pizza to them. Talk about delighting the customer. The parents love it because they don't have to take time to stop and cook a meal, and the kids love it because they get to eat all the pizza they can. Our total cash outlay with food and drinks usually doesn't exceed more than $20. Considering that the client just purchased a brand-new $350,000 home from us, what's another twenty bucks?

The Harmons summarize the concept of outer-circle thinking with a quote from David Freemantle, an English expert on the subject. Freemantle maintains the following:

> One of the most exciting aspects of customer service . . . is to discover innovative little ways of pleasing the customer even more. This can be a real test for any progressive customer caring company. The provision of unsolicited little extras is a creative and challenging opportunity all staff can enthusiastically respond to. It enables people to be themselves in a way that is pleasing to the customer. It enables staff to put themselves out for the customer.

In summary, remember that the cost to keep or retain customers is a small fraction of the cost of replacing them. Positive changes in tenant retention are correlated directly with positive changes in service and value, whether they are real or perceived. By implementing the three principles discussed in this chapter—the Golden Rule, increasing visibility, and concentric circles—your real estate investment company is certain to enjoy a greater level of success, as well as a greater level of personal satisfaction.

How to Find, Qualify, and Keep Good Tenants

The credit belongs to the man who is actually in the arena; whose face is marred by dust and sweat and blood; who strives valiantly; who errs and comes short again and again; who knows the great enthusiasms, the great devotions, and spends himself in a worthy cause; who at the best knows in the end the triumph of high achievement; and who at the worst, if he fails, at least fails while daring greatly.

—THEODORE ROOSEVELT

8

Lease Agreements for the Smart Investor

As a real estate investor in the business of managing rental properties, you should have a carefully drafted residential lease agreement signed by your tenants each and every time you rent or lease your property. A written lease agreement sets forth the obligations of both the owner and the tenant and establishes the contractual basis that forms your legal relationship. The agreement is used to outline the specific duties and responsibilities to be performed by both you and your tenant.

There are essentially two types of agreements—a month-to-month rental agreement and a fixed-term lease agreement. The primary difference between the two is the period of time being rented or leased. In a month-to-month rental agreement, the duration or period is established as a single month, after which the agreement renews automatically, or monthly. The short-term nature of this type of agreement lends itself to markets where tenants are unwilling to rent for longer periods of time. It also may be, perhaps, that the property is in a very tight rental market where the occupancy rate is high, thus placing upward pressure on rates, and the owner does not want a long-term lease so as to take advantage of price increases. The primary advantage to the owner using a month-to-month agreement is that he or she is not locked into anything on a long-term basis, thereby giving him or her greater flexibility to increase rents or to sell the property if he or she so desires. The disadvantage is that the owner may experience higher turnover as a result of the shorter term.

A fixed-term lease agreement, conversely, covers a longer duration of time, usually lasting no less than 6 months and often 12 months or more. The long-term nature of this type of agreement lends itself to markets where tenants are willing to lease for longer periods of time and desire a more secure living arrangement. This type of rental market tends to be more stable and is not subject to significant rate increases in the short term. The primary advantage to an owner using a lease agreement is that he is likely to experience lower turnover as a result of the longer term. The disadvantage to the owner is that he is locked into a long-term lease, thus decreasing his flexibility to raise rents or to sell the property if he so desires.

Although there are just about as many lease agreements as there are investors, most of them share all the basic components needed to make an agreement binding. Where they differ, however, is in their length and complexity. While some lease agreements are relatively brief and cover only the basics, others are extremely comprehensive and try to cover almost every conceivable situation that could arise. One logically could conclude that the more thorough the agreement, the more protection is afforded the owner. Although this may be true in general, no lease agreement is airtight. Drawing on my own experience, I'm of the opinion that more is better. It is better to identify contractually the obligations and responsibilities of both the owner and the tenant ahead of time rather than to leave the interpretation of a lease agreement to the courts in the event of a dispute.

Following is a discussion of some of the primary components of a residential lease agreement While it is fairly thorough, by no means should it be considered exhaustive. Keep in mind that many laws governing tenancy vary from state to state, so what may be applicable in one state may not be in another. Be sure to check with your attorney regarding any laws that may be particular to your state or area.

Residential Lease Agreement

1. Parties. All adults who will be living in the dwelling should be required to sign your lease agreement. When two or more adults sign a lease agreement, they become cotenants and, as such, are both responsible for all obligations set forth in the agreement. The lease agreement furthermore should contain specific language stating the cotenants are "jointly and severally liable." This clause affords the owner an added measure of protection in that he now has the option to hold all the adults who have signed the lease agreement jointly liable, as well as individually liable, for the payment of rent, damages, late fees, and all other obligations set forth in the agreement. If, for example, one tenant moves out and cannot be located, the owner has the legal right to hold the remaining tenant responsible for any uncollected rents or charges that may be due.

2. Property Address. The property address is the location of the dwelling the tenant will be leasing and should include the physical street address, as well as any apartment or unit number, if applicable, along with the city, state, and zip code. It's also a good idea to include in this section any additional property that the tenant may be leasing, such as a storage locker or other type of storage facility, a boat slip, any furniture if the premises are furnished, or anything else that you may deem appropriate. Being specific in this section will help to alleviate any disputes that may arise regarding what is included and what isn't included in the lease agreement.

3. Limits on Use and Occupancy. This section is used expressly to establish who may occupy the dwelling. If the dwelling is a "single-family dwelling," it should be limited to one family, unless the owner agrees otherwise. All adults living there, along with their children, should be clearly listed in the agreement. Adults usually are limited to one or two parents in the case of a family with children but may include an occasional relative. Other tenants may include a group of friends who are rooming together, but once again, this should be identified clearly in the lease agreement. This section is used to protect the owner from a revolving-door policy or, worse yet, an open-door policy in which two or three families occupy the dwelling at any given time. More people means more wear and tear on the property. Almost everyone has guests or relatives come into town occasionally, and this is perfectly acceptable. The occupancy section contains a provision for this that allows guests to stay up to a predetermined number of days established at the time of signing. This prevents tenants from taking advantage of the owner by stating that their friend or relative, who happened to move in three months ago, is only a temporary guest. The occupancy section also provides for a daily rate that can be applied in the event someone does appear to be staying on an ongoing basis. In one apartment building I used to own, I had one manager in particular who knew every single tenant, as well as all their children. If she noticed an extra adult or two who appeared to be coming and going on a daily basis, as if to work, she promptly charged the tenant the extra daily rate. Even at $5 a day, this added an extra $150 to the monthly rent on that particular unit. The tenants didn't mind. After all, where else can you stay for only $5 a day?

4. Term of Lease. This section is used to stipulate the period of time the tenancy is to remain in force. If the month-to-month option is selected, then the tenancy begins on the day specified in the agreement and will continue thereafter until either party gives the other the required notice, as embodied in the agreement. If the fixed-term option is selected, then the tenancy begins on the day specified and will continue for a fixed period thereafter, usually no less than six months. The agreement also stipulates that the tenant is responsible for all rent due for the entire lease period even if he vacates the dwelling prematurely.

5. Payment of Rent. This section is used to denote all the terms and conditions having to do with the timely payment of rent. The amount of the rent is clearly specified and is done so in monthly amounts, since this is how it will be paid. In addition, the agreement states that rent is due and payable in advance on the first day of each month, as well as what forms of payment are acceptable, who the payment should be made to, and where the payment should be delivered. Finally, this section is used to establish that the tenant's rights as related to the agreement are predicated on the prompt and timely payment of rents as they become due.

6. Penalties. This part of the lease agreement is used to specify any penalties that will be imposed for failure to pay rents on time. Since section 5 states that rents are due and payable on the first day of the month, any rent payments made after that day are considered late, and a penalty is imposed as set forth in the agreement. Furthermore, additional penalties are applied for each and every day the rent remains unpaid. The inclusion of additional penalties is very important. Otherwise, if a tenant was charged only a one-time late charge of $25, for example, then it wouldn't make any difference if he paid on the second day of the month or the fifteenth day of the month. It is better to protect yourself by giving the tenants a disincentive for paying late.

When I first got started in the rental business years ago, tenants who knew the ropes were able to take advantage of my youth and inexperience, and I therefore was subjected to all kinds of excuses about why they couldn't pay the rent on time. After I got the hang of things, however, I no longer tolerated their wildly imaginative excuses and became a strict enforcer of collecting the rents on the day they were due. One key element to keep in mind is the need to clarify from the very outset what your policy is. This is *not* the section to gloss over with tenants. You must make every effort from the beginning of the tenancy to manage the tenant's expectations. In other words, communicate clearly to them what you expect and when you expect it, and then be prepared to enforce it. Don't be surprised if some tenants put you to the test the first month or two. After they learn that you mean business, however, they usually come around. This doesn't mean that you have to be mean or ugly with the tenants but rather firm in your position and expectation of the timely payment of rent.

7. Deposit. The amount of the security deposit is stipulated in this section, along with what is required in order to be entitled to a refund. The amount of the deposit varies widely depending on such factors as the clientele being leased to and local market conditions. For example, it is not uncommon to see such signs as "No Deposit Required" posted outside many low-income apartment buildings. The majority of tenants renting low-income housing often live paycheck to paycheck and cannot afford any amount of deposit. On the other hand, deposits for middle- to upper-income housing often are a minimum of the equivalent of one month's rent and many times as much as two month's rent. Market conditions also may play a factor in determining how much of a deposit you are likely to get. I remember in the middle to late 1980s the glut of newly built apartment complexes in Houston. An easy money policy coupled with strong tax incentives led to an oversupply of housing that consequently pushed vacancy rates into the stratosphere. Not only were apartment owners not requiring any deposit, but they also were offering giveaways such as first-month free rent. Determining the proper amount of deposit to collect in your area is easy enough to do simply by calling to inquire about a few of the rental properties that are comparable to yours. It only takes a few phone calls to quickly learn the most appropriate amount of deposit to collect for a rental property in your area.

The deposit portion of the agreement also stipulates that in order to be entitled to a full refund of the security deposit, the tenant must leave the dwelling in the condition in which it was first leased. The owner is expressly granted the right to use the deposit to defray any costs resulting from negligence, damage, or failure to clean the dwelling. The agreement furthermore states that the tenant may not apply any part of the deposit to rent.

One final note regarding security deposits that you should be aware of pertains to purchasing a rental property that already has a tenant in it. As the new owner, you will be responsible for returning the tenant's deposit to her when she eventually vacates the premises. The time for you to collect that deposit is when you close on the property. You should receive a credit at closing equal to the amount of the deposit held by the seller. Of course, it's a good idea to have a copy of the existing lease between the seller and your soon-to-be tenant because this also will enable you to verify the amount of the deposit.

8. Assignment and Subletting. An *assignment* of a lease or rental agreement means that an individual would have the right to assign, or turn over, his or her obligations under the terms in the lease agreement to another person. It is important to include terminology that precludes tenants from having the right to assign their rights over to someone else without the owner's prior written consent. Just as the original tenant was required to fill out an application and to undergo the appropriate background checks, so should the new tenant assuming responsibility for the lease. This clause protects the owner by giving her the right to reject an assignment of the lease to a potentially undesirable tenant.

Subletting means that the original tenant can sublet, or lease, the dwelling or any portion thereof to another person. A college student who rents a three-bedroom house, for example, and is the sole tenant on the lease agreement containing no subletting clause potentially could invite two or more additional college students to rent rooms directly from him. This clause protects the owner by giving him the right to reject any and all subletting of the lease to a potentially undesirable tenant.

9. Utilities. This section stipulates who will be liable for the payment of any and all utility bills associated with the dwelling. Depending on the type of rental property, the tenant may be responsible for all the utilities or some portion thereof. If it is a single-family dwelling, chances are that the tenant will be responsible for all the utilities and pay for them directly. The agreement also contains a provision to list any utilities for which the owner will be responsible. Specifying who is liable for the utilities is important because it safeguards the interests of both the owner and the tenant.

10. Maintenance of Dwelling and Property. This section is included in the lease agreement to outline the responsibilities of the tenant with respect to repairs and maintenance of the property. The first provision in this section stipulates that the tenant will be liable for a predetermined amount or value of repairs. It states, "Tenant agrees to pay the first $_____ of all minor repairs and furthermore agrees to report promptly any and all major repairs." More than anything else, this clause will help to minimize the number of service calls the owner or his handyman will have to make for minor repairs.

The maintenance section of the agreement outlines an additional 12 provisions that require the tenant to maintain the dwelling by keeping it in good repair. Item number 12 in this section is one modification I added as a result of the thoughtless actions of a tenant. One day while I was doing a drive-by inspection of one of my rental properties, I noticed a large satellite dish attached to the roof. Closer inspection revealed that the dish had been bolted or nailed right into the roof and had punctured holes in it in the process. This is the kind of thing an owner just loves to see—holes made in the roof of a building by a brainless tenant. I promptly sent out a notice prohibiting the installation of any items such as this and added language to the lease agreement stating that the tenant expressly agrees "to not install antennae, satellite dishes, or any other attachments to the dwelling, including but not limited to the roof." I'm sure that over the course of years in your own experience you, too, will encounter similar occurrences and will find the need to modify your own lease agreement.

11. Entry and Inspection. This clause gives the owner the right to make periodic inspections of the property to ensure that it is being maintained in accordance with the agreement. Although notice is not required, the lease agreement stipulates that the inspections are to be made "during reasonable times." This would indicate that an owner cannot just show up in the middle of the night and expect access to the property to do a routine inspection. Most repairs and inspections are done during the normal workday and often while the tenant is away. Since the owner retains a set of keys to all the properties, she can gain access as needed, but again, while respecting the rights of her tenants by not barging in unsuspectingly in the middle of the night.

12. Right to Quiet Enjoyment. Your tenants are entitled to a right to quiet enjoyment, which means in part that as the landlord or owner, you have the responsibility of helping to maintain peace and order. If the residence is a single-family dwelling, this may be difficult to do because you are likely to have little control over what the neighbors may be doing except to assist by notifying the police, which is really something the tenants can do themselves. On the other hand, if you own apartments and some of the tenants are loud and obnoxious and are disturbing the other tenants, it is up to you or your manager to restore peace and order. The right to quiet enjoyment also stipulates that the tenants signing the lease agreement must abide by the same rules so that others may enjoy this right. Other violations of the right to quiet enjoyment include possessing or selling illegal drugs, creating a nuisance by interfering with others, drunken behavior, and the playing of loud music or broadcast programs.

13. Locks. This provision stipulates that the tenant has inspected the locks and agrees that they are in good working order and are sufficient for the protection of his or her property. It also specifies that the tenant will not change the locks without the owner's prior written permission. It's a good idea to keep the name and number of a locksmith handy who can rekey the locks each time a tenant moves out. Changing the locks is not very expensive to have done and will help to reduce the risk of unlawful entry by the previous tenant.

14. Possession. The section on possession addresses both the tenant's and the owner's obligations. It stipulates that after signing the lease agreement, if the tenant fails to take possession of the dwelling, she still can be held responsible for complying with all the terms and conditions outlined in the agreement, including the payment of rent. The owner has an obligation to deliver possession of the premises to the tenant, and if for any reason beyond his control he is not able to do so, then the owner's liability is limited to a refund of the tenant's deposit. The tenant, in turn, shall have the right to terminate the agreement.

15. Lead-Based Paint Disclosure. The Residential Lead-Based Paint Hazard Reduction Act, also known as *Title X,* was enacted in 1992 with the intent to reduce the hazards caused by lead-based paint, especially in houses built prior to 1978. The act requires owners to disclose any knowledge they possess relating to the presence of lead-based paint that may have been used in the dwelling to be rented. The act also requires that the following language be used to notify tenants of the dangers of lead-based paint:

> Housing built before 1978 may contain lead-based paint. Lead from paint, paint chips and dust can pose health hazards if not taken care of properly. Lead exposure is especially harmful to young children and pregnant women. Before renting or leasing dwellings built prior to 1978, landlords must disclose the presence of known lead-based paint and lead-based paint hazards in the dwelling. Tenants must also receive a federally approved pamphlet on lead poisoning prevention.

The lease agreement should provide a place for both the tenant and the owner to initial acknowledging that the tenant has received and understands the disclosure and that the owner has made the disclosure as required by law.

16. Termination of Tenancy. The termination-of-tenancy clause gives the owner the right to terminate the lease agreement should the tenant fail to comply with any term or condition outlined within it. It further allows the owner to take action as deemed necessary should the tenant falsely misrepresent any material fact or facts on the application, provided that appropriate notice is given to the tenant as required by law.

17. Abandonment. The abandonment clause stipulates what action the owner may take in the event a tenant abandons, or vacates, the dwelling. *Abandonment* refers to a tenant who moves out prior to expiration of his lease agreement without giving any notice whatsoever to the owner. The owner typically discovers that the rental property has been abandoned after a week or so when no lease payments have been made and telephone calls go unreturned. This prompts a visit to the premises, which is often found in disrepair and looks like someone left in a hurry and with no regard for the owner's property.

In the event the property becomes abandoned, the lease agreement stipulates that the owner shall have "the right to enter and repossess the dwelling and attempt to rent the property at fair market value." It also states that the tenant shall be responsible for all remaining rent as set forth, as well as any damages, cleaning charges, and costs to lease the dwelling again. The abandonment section furthermore gives the owner the right to sell any personal property left behind by the tenant after allowing 30 days for him to reclaim it. If the tenant returns to reclaim his personal property, he may do so only after satisfying all outstanding obligations to the owner. If the tenant fails to return, then the owner may use the proceeds from the sale of the personal property to apply toward moneys owed by the tenant.

18. Additional Provisions. This section can be used to include any additional provisions or requirements by either the owner or the tenant not already covered within the body of the lease agreement. For example, the owner may agree to provide lawn mowing and landscaping services at an additional charge for the dwelling the tenant will be occupying. The parties may, for example, agree to a preset amount of $75 per month payable in advance at the same time the rent is due, which is on the first of the month.

19. Entire Agreement. This section is vital to the integrity of the agreement in that it stipulates that the lease agreement represents the *entire agreement* between the owner and the tenant and that no other representations have been made orally. This section is important to bind the parties to the agreement in the event that either party may have implied something that may have been inconsistent with the lease agreement. I know from my own personal experience the importance of "having it in writing." I once had a developer who seemed like a very trusting individual tell me before signing an agreement that our written contract "was just a piece of paper" and really didn't mean anything. As it turns out, we had a disagreement based on something he stated orally that was not contained within the contract. He stated that he never made any such claim, and the first place he turned to was the contract, which did not contain his oral promise. If any disagreements arise between the parties, the first thing the courts will look to is the lease agreement. Regardless of what either party may have promised orally, if it is not expressly stated in the agreement, chances are that it will not be upheld in a court of law. The tenant furthermore acknowledges that he has read and agrees to this provision.

20. Default. Section 20 stipulates that the "failure to comply with one or more of the substantive or procedural terms" shall constitute a default of the entire agreement and sets forth the rights of the owner to act in the event such a default occurs. Should the tenant default, the owner is entitled to the immediate right of possession because default provides due cause to evict the tenant. Finally, the prevailing party is entitled to recover costs spent on reasonable legal fees.

21. Validity of Each Part. Section 21 states, "If any portion of this Agreement is held to be invalid, its invalidity will not affect the validity or enforceability of any other provision of this Agreement." In other words, just because one section or portion of the lease agreement is determined to be invalid and subsequently not upheld in a court of law does not render the entire agreement invalid.

22. Indemnification. Section 22 is the last section of the agreement and contains a provision to indemnify, or hold harmless, the owner from acts of negligence by the tenant or one of the tenant's guests that may have caused injury or death to the tenant or any other person residing with the tenant. This provision does not attempt to absolve the owner from legal liability for any acts of negligence caused by the owner but rather to protect him from acts caused either directly or indirectly by or related to the tenant or her guests. The indemnity clause does contain language, however, stipulating that the owner "shall not be liable to Tenant, Tenant's guests, or other occupants or persons on the Premises for personal injury, property damage or other losses to such persons or their property caused by other persons, theft, burglary, assault, other crimes, fire, water, wind, rain, smoke, or any other causes." Although portions of this clause may or may not be upheld in some states because of the "validity of each part" language contained in section 21, the rest of the agreement remains valid.

In summary, while there are almost as many different lease agreements as there are real estate investors, most of them share the basic elements needed to make an agreement binding. Whereas some lease agreements are simple and brief and cover only the basics, others are much more comprehensive and try to cover almost every conceivable situation that could arise. Remember that it is better to identify contractually the obligations and responsibilities of both the owner and the tenant from the outset rather than to leave the interpretation to the courts in the event of a disagreement.

If a man is called to be a street sweeper, he should sweep streets even as Michelangelo painted or Beethoven composed music or Shakespeare wrote poetry. He should sweep streets so well that all the hosts of heaven and earth will pause to say, "Here lived a great street sweeper who did his job well."

—MARTIN LUTHER KING, JR.

9

Eight Smart Ways to Increase Rents by Making These Improvements

As a real estate investor, it is obviously in your best interest to determine how to increase the rent of your property while simultaneously spending the least amount of money to do so. Since the amount of rent charged on a rental house is a function of several factors, you must take each of them into consideration. For example, before purchasing the property, you carefully considered its location, including the neighborhood, schools, and proximity to major employers. You also took into consideration the age and condition of the property. Once you've purchased the rental unit, there's nothing you can do to change its location; however, there are many things you can do to improve its condition. Before investing a lot of money in property improvements, though, it is helpful to know where to get the greatest value for each dollar spent. From purely an investment standpoint, you are seeking to get the greatest return on your invested capital. For example, if you spent $1200 on painting the exterior of the house and subsequently increased the rent by $10 per month, the return on investment (ROI) would be 10 percent as follows:

$$\text{ROI} = \frac{(\$10 \times 12 \text{ months})}{\$1200} = 10\%$$

The more rental income that can be justified for property improvements, the greater the return will be on your invested capital. While some property improvements can be very costly, others don't cost much at all. Anything that can be done to enhance the appearance of the rental property almost always can justify an increase in the rents. The rate charged, however, must be in balance with competing properties in your market. If your property is already renting at the upper end of the market for comparative properties, spending money on additional improvements hardly can be justified. Be careful not to overimprove the property. Remember that this is an investment, and you must treat it as such. In this chapter we will examine eight easy, low-cost improvements that can be made to any rental property to increase rents (see the following box).

Eight Improvements You Can Make to Increase Rents

1. Good first impressions
2. Landscaper's delight
3. Fancy fencing
4. Room to stow
5. Room with a view
6. Flattering floors
7. Lighting the way
8. Clean kitchens

Good First Impressions

I'm sure you've heard the expression before that you only get one chance to make a first impression. Well, guess what? This is especially true when it comes to rental property. If a prospective tenant comes to view a house where there is trash and debris scattered around, the paint looks like it's about to peal off, the roof is discolored, and the shutters are hanging down, he or she may very well keep right on driving.

A rental property's appearance is absolutely one of the easiest and least costly improvements that can be made to produce immediate results. It's just like buying a used car. If a car is dirty on the outside and filthy on the inside, chances are that the customer may not be interested in buying it. In fact, the seller even may have to pay someone just to take it away. On the other hand, if the car is bright and shiny and clean, the seller is likely to command a premium for it.

Cleaning up trash and debris from a property is easy to do and doesn't cost very much either. If there are junk cars or engine blocks lying around, throw them out. Get rid of all that unsightly junk. You want the outside of the property to be inviting to prospective tenants. A lot of stuff lying around the outside is a poor reflection on the entire property, so get that junk cleaned up.

Painting both the interior and exterior of a house is another inexpensive way to greatly improve its appearance. Although painting a house is somewhat labor-intensive, it's a job that can be tackled by almost anyone. If you're not into painting, the work can be hired out at a fairly low cost. Be sure to shop around, though, because labor prices vary widely. In my younger days I used to not think twice about grabbing a paintbrush and roller and taking on a job like that. I've painted more houses inside and out than I care to remember. Now that I'm a little older, however, I don't think twice about calling a painter to hire the work out. It's truly amazing what a fresh coat of paint will do for a house because it will go a long way toward sprucing up the property's overall appearance. Primary advantages of painting a rental house are that it doesn't cost very much, it's easy to apply, and it can be done in less than a week.

Cleaning asphalt shingles on a roof also can go a long way toward improving the appearance of a house. Contrary to what most roofing companies would have you believe, when an asphalt roof is several years old and begins to look dirty, it can be cleaned easily with a solution sold by most hardware stores. Most shingles have a minimum of a 20-year life, and some are guaranteed to last for up to 30 years. After as few as 3 to 4 years, however, the shingles can begin to build up a deposit of mildew that from the ground makes them appear old and worn. At first glance you may think that they need to be replaced. If the shingles are not more than 10 years old or so, chances are that they only need to be cleaned, provided, of course, that the roof is not leaking. I once owned a 24-unit apartment building in which the roof looked like it needed replacing when I first bought it. There were several large trees around the apartment buildings that also contributed to the buildup of deposits on the roof. I asked the seller how old the roof was. He stated that the shingles were only 5 to 7 years old or so and that they had a 25-year life. I determined that I could get by with cleaning the roof rather than replacing it. As I recall, I spent around $1000 to have the roof professionally cleaned. To have it replaced would have cost me 10 times that much. This was the first time that I had ever done this, but I must tell you, I was very impressed with the outcome. The roof looked brand new at a fraction of the cost of replacing it.

Landscaper's Delight

Landscaping is another low-cost way to greatly enhance the appearance of your rental property. It can encompass mowing, trimming, hedging, pulling weeds, planting shrubs, or creating a breathtaking visual splendor. One primary advantage of using landscaping to dress up a property is that the scope of work to be completed can be adjusted to fit almost any budget. If you have a very small budget, for example, you may just have the lawn mowed and the weeds pulled. On the other hand, if your budget is somewhat larger, you may consider bringing in some flowering plants and blossoming trees. In *The Complete Guide to Buying and Selling Apartment Buildings*, I wrote about one particular 22-unit apartment building I had purchased that needed quite a bit of landscaping work. The story is as follows:

> The property was a real eyesore when I bought it. My intent was to clean it up and make it as aesthetically appealing as I could for the least amount of money possible. This is not to imply that I am cheap. As an investor, my goal was to maximize the utility of each and every dollar spent on the project. I took the time to get several bids from contractors on all work performed and did not hesitate to spend as necessary within the budget I had established prior to the purchase.

Over the next sixty to ninety days, the contractors stayed busy getting the property cleaned up. The very first people I put to work were a professional landscaping crew. You'd be amazed at what a difference simply mowing down the weeds can make. They didn't stop there, though. They trimmed all the hedges, edged along the sidewalks, and cleaned up the grounds. I also had the landscaping crew bring in several truckloads of fresh mulch to place all around the bushes and hedges. By signing an annual contract with them, they assumed responsibility for all mowing, hedging, and edging on a weekly basis and at a very reasonable rate.

There were large, beautiful trees planted in between each of the driveways, but they were so overgrown they too had become an eyesore. A tree trimming service promptly alleviated that problem. Within a single day, they had all the trees trimmed and most of the branches hauled away.

In short, whether you spend a lot or a little, improving the landscaping of a rental house will go a long way toward beautifying the overall appearance of the property. Your tenants will gladly pay more for a house they can live in and be proud of the way it looks.

Fancy Fencing

Improvements to fencing also can go a long way toward enhancing not only the appearance of a rental property but also its functionality. Although not all houses have fences, there are many areas in which every house in an entire neighborhood is built with a fence. This is especially true of new construction. Again, the prevalence of fencing will vary by area. I have lived in areas where every house in the neighborhood has had a fenced yard, and I've also lived in neighborhoods where fences weren't allowed at all with the exception of those required by law for swimming pools. If the fence is made of a wood product such as cedar, for example, after many years it begins to look worn and run down. If the wood is still in good condition, the fence can be power washed and then stained to make it look like new again. This process is very inexpensive and can make the fence look like new for years to come. Other fences made of wood can be painted to achieve similar results. Decorative slats and accessories are also available if you choose to go with the "fancy fencing" look. If the wood is beginning to show signs of deterioration, it may be time to replace it. Replacing a fence made of cedar or a similar wood product is much more expensive than painting or power washing. If the fence has deteriorated to the point to where it is no longer usable and you cannot justify the expense of replacing it, tearing it down and hauling off the debris are another inexpensive alternative. Whether you choose to remove the fence completely or replace it will depend in part on what is the norm in that particular neighborhood. If all the surrounding houses have fences, chances are that yours will have to be replaced to comply with the association rules and bylaws.

Room to Stow

Believe it or not, increasing the amount of available storage space a rental property has can justify an increase in rents. Everybody needs a place to put their stuff, including tenants. The more space they have to put it, the happier they are. I know of two brand-new condominium units that sat on the market unsold for almost two years primarily because they lacked adequate storage space. After looking at the units, both of which were very nice on the inside, I asked the sales agent why they hadn't sold yet. She replied that almost without fail, the negative feedback she received was directed at the lack of closets and additional storage areas, such as a garage, attic, or basement.

Creating additional storage space is very easy to do, especially on the outside. You can purchase a ready-made shed or storage closet, for example, from almost any home improvement store to add space instantly. Or if you prefer, a more permanent storage shed such as one made from wood products can be constructed. These types of sheds also can be designed to match the color scheme of the house. Some homeowner's associations may restrict the use of outside storage sheds, so be sure to check with them before spending any money. Sheds such as these are especially popular with men because they tend to own such things as ladders and shovels or lawn mowing equipment. After having shown numerous houses to couples, I can tell you that one of the first things men like to look at is the garage, and running a close second is some type of storage shed. Most women, on the other hand, prefer to look at the kitchen and, in particular, the cabinets. In both instances, couples are looking to see if there is enough space to store their belongings. Therefore, whether people are looking to buy a house or to rent it doesn't matter, and whether it's a man or a woman doesn't matter either. They all want a place to put their stuff.

One additional idea to consider to increase the revenue stream of your rental property is to create storage space with the idea of renting it out. That's right. Rather than just give the space away to the existing tenant, you agree to rent it out at an additional charge. The idea is to build a storage shed or building large enough to store items of value such as a boat, camper, or recreational vehicle (RV). This will depend on the neighborhood in which your rental property is located and whether or not the association bylaws will allow storage facilities such as these. It also will depend on the size of your lot and whether or not there is room to put a building on it. If the tenant living in the house isn't interested in renting the building, don't let that stop you from putting up a building and leasing it to someone else. Your tenant is not likely to object because people who store boats and RVs usually get them out of storage only every now and then. Even if they do, too bad. The property is yours to do with as you wish so long as it complies with all the local laws and ordinances.

Room with a View

Anything that can be done to improve a tenant's view will make your rental property more valuable to them. What a tenant sees each morning as she looks out the window, for example, can have a significant impact on the way she feels about living there. Of course, you want the tenant to feel good about living there. In fact, you want the tenant to feel great about living there. If a tenant wakes up every morning and looks out the front window only to see a chemical plant across the street bellowing plumes of smoke up into the air, she probably isn't going to feel that good about it. On the other hand, if the tenant wakes up and looks out of her window to enjoy a visual panorama of the ocean, she is much more likely to feel good about where she is living. Since not all properties will have the advantage of being located next to natural scenery such as lakes, oceans, or mountains, it is up to you to be a little creative. You could, for example, plant flowers and shrubs in strategic locations around the house. Perhaps there is a room that needs more light and would benefit from a larger window or even a skylight. Use your imagination, and walk for a moment in the shoes of your tenant. Ask yourself what your tenant sees now and what he or she might prefer to see instead.

I once owned a rental property that was across the street from a rather large and hideous-looking apartment complex. The building was in disrepair, and judging by the way it looked, it hadn't seen a coat of paint in at least 20 years. The bottom line is that it was a real eyesore for my tenants. It just so happened that there was a six-foot-high chain link fence between my property and the apartments. As you know, you can see right through a chain link fence, so although it was effective at keeping the vagrants from next door away, the fence did little to block the view of the building. Since the fence was a full six feet in height, I determined that there must be some way to use it to help obstruct the view of the neighboring property. I contacted a local fence company that recommended some inexpensive plastic slats or strips that could be inserted and woven from top to bottom through the links on the fence. The plastic strips were about two inches wide or so, just the right size to be held securely in the fence, and came in a choice of white, tan, or green. Since the fence ran lengthwise across a grassy, green field, I chose the green slats so that they would blend in better. I paid the company for the plastic inserts, and it, in turn, sent out a crew of two men a few days later to install them. The crew did a great job, and the fence already looked much better and was quite effective at obstructing the view of the neighboring property. I decided to take the process one step further, however, by planting a row of flowering bushes across the fence. Although the plants I bought were four feet tall at the time, they were known to be hardy plants that grew quickly, so it would only be a matter of time before they grew in thick and full of beautiful flowering blossoms. Now when my tenants looked outside, instead of seeing an unsightly apartment complex across the street, they saw an enchanting fence colored with magnificent ruby red blossoms, truly a visual delight. Use your imagination, and you, too, can give your tenants a room with a view.

Flattering Floors

Every rental property will at some time or another need to have the flooring cleaned or replaced. The appearance of the flooring will make a big difference in the way the unit shows when it is time to lease it out. If the carpets are dirty, stained, and have numerous burn holes in them, it is an immediate turnoff for prospective tenants. Nobody wants to walk around in their bare feet on something like that day after day. Even if the flooring is a little worn, as long as it is neat with freshly cleaned carpets, the house will show much better, and you'll be able to justify a higher rent than you otherwise would be able to.

Most houses have a combination of primarily carpet and vinyl flooring. Some may have a little tile in the bathroom or perhaps hardwood in the entryway, but for the most part it's a combination of carpet and vinyl. You should expect a minimum life of five to seven years for the carpet. This depends on several factors, however, including how frequently the tenants move (turn over), whether or not they have kids, whether or not they have pets, and whether or not they're slobs. Pardon the bluntness of that last point, but let's face it, some people are just plain slobs when it comes to personal housekeeping habits. Pets, too, can be brutally hard on carpeting, especially if they're not housebroken. After a tenant moves out, you'll need to make a thorough inspection of the carpet room by room to determine if the carpet just needs to be cleaned or will need to be replaced. If the carpet does need replacing, you should be able to find a durable economy-grade carpet that won't break the bank and at the same time will stand up to the abuse that it is certain to endure. I recommend shopping around at several carpet stores because sometimes you can find perfectly good remnants at a fraction of the price of the standard brands of carpet. Keep in mind that you're not buying carpet for your own personal residence, something that you may be a little more particular about. You're buying carpet for an investment property in which your main goal is to find something that doesn't cost much, is durable, and looks decent. Avoid light-colored carpets also, such as light tans and grays. I suggest using something a little darker that will hide stains and dirt better. Don't use too dark of a color, though, because you want the house to look bright and cheery.

Vinyl flooring is much more durable and much easier to clean than carpet. A decent grade of vinyl should last a minimum of 10 years or more. Once again, this depends largely on the tenants who occupy your rental property. For the most part, spills and dirt can be cleaned easily, and the floor can be made to look like new with little effort. Be careful moving appliances in and out of the kitchen area, though, because they can tear the vinyl. Nicks and small tears are acceptable, but if they get too bad, you may need to go ahead and replace the vinyl. Like the carpet, keep the colors bright and cheery without getting too wild or exotic with the design. By making an extra effort to keep the floors in good condition, your rental property will show better, and you will be able to justify a higher rent for it as a result. The results will absolutely flatter you.

Lighting the Way

Replacing or upgrading the lighting is another low-cost way to improve a rental property. Providing attractive-looking light fixtures throughout the house, complemented by ceiling fans in the bedrooms and family room, if possible, will be very appealing to prospective tenants. As a builder of new homes, my suppliers furnish me with nice looking lighting packages for an entire house that are very reasonable in cost. Most home improvement stores have a decent selection of low-cost lighting that can be used to replace the existing fixtures in a house. Although you don't have to be an electrician to replace light fixtures, you should take the necessary precaution of turning the circuit breakers off so that you don't end up electrocuting yourself.

Ceiling fans are also popular among tenants and can be purchased for just a little more than a light fixture. Tenants appreciate having ceiling fans because they provide two additional benefits to them. First of all, they provide a greater level of comfort through better cooling and greater air circulation, and second, ceiling fans can save the tenants money by allowing them not to have to run the air conditioner as much. In short, upgrading the lighting in a rental property is easy and inexpensive to do and will provide your tenants with an added measure of comfort they may not otherwise enjoy.

Clean Kitchens

Second only to the family room, most people spend more time in the kitchen than in any other room in the house. The kitchen is where families come together several times throughout the day. They start their day in the kitchen and bring their day to a close in the kitchen, whether it's at the dinner hour or at a late-night snack just before bedtime. The consumption of food, which is fundamental to sustaining life, necessitates our coming together periodically throughout the day. Since the kitchen represents such an important part of our lives, it makes sense to have one that is clean, bright, and refreshing. A cheery kitchen helps to set the tone for the day and will help your tenants to feel good about living in your rental property. Remember, the better they feel emotionally and psychologically about where they live, the longer they are likely to stay. As the owner, you will benefit through a reduction in tenant turnover.

There are several things you can do to improve the appearance of a kitchen. The quickest and least expensive improvement will be to ensure that everything in the kitchen is spotlessly clean. This includes the floor, the cabinets (inside and out), the drawers, and most especially the appliances. A can of oven cleaner will do wonders for a dirty stove, and a mild solution of soap and warm water will clean almost any refrigerator. Don't overlook the microwave or dishwasher either. If you've ever owned rental property before, you already know that when prospective tenants walk through with you to look at the unit, they will open almost every door in the house. This includes those in the kitchen. If the cabinets or appliances are dirty on the inside, the tenant may decide to tell you something like "I'll think about it" and keep right on looking. If the appliances are old and beyond repair, I don't hesitate to replace them with new ones. Some property owners prefer to buy refurbished appliances, but for the small difference in cost, I favor purchasing brand-new ones. For a few extra dollars, I know, for example, that if there is a problem with the dishwasher, since the unit comes with a warranty, all I have to do is call the appliance store from which I purchased it, and the store will send out a repairperson to fix it. Furthermore, you should be able to expect a minimum of 10 years out of your new appliances. By spending a little more now on brand-new ones rather than trying to save a few dollars on refurbished units, you're likely to come out ahead anyway. Don't be penny wise and pound foolish.

If the rental property is older than, say, 20 to 30 years, it may be time to update the kitchen. Old and outdated kitchens can be brought back to life with new cabinets. I've seen older-style cabinets that were beat up or dark and dingy looking, some of which the previous owners had tried to clean up by slapping on a coat of paint or even covering them with cheap contact paper or wallpaper. Although replacing the cabinets is more expensive than replacing an appliance or two, the money spent on modernizing a kitchen will go a long way with your tenants. Cabinets vary widely in both price and quality, so be sure to do your homework by shopping around. Good-quality cabinets that are available at the lower end of the price range typically are made of a light- to medium-stained oak. White cabinets, also known as *white bay,* usually cost a little more than do the light oak. The next most expensive cabinets are those made of maple, which are then followed by cherry at the top of the line. I recommend using the light-oak cabinets for two reasons. First, they are the least expensive, and second, they tend to be the most popular because they are considered to be neutral in color. If your rental property is a higher-end unit, however, you may want to consider spending a little more money on nicer cabinets.

In summary, making any one of these low-cost improvements to your rental property is a great way to justifiably increase the rent you can charge for it. Remember, though, that the rate charged must not be out of balance with competing properties in your market. Remember also to treat property improvements as an investment of your capital. Your objective should be to earn a reasonable rate of return for every dollar spent on property improvements. Finally, be careful not to overimprove the property by exceeding what the market or tenants will expect in a given area. For even more ways to improve your rental property, you may want to consider picking up a copy of another book I wrote entitled *101 Cost-Effective Ways to Increase the Value of Your Home.*

The quality of a person's life is in direct proportion to their commitment to excellence, regardless of their chosen field of endeavor.
—VINCE LOMBARDI

10

How to Decrease Expenses the Smart Way

To improve the net income from a rental property, an investor must do one of two things—either increase the revenues or decrease the expenses. The profitability of an investment property is a direct function of how revenues and expenses are managed. In Chapter 9 we examined several ways to improve a rental property that would enable an investor to justify increasing the rent and thus improve the revenue side of the equation. In this chapter we'll study several methods of decreasing a rental property's expenses by implementing various changes that would have an impact on the expense side of the equation. Using a combination of increasing income while simultaneously decreasing expenses is a sure way to improve the profitability of your rental property. The following box illustrates our approach.

Six Money-Saving Ways to Slash Expenses

1. Pass the buck
2. Hire the handyman
3. Utilize utilities
4. A taxing matter
5. Dialing for dollars
6. Management 101

Pass the Buck

One easy and effective way to decrease expenses and immediately begin saving $25 to $50 each and every month is to *pass the buck*. This phrase refers to shifting responsibility from one party to another. In this case, it is the rental property owner who is shifting the responsibility of the first $25 to $50 of repair expenses to the tenant. The best time to do this is at the initial signing of the lease agreement. In the repairs and maintenance section, you simply stipulate that the tenant is responsible for paying for all minor repairs that cost $50 or less, or whatever amount you deem to be appropriate. Using this approach has several advantages to the owner. First, it will save her money each month, and second, it will save her time. Although minor repairs may not cost the owner very much in terms of money, they certainly can cost her in terms of time. Imagine if you got called every time there was a clogged sink or a stopped-up toilet. Then multiply those phone calls times 10 or 20 rental properties, and you can see where making these types of minor repairs will get old fast. By passing the buck to the tenant, you are also empowering the tenant to take a degree of responsibility for the premises in which he or she lives. If the tenant knows that he has to repair something if he breaks it, then maybe he will be a little more careful not to break it in the first place. Most tenants won't mind a clause in the lease agreement requiring them to be responsible for the first $50 or so of minor repairs. If the tenant does balk at it, however, just explain to him that the cost of minor repairs has been factored into the monthly rent and that without the repair clause, the rent would be $50 more per month.

Hire the Handyman

When it comes to making needed repairs on a rental property, investors have three choices. They can either make the repairs themselves, pay a professional to make them, or hire a handyman. Although each method has its advantages and disadvantages, hiring a handyman to repair your rental property often makes the most sense. Chances are that you are pretty handy with tools yourself and are likely to have tackled a few home improvement projects at one time or another. The chief advantage of making repairs yourself is the money you'll save by not having to pay someone else. If you only have one or two rental properties and also have the time, then this is probably a good choice for you. On the other hand, if you own several properties, it will become increasingly difficult to keep up with all of them. Time is your chief constraint. Investors also should consider that if they're spending all their time repairing houses, they will have very little time left to buy and manage them. Are you in the business of buying, managing, and selling rental properties, or are you in the business of making house repairs? You and only you can decide this.

The primary advantage to hiring a professional company to make repairs is the level of expertise that company provides. An air-conditioning unit or a furnace that needs replacing, for example, warrants the services of licensed professionals who can replace the old equipment and subsequently test the new equipment to ensure proper operation. Major repairs such as this should be left to the pros and not the amateurs. On a smaller job, such as lighting the pilot light on a furnace, however, paying top dollar for a professional company hardly makes sense.

Then there's the handyman. The primary advantage of hiring a handyman is that he can perform just about any kind of light to moderately difficult repair or maintenance. I'm sure you've heard the axiom "jack of all trades, master of none." This aptly describes exactly the type of individual you are looking for about 80 percent of the time. Most of the upkeep and maintenance on a house can be made by a handyman and does not warrant calling in the pros. Using a handyman offers two main advantages. First and foremost, a good handyman will save you money because he often works independently and doesn't have the overhead that larger commercial outfits do. Having access to a competent handyman also can save you time. Instead of having to call out a different trade or service every time something needs to be repaired, you simply call your handyman, who can repair most anything. The primary disadvantage of using a handyman is that while such people typically have a broad base of skills, they do not specialize in any one thing. Once again, though, when you need a specialist, you simply call one.

Utilize Utilities

Depending on the area in which your rental property is located, and depending on the type of unit it is, as the owner, you may be the one paying all the utility bills. It may be, for example, reasonable and customary for owners in some markets to be responsible for paying the gas, electric, water, and sewer bills. If the utility bills are left in your name for whatever reason, you can charge the expenses back to the tenant each month and get reimbursed for any costs you may have incurred. The other option is to have the tenant put the utilities in his name and be directly responsible for them. Regardless of how you do it, if at all possible, shift the responsibility of paying the utility bills to the tenant. Since there is no incentive for tenants to conserve energy if they are not the ones paying for it, operating expenses almost always will be higher than they should be. Tenants naturally will reason that it's okay to go to work all day long on a hot summer day and leave the thermostat set at 65 degrees so that it will be nice and cool when they return. And why shouldn't they? After all, they're not the ones paying the utility expenses; the owner is. It is becoming more and more common, especially for single-family houses, to have the tenants be responsible for paying all the utility bills. Chances are that they already are in your area.

In many states, the gas and electric bills follow the tenant, but the water and sewer bills do not. This means that if a tenant fails to pay the last month's utility bill, the gas and electric companies will pursue the tenant to collect any past due amounts. The water and sewer companies, which most often are controlled by local municipalities, however, will pursue the owner to collect past due amounts. If the bill is not paid, they may even attach a lien to the property so that when it is eventually sold, any outstanding balances along with late penalties and interest will be collected. If this is the case in your area, you can take precautionary measures by agreeing to retain the tenant's deposit on vacating until such time as they provide evidence that the final water and sewer bills have been paid. All the tenant needs to do is simply provide you with a receipt showing that the account has been paid in full to be entitled to a refund of her deposit.

Once again, if the rental property you own is a single-family house, chances are that the tenant is already paying for the utilities. On the other hand, if your rental property is an older multifamily property such as a duplex, triplex, or fourplex, there's a good chance that it may be master metered. Properties that are master metered are typically "all bills paid," meaning that the tenant does not pay any of the utility bills and that the owner is responsible for them. Converting a property from master metered to submetered is fairly easy to do. There are, in fact, companies that specialize in providing utility services such as this that have their own licensed electricians and can retrofit almost any property with a turnkey submetering system. The sooner you convert your property, the sooner you'll begin reducing operating costs by a significant margin. To get existing tenants to buy into the program, you may have to reduce their rents slightly, but you'll still come out ahead. If the average utility bill on a per-unit basis is $50, for example, then I suggest reducing the tenant's rent by a factor of approximately 70 percent, or $35. This leaves a net savings of $15 per unit per month to you. Since the tenant is now in charge of paying the utility bills, chances are that he will modify the way the thermostat is regulated by a factor of 30 percent or so, which means that the new utility bill now will be $35, the same amount the rent was reduced. The tenant breaks even, and the owner realizes a net savings of $15 per month. Although this may not sound like much, if you multiply this savings times 10 or 100 units over one, two, or three years, the savings can really add up and will contribute directly to the owner's bottom line.

A Taxing Matter

Property taxes represent a large portion of the operating expenses on any rental unit. Reducing the tax liability by even 5 or 10 percent can mean a significant savings to the owner. Reducing a $3000 tax liability by 10 percent, for example, would yield an annual savings of $300, or $25 per month. I don't know about you, but I prefer to keep as much of my money as possible rather than giving it to Uncle Sam. Reducing the tax liability on investment property is not always easy, but it can be done. In fact, it can be done with little to no effort by the investor. Real estate property values are reassessed periodically for one reason or another but most often when a property is transferred from one individual or party to another, usually triggered by a sale. If the owner of the real estate believes that the newly assessed value is too high and is out of line with the market, she may file a notice of protest. The owner will be granted a hearing, at which time she may present evidence as to why the new tax value is too high. The tax assessor or treasurer can accept the owner's claim, reject the owner's claim, or do anything in between.

If you don't want to file the protest personally, there are many companies that specialize in representing property owners in tax protests. These companies are very familiar with the laws and corresponding market values and often know the best approach to use to reduce the assessed value. Most companies that provide this type of service only charge the client if they are successful in reducing his taxes. This gives them a strong incentive to represent the client to the fullest extent because the only way they get paid is if they win the case. Fees typically are charged as a percentage of the total the client saves on his taxes for a given period. I don't know about you, but I get solicitations from companies that provide these services on a routine basis, and as a matter of fact, I have even used one to represent me on an apartment building I had purchased recently. The tax assessor's office had raised the assessed value on my apartments by about 25 percent, which would have meant an increase of several thousand dollars each year in taxes. The firm I hired to represent me did so successfully, and although the assessed value was still increased, it was by a much smaller margin than was proposed originally.

Dialing for Dollars

One of the easiest ways to save money on a rental property is by doing what I refer to as "dialing for dollars." This simply means to get on the telephone and start calling around to do some comparison shopping. People do comparison shopping every day when they compare grocery prices from one store to the next or gas prices from station to station. Talk about a commodity that is price sensitive. Gas stations all across the country vividly display the price per gallon of gasoline. Moreover, as consumers, we tend to drive an extra mile or two and sometimes more just because we know the price of gas is 3 cents cheaper at a particular station. If we are willing to go out of our way to save 50 cents on a tank of gas, don't you think that it makes sense to comparison shop for your rental property by calling different trades, vendors, and suppliers? Of course it does. As a builder of new homes, I am on the phone negotiating for the best price and terms from my trades and suppliers. Building a house involves many different labor trades and various materials that must be managed throughout the entire construction phase. If I am not careful to control costs, the house will go over budget and thus reduce my company's profit margin. Price variances are scrutinized carefully and must be explained fully so that they don't recur.

The following is an example of dialing for dollars I wrote about in *The Complete Guide to Buying and Selling Apartment Buildings*. I was shopping for property insurance at the time for a small apartment building.

The cost of insurance will vary widely among agents. You should look for an insurance agent who specializes in commercial real estate. While there are many agents who provide auto insurance, homeowner's policies, and life and health insurance, there are also those who specialize in providing commercial services. Let's look at an example of what the difference between these types can mean to you. The owner of a 22-unit property I had under contract was paying about $4500 per year for property and liability insurance. I got a quote from an agent who had been providing my auto and homeowner's insurance for years. She offered the same coverage to me for $5200. The mortgage broker I was working through at the time suggested I call another agent who specialized in providing commercial insurance. When he quoted me $2400 for the exact same coverage, I had difficulty containing my enthusiasm over the phone. While I thought this was an exceptional deal, I didn't want to let him know that's what I thought. I have been using this particular agent ever since and have been quite satisfied. Depending on the level of coverage your lender requires, you should be able to insure your property for about $100 per unit per year on average.

So there you have it. I had a choice of paying $5200, or I could get identical coverage for less than half of that at only $2400. As is clearly evident from this example, it pays to go dialing for dollars.

Management 101

At some point in your real estate investment endeavors, out of necessity, if nothing else, you are likely to make the transition from self-management to professional management. As you add more and more rental properties to your portfolio, it will become increasingly difficult to keep up with the many responsibilities for all of them. Hiring a professional property manager will relieve you of having to be involved with the day-to-day operations of managing or leasing and will leave you more time to focus on building a solid portfolio of rental properties.

Hey, wait a minute. This chapter is supposed to be about decreasing expenses, not increasing them, you say. Well you're exactly right. Transitioning from self-management to professional management will increase operating expenses. You must decide, however, what your greatest value is to your investment company. In other words, what skills and attributes do you possess that add the most value to your organization? How can you personally make the greatest contribution to building your company? Is it as a property manager who has to deal with the daily operations of keeping all the rental units fully leased and making sure the tenants are happy? Or perhaps you prefer to spend your time on the maintenance and upkeep of all your properties. Now let me pose another series of questions to you. How much would it cost to hire a property manager? How much would it cost to hire a maintenance man or handyman? Now, for the last question: How much would it cost to hire someone who is capable of taking your place? The answer should be obvious to you, but in case it isn't, let me just say that it wouldn't cost anything because you cannot be replaced. That's right; you are irreplaceable when it comes to building your own organization. You are the mastermind of your company. Only you can lead the way and create the kind of business that will give you the most joy and satisfaction. With each and every rental property purchased comes an increase in knowledge and experience. Any fears you may have had in the beginning stages of creating your company have long been overcome with courage, for when the forces of fear and courage collided with one another, you were willing to choose the road less traveled, the noble path of courage.

How to Decrease Expenses the Smart Way

Recognizing that it is you who can lead your organization to realize its greatest potential leads us to conclude that somewhere along the way it will become necessary to engage the services of a property management company or to hire your own manager. There are advantages and disadvantages to both approaches. The primary advantage of hiring a management company is that it already has all the management systems in place. Management firms typically have on staff experienced individuals capable of providing a full range of services, including leasing, managing, maintenance, and accounting. Property management companies are most often compensated on a percentage schedule based on the total revenues collected. Fees range from about 3 percent to as high as 10 percent depending on factors such as the number of units to be managed, whether or not they are clustered together in a close proximity to each other, and the level of services to be provided. If an investor has, for example, just one property to manage, she could expect to pay at the upper end of the range, or 10 percent. On the other hand, if she has 50 units or more, then 3 to 5 percent is more in line with most markets. If the units are spread out over a large metropolitan area, an investor could expect to pay a little more, but if they are all in the same general vicinity, the same investor likely would pay less. Finally, if an investor desires a full range of services, he can expect to pay a higher rate, but if he only needs leasing services, for example, he could expect a lower rate.

One primary disadvantage of using a property management company is that you give up a degree of control that you might otherwise have with your own personal manager. It is easy to lose touch with much of the daily operations because another firm has assumed those responsibilities, but then again, this is what you are paying the firm for. As the investor-owner, however, since you may be more in tune with some problems that otherwise might arise undetected by the management firm, you should take extra care to alert the firm to any situations that may require special attention.

If you decide to hire an individual who will be responsible for managing your property and no one else's, you retain an added measure of control that you otherwise wouldn't with a management company. You may be able to save money with a personal manager also because sometimes such a person can function in multiple roles. For example, your manager may be able to lease the property, manage it, and perform some of the light maintenance. This will depend in part on the skills your manager has and also on the number of properties there are to be managed. Since your manager more than likely will report to you on a daily basis, as the owner, you will retain a greater degree of control over your portfolio and will be able to respond more quickly to special situations as the need arises. A primary disadvantage could be that the management function remains in-house and perhaps leaves you closer to the daily operations than you care to be.

In summary, there are many ways to trim the operating expenses of your rental properties. Each and every line item under the "Operating Expenses" heading of the income statement should be examined for the possibility of cost cutting. Over time, you will come to know what costs to expect on average to operate a rental property and where the greatest potential to save money lies.

We hold these truths to be self-evident: That all men are created equal; that they are endowed by their Creator with certain unalienable rights; that among these are life, liberty, and the pursuit of happiness.

—THOMAS JEFFERSON

11

How to Manage Tenants the Smart Way

O ne of the most important things to remember in the rental property business is that in order to be a good property manager, you also have to be a good people manager. An effective property manager must be able to resolve a myriad of problems on a regular basis, sometimes daily, depending on the number of rental units that are owned. A good manager should have above-average communication skills and excellent human relations skills. In addition, the manager must be intimately familiar with the rules and regulations established for the dwelling and also be able to enforce them consistently as needed. Finally, the manager must know how to collect the rents effectively when they are due and must know how and when to raise the rents.

Your Role as a Manager

Managing rental property requires a unique blend of skills and talents that can be acquired through both training and experience. One of the most important aspects to recognize in your role as a manager is the difference between managing property and managing people. As a manager of property, there is no human or emotional element to contend with. Conversely, as a manager of people, there is quite naturally a human and emotional element involved. Procuring a contractor to paint your rental unit is quite easy to do. Settling a dispute or resolving a conflict with a tenant, on the other hand, can be a bit more challenging.

Treating tenants with respect should be a standard business practice for all real estate managers. Recall that in Chapter 7 we discussed the principle of the Golden Rule, which states that we should do unto others as we would have them do unto us. As a customer yourself entering into any place of business, certainly you like to be—and expect to be—treated in a professional and courteous manner. Your tenants are no different, so be sure to treat them with respect. Does this mean that you have to give in to every whim and demand a tenant may place on you? Of course it doesn't. Adhering to the Golden Rule does not mean that as an investor and property owner you disregard prudent business practices. Accommodating the tenant must be tempered with your needs as an investor. It's okay for a tenant to ask for additional services, for example, that a manager normally would not include in the rent. It's also okay to say "no" when the situation demands it.

Managing tenants is in a way very similar to managing children. As parents, from the time our children are old enough to begin understanding us, we establish rules and guidelines for them to follow. We don't dare wait until they are teenagers to provide guidance and direction. By then it is much too late. We instead begin setting boundaries when they are very young, and if your children are anything like mine, they will push the envelope of those boundaries as far as you will let them. As parents, however, we have an obligation to enforce the rules we set for them. To shirk our responsibility would be to our children's detriment and, if left unchecked altogether, eventually would impair their ability to function in society as adults. Furthermore, our children would be led to believe that we don't really care about them if we let them get away with whatever they want. In addition, the enforcement of rules also must be applied consistently rather than randomly. Our children should know and come to expect that when they disobey, punishment surely will follow. Conversely, when our children comply with the rules and stay within the boundaries set for them, they have no need to fear retribution of any kind whatsoever. In fact, as their parents, we'll bend over backwards to help them and work with them and love them as long as they obey the rules. Just as flowers thrive when basking in the sunlight, so do our children flourish when bathed in showers of praise. And just as a turtle withdraws into the safety of its shell when threatened by menacing predators, so do our children retreat from life when intimidated by abusive caretakers.

And so it is with our tenants. As property managers, we must establish the rules and guidelines from the very outset. To wait until our tenants are three or four months into a lease potentially could mean disaster. Their boundaries must be set at the beginning of the tenancy. And like our children, our tenants sometimes will absolutely push the limits of their boundaries. As managers, we have the responsibility to enforce the rules however difficult that may be. To allow our tenants to go unchecked would lead them to believe that we don't really care about them or about what they do. And again, like our children, we must be prepared to enforce the rules consistently. Our tenants must come to know that when they disobey or don't follow the rules, a penalty will be imposed. On the other hand, as long as they comply with our expectations, they have no need to fear, and in fact, as their property managers, we will bend over backwards to help them. Finally, when tenants are treated with respect, they respond in kind. Conversely, when they are spoken to in a demeaning manner, they become resentful and uncooperative.

To summarize, apply the Golden Rule whenever possible in dealing with tenants. Treat them with the same degree of courtesy and professionalism with which you like to be treated. Establish rules and guidelines from the outset, and be prepared to enforce them when needed.

How to Collect Rents When They Are Due

Collecting the rents when they are due sometimes can be one of a manager's biggest challenges. There are certain steps you can take, however, to make your life easier as an owner when it comes to collecting the money that is rightfully yours. They include properly qualifying the tenant, managing their expectations, and consistently imposing penalties when tenants fail to comply.

In Chapter 7 we discussed several methods used to qualify tenants properly. If a tenant has good credit, for example, then she has demonstrated over the years her ability to pay on time. Poor credit, on the other hand, is reflective of an individual who is habitually delinquent with payments. Verification of employment and income is also important and should not be overlooked. Finally, verification of a tenant's most recent rental history is essential to qualifying him for tenancy. Once again, if the tenant has shown that he can pay on time with a recent landlord, chances are that he'll pay on time in your property too.

Once a tenant's qualifications are verified to the owner's satisfaction, the next step is to manage the tenant's expectations. In other words, the rules for payment of the rent each month must be established before the tenant ever moves in. The property manager should provide a written policy, usually contained within the lease, that clearly and in no uncertain terms identifies exactly *how much* rent is to be paid, *who* it is to be paid to, *where* it is to be paid, and finally, *when* it is to be paid. The *when* is especially important. If the lease agreement states that the rent is due on the first, then this means that it is due on the first and not on the second, not on the third, and so on. The first means the first. Managing the tenant's expectations means that the rules for payment of the rent must be communicated clearly. In addition to providing the language in the body of the lease agreement, the payment expectations should be discussed with tenants verbally as well. Don't make the mistake of saying something like, "Well Mr. T, the rent's due on the first, but as long as I get it by the second or third, that'll be okay." You've just set yourself up so that you'll likely never get paid on the first and will be lucky if you get paid by the second or third. The tenant will infer from your remarks that the rent really is not that important and that he can pay it whenever it is convenient.

Finally, to facilitate the collection of rents when they become due, a penalty should be imposed if they are late. If there is no penalty or late charge, then there is no reason to pay the rent on time. Furthermore, the penalty should be set high enough to be an effective disincentive not to pay on time. If it is set too low, the tenant may not mind paying the penalty if it means buying a few extra days before having to cough up the rent money. Late charges often are comparable to the going rate banks charge for bounced checks. For example, if most of the banks in your area assess a $35 fee for a bounced check, this is fairly close to where you should set your late fee. An additional late charge also should be imposed for each and every day the tenant continues to be late. For example, you might charge an extra $10 per day every day the rent remains unpaid.

Some managers like to give a two- or three-day grace period before imposing a penalty. Using a grace period system, however, is akin to saying that the rent is due on the second or third rather than on the first. If the rent is due on the first, then it is late on the second. If the rent is late, then the penalty must be imposed. If a tenant pays one day late, on the second, for example, he may try to persuade you into waiving the late fee by saying something like, "Can't you just waive the late fee this one time? I'm only one day late." To cede to the tenant's request is asking for trouble because you are setting yourself up for another late payment the following month. Instead, you should politely but firmly remind the tenant that he agreed to pay the late charge when the lease agreement was signed. You also can explain that charging the late fee is part of your policy and that you have no choice. Imposing and collecting late charges must be done consistently and unwaveringly.

One way to emphasize the positive aspects of paying on time rather than focusing on the negative aspects is to give your tenants an incentive in the form of a discount. For instance, rather than threaten the tenant with additional charges for paying late, give him a discount for paying early. Here's how it works: Let's say that the day you would really like to collect the rent is on the first of the month and that the amount of rent you want to collect is $675. Tell the tenant that her monthly rent is $700 and that it is due and payable on the third day of each month. Then tell her about your wonderful discount program, which is that if she pays by the first, she will receive a $25 discount. I have used this approach many times, and I can tell you that tenants will work harder to pay their rent early and receive a discount than they will to pay on time and run the risk of paying a late charge if delinquent.

Although collecting the rents on time each and every month sometimes can be a bit of a challenge, following the guidelines discussed here will greatly improve your odds of getting paid each month. Be sure to properly qualify tenants before they move in, manage their expectations from the very beginning, and consistently impose a penalty when they fail to comply. By applying the methods described in this section, you're certain to collect the rents that are rightfully due to you on a more timely and consistent basis.

When and How to Raise Rents

Although raising a tenant's rent is not always the most pleasant task, there are certain steps that can be taken to minimize the trauma of a rent increase. The first step to take is to be sure that you are in compliance with state and local ordinances that govern changes in tenancy such as rent increases. Most laws require that the time required to give notice be equal to or greater than the period of tenancy covered in the lease agreement. In a month-to-month rental agreement, for instance, a one-month notice normally is called for. If the lease agreement is for one year, however, this does not mean that a whole year is needed to give notice because at the end of the one-year period the lease agreement expires. When and if it renews, rents can be increased at that time. If a tenant who has been renting for several years originally signed a six-month or one-year lease agreement and is now renting month-to-month, an increase can be given with a one-month notice.

In addition to rent increases given on renewal of a lease agreement, they also should be timed to correspond with recent property improvements, if possible. Anytime an improvement has been done that is noticeable or visible to the tenant, an increase in the rent can be justified. Property improvements such as painting the house or building, putting in new landscaping to beautify the premises, or installing new heating or air-conditioning equipment are all worthy of rent increases. The reason to time an increase to correspond with improvements is that it helps to justify in the mind of the tenant a need for the raise. In other words, tenants feel like they are getting something for their money, some added benefit of value.

If the improvements to the property are quite substantial, they may justify an equally substantial increase in the rent. If the tenant is living in the property at the time the improvements are made and the rent is raised so high that the tenant can no longer afford it, he or she may in fact choose to move. As the owner, you must be prepared for this. There is no reason to despair, though, because the next tenant who rents the dwelling should be able to afford it because he or she will be responding to an advertisement with the new higher rental rate in it. If a major rehab for the property is being done, it may make sense to do it in between tenants. The tradeoff, of course, is the loss of income during the time the work is being completed. If the dwelling is a larger multifamily property, it is better to try to schedule the work to be performed while the tenants are still living there so as to avoid a total loss of revenues. Collecting rental income from the property while making improvements is the ideal situation because it allows the owner to offset the carrying costs associated with the property, such as the monthly principal, interest, taxes, and insurance (PITI).

Finally, there's the "Grinch who stole Christmas" method of raising the rents. This method is timed around two significant annual events, the first one being the Christmas holiday and the second one being the beginning of a new year. Tenant turnover tends to be very low during the months of November and December primarily due to the Thanksgiving and Christmas holidays. Most people are focused on spending time with their families and enjoying the holiday season and therefore are not preoccupied with moving. The notice of change in tenancy for the rent increase should be given no later than the first day of December so that the increase will become effective on the first day of January, which is also the first day of the new year. Yes, I know, the rent increase is being given right in the middle of two major holidays. Although giving notice at Christmastime initially may cause your tenants to think of you as the "Grinch who stole Christmas," by the end of the month they've had some time to digest the news and still enjoy their holiday. There's a good chance that since the tenants have been busy with Christmas, they haven't taken time to shop for another place to live, so they are likely to remain at least through the month of January.

The second reason for year-end timing has to do with property taxes. On the first day of January (even though it's a holiday), property values are reassessed, which is a polite way of saying that they go up. If your experience has been anything like mine, chances are that you've never received an assessment notice stating that your taxes are going down. Since the propensity for tax assessments to increase is quite high, the related increase in the amount of taxes you will have to pay can be used to justify the increase in rents. I recommend including some language in the notice of change in tenancy to your tenants to help them understand exactly why their rent is going up. In this case, since it's Uncle Sam who is responsible, blame the increase in rents on him. Let the government be the bad guy, not you. Your tenants will be much more understanding if they believe that there is a valid reason for the rent increase. Since everybody knows that taxes go up, be sure to tell your tenants so that they can blame the proper party for the increase.

Raising a tenant's rent is not always easy to do, and as the owner, you are not going to win any popularity contests in the process. Remember, though, that you are responsible for managing an investment and that you're not trying to win any contests, except the contest of life. It is up to you to manage your investment property in the most effective and profitable manner possible. Let's face it, whether rents are increased at the time of a lease renewal, when property improvements have been made, or at Christmas time, the tenants aren't going to be very excited about it, so as the owner, you may as well raise them when it best suits your needs.

How Much to Raise Rents

Now that you know when to raise your tenant's rent, the question naturally arises as to how much they should be or can be raised. The answer is, it depends. While some investors contend that there are general rules of thumb on how much to increase a tenant's rent, there are often extenuating factors to which no general rules apply. How much rents can be increased depends on the market environment you're competing in and the relevant market rates, whether or not any improvements have been made to the property, and your sensitivity to fluctuations in occupancy levels.

In Chapter 4 we did an in-depth examination of how to calculate a rental property's market rents by comparing it with several other similar properties. In Exhibit 4-2, information such as rental rates, amenities, and square footage was compiled for a total of 10 houses considered to be comparable to the subject property. The monthly rent was then broken down for each house to an average rate per square foot, and finally, an average monthly rent per square foot was calculated for all the properties combined. The result was then used to help set the monthly rental rate for the subject property. Another method suggested in Chapter 4 to determine market rates was to contact a local property management company. Regardless of which method is used to assess the most accurate rental rate for your property, the most important thing is to understand where your dwelling is priced relative to the market.

If, for example, the majority of properties similar to yours are renting for $850 per month and yours is renting for only $775 per month, you know that a $75 per month increase is justified. Whether or not you increase the rent all at once will depend on a number of things. If your tenant has just moved out and you are getting the property ready to be leased again, by all means bring your rents in line with the market. If, on the other hand, you've had a tenant living there for the past 5 or 10 years who has been paying the rent like clockwork, you may want to increase the rent in a tiered fashion over time. For example, you could increase the rent by $20 every 6 months until the rent is more in line with the market.

Another factor to consider is the overall occupancy rate in your area. If the rental market is soft and vacancies are above average, you should consider either leaving your property priced just below the market or improving it so that it has slightly more to offer than comparable properties. Either way, you come out ahead because your property is likely to rent more quickly and thereby reduce your vacancy rate.

In addition to increasing rents based on comparable properties and the strength of a particular market, your decision also must be balanced with your degree of sensitivity to occupancy levels. If, for example, your cash reserves are not adequate to sustain the property's carrying costs during a vacancy, then it is probably wise to reduce the rate to just below market so as to minimize the loss of income. If, on the other hand, your tolerance for vacancies is higher and your cash reserves are sufficient to sustain the property's carrying costs, then you may consider increasing the rental rate to market or slightly above. Once again, these decisions must be balanced with local market conditions. It certainly doesn't make sense, for example, to hold out for an extra $25 per month in rent if it takes an extra month to rent the property. Assume, for example, that Investor Smith holds out for $800 per month, whereas Investor Jones is willing to accept $785 per month. Assume also that while Investor Jones is able to lease her property right away, it takes Investor Smith an additional 2 weeks to lease his property. Let's look at the math in this example:

Investor Smith: $800 per month × 11.5 months = $9200

Investor Jones: $785 per month × 12.0 months = $9420

Difference: +$220

In this example, as it turns out, less is more. In other words, by being willing to accept $15 per month less than Investor Smith, Investor Jones was able to earn an additional $220 for the year in rental income because of the lower vacancy rate she was able to achieve. In summary, therefore, balance the amount of your rent increases with local market conditions and be careful not to be penny wise and pound foolish.

To put the world right in order, we must first put the nation in order; to put the nation in order, we must first put the family in order; to put the family in order, we must first cultivate our personal life; we must first set our hearts right.

—CONFUCIUS

SECTION 3

How to Sell Rental Properties the Smart Way

12

Five Smart Ways to Enhance Your Rental House's Marketability

Whether you've owned your rental property for 1 year or 10 years, the time eventually will come when you will want to sell it. By any measure of historical standards, regardless of how long you've owned your investment property, chances are that it has increased in value. There are many methods you can use to increase the overall marketability of your rental property and to increase the exposure it receives. As the following box shows, some of these methods include beginning with the end in mind, maximizing your exposure, selling what the buyer wants to buy, pricing your rental property to sell, and sweetening the pot.

Enhance Your Property's Marketability

1. Begin with the end in mind.
2. Maximize your exposure.
3. Sell what the buyer wants.
4. Price your house to sell.
5. Sweeten the pot.

Begin with the End in Mind

Smart investors know that to improve significantly the eventual resell and marketability of a rental property, they must carefully consider a variety of factors that may affect their ability to do so. Proper planning from start to finish is essential to be successful in this business. This includes planning for the sale of rental property. The proper planning of an exit strategy is as important as, if not more so than, the preentry strategy. Ideally, investors should begin thinking about how to sell a rental property even before it is purchased—that is, they should begin with the end in mind.

To begin with the end in mind, you must take the time to formalize a business plan for your real estate investments. Whenever you travel in your car from one place to another, you always have a destination in mind even before you get into the car. If you didn't, chances are that you wouldn't be driving anywhere. Investing your valuable capital in real estate is no different. To say that maybe you'll buy one house here and another one there whenever you happen to find a good deal simply isn't enough. Before you even think about purchasing, you should consider what your exit strategy, or sales strategy, will be when the time comes for you to dispose of your rental property. Points to consider include, but are not limited to, the following:

- Investment time horizon
- Location and neighborhood
- Growth trends in the area
- Economic environment
- Interest-rate environment
- Demographic shifts or trends
- Changes in land use through rezoning

You should consider the effect each of these items may have on your rental property not only at the time of purchase but also at the time of sale. You must be forward-thinking when applying an investment strategy. As a smart investor, you should make every effort to plan for the eventual resale of a rental property by anticipating certain market factors that may influence the marketability of the house. Carefully reviewing all the elements that affect your decision and making certain assumptions about them will greatly improve your ability to dispose of the property successfully and maximize its respective profitability. As a smart investor, you already know that by failing to plan, you are also planning to fail, so stay smart by beginning with the end in mind.

Maximize Your Exposure

Recall that in Chapter 3 we discussed eight terrific ways to locate great rental properties. Well, guess what? You can use most of those same methods to sell your property, too. To sell any type of real estate, I recommend that you do everything possible to maximize the property's exposure. The more people who know that your property is for sale, the more likely you are to sell it. By maximizing the property's exposure, you are increasing the probability that it will sell quickly and at a price that represents full market value.

The following list is a quick recap of some of the methods found in Chapter 3, along with a few others, that can help to increase the exposure of a rental property:

- Classified advertisements
- Real estate magazines
- Web sites
- Small corrugated signs
- Real estate agents and the Multiple Listing Service (MLS)
- Professional affiliations
- Handouts and flyers

Placing an advertisement in the classified section of the local newspaper is one cost-effective method of marketing your rental property for sale. I suggest listing only the essentials in a classified ad, such as the property's location, number of bedrooms, price, and a telephone number to call. The ad should be written in a crisp and concise format without being too wordy. The idea is to whet the reader's appetite by giving her just enough information to pique her curiosity. I like to include the price also because doing so weeds out a lot of the buyers who may not be qualified or who may qualify but want a more expensive house. One limitation of classified ads is that depending on the newspaper, the readership may be limited to the immediate area. Larger papers provide greater exposure, but since there are more ads in the real estate for sale section, it makes it more difficult for your ad to stand out. You can compensate for this shortcoming by paying a little extra to highlight in bold, for example, the heading of your ad.

Real estate magazines also can be a great way to market your house. These magazines often are conveniently placed near grocery stores, hair salons, real estate offices, and gas stations. The advertising rates are often comparable with those of a classified ad in the newspaper. If you are using a real estate agent to represent you, make sure that your property is one that gets featured in the magazines. These publications differ from classified ads in that they have a lot more display ads in which you can include more information about your property, as well as a photograph.

Another great way to increase the visibility of your rental property is by making it available for all the world to see on a Web site. If your real estate investment company already has a Web site, it's easy to include a page that features the houses you have available for sale at any given time. Don't underestimate the power of the Internet. It can attract prospective buyers from all across the country and, for that matter, from all across the globe. Just a few weeks ago, my company, Symphony Homes, sold a house site unseen to a buyer from Australia. The buyer, who will be relocating to this area in a few months, found my company online by doing a search. After looking at some of the photos in the photo gallery of houses that have been built already, he fell in love with one of our most popular models, The Mozart, and decided that it was the house he had to have. My sales agent did a purchase agreement via fax machine, the buyer overnighted the earnest money deposit, and the company since has begun construction of his magnificent new home. Exhibit 12-1 presents an example of how to market your property using the Internet.

Signs are another great way to tell people about your house. They are fairly inexpensive and usually don't require more than a few days to have made up if you're having custom signs printed. Local hardware stores often carry "For Sale" signs that you may want to consider also. The signs, which can be placed almost anywhere, can be used to direct passersby into the neighborhood where the house is located if it is off the

Five Smart Ways to Enhance Your Rental House's Marketability

Exhibit 12-1   Uniform residential appraisal report

beaten path. Real estate agents use them quite often to inform motorists of open-house events.

The Multiple Listing Service (MLS) is an essential tool to provide your rental property with maximum exposure. This means, of course, that you will have to list your property for sale with a licensed real estate agent, unless you happen to be a licensed agent yourself. When your house is

Exhibit 12-1   Uniform residential appraisal report (*Continued*)

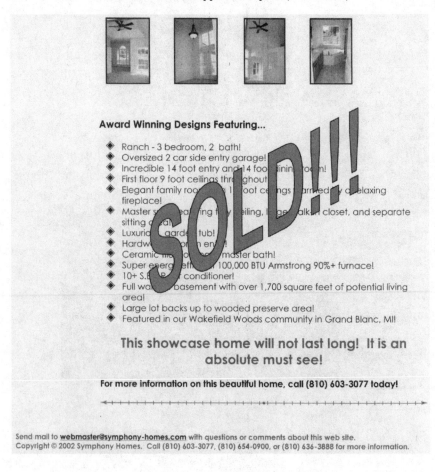

Award Winning Designs Featuring...

- Ranch - 3 bedroom, 2 bath!
- Oversized 2 car side entry garage!
- Incredible 14 foot entry and 14 foot dining room!
- First floor 9 foot ceilings throughout!
- Elegant family room with 11 foot ceilings warmed by a relaxing fireplace!
- Master suite reaching tray ceiling, large walk-in closet, and separate sitting area!
- Luxurious garden tub!
- Hardwood floor in entry!
- Ceramic tile floor in master bath!
- Super energy efficient 100,000 BTU Armstrong 90%+ furnace!
- 10+ S.E.E.R. air conditioner!
- Full walkout basement with over 1,700 square feet of potential living area!
- Large lot backs up to wooded preserve area!
- Featured in our Wakefield Woods community in Grand Blanc, MI!

This showcase home will not last long! It is an absolute must see!

For more information on this beautiful home, call (810) 603-3077 today!

Send mail to **webmaster@symphony-homes.com** with questions or comments about this web site.
Copyright © 2002 Symphony Homes. Call (810) 603-3077, (810) 654-0900, or (810) 636-3888 for more information.

placed in the MLS, you gain immediate access to hundreds and even thousands of sales agents who have a potential interest in your property. Any one of them may have a prospective buyer with whom they are working who may be interested in exactly what you are selling. You cannot afford not to have your investment property listed for sale in the MLS. If you are not a licensed real estate agent already, I recommend that you find a top-producing agent who has a proven track record. The most important thing for you to do is to maximize the visibility of the property you are selling so that you can gain ready access to as large of a pool of buyers as possible. Working with a competent agent is one of the best ways to do this.

Membership in any type of professional organization such as a real estate investment club will provide you with a ready pool of buyers who may be interested in your property. Be sure to tell as many of the members as you can about the availability of your house. The club also may have a newsletter that is published periodically that you can advertise in. In addition, many clubs have Web sites that will allow members to post their listings on. Finally, you can distribute flyers that describe your rental property to members when they attend club meetings.

Circulating handouts at investment club meetings is just one of many places your flyers can be distributed. Flyers can be posted just about anywhere you can think of, including grocery stores, church bulletin boards, office buildings, convenience stores, and the local pizza parlor. One advantage of using flyers is that you can provide a lot of information on them, including a photo of the house. Also, copies are fairly inexpensive to make, so using flyers won't cost you much. In addition, you can provide information on one side of the flyer about the house you are selling and include information on the other side of the flyer to promote your real estate investment company. Exhibits 12-2 and 12-3 are examples of flyers I use to promote my company and one of the many fine homes my company offers.

In summary, there are many tools at your disposal to market your investment property. The more people who know that your house is for sale, the greater your chances become at getting it sold quickly, and the more likely you are to get a price that represents fair market value for it. Whether you're selling a house or selling a car, the more tools you use to increase its exposure, the more effective you will be.

Sell What the Buyer Wants

Smart investors know that to improve the salability of rental properties, they must offer a product that people want to buy. As simple as this may sound, this is an important point that shouldn't be taken lightly. One point to consider before investing is to determine which neighborhoods in your area have houses in them that are selling in the shortest average number of days. The type of location best suited for selling your properties in a timely manner is a neighborhood that typically is between 10 and 30 years old.

Exhibit 12-2

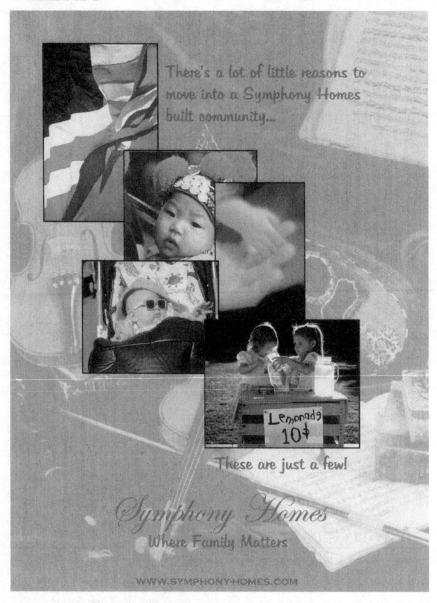

Five Smart Ways to Enhance Your Rental House's Marketability

Exhibit 12-3

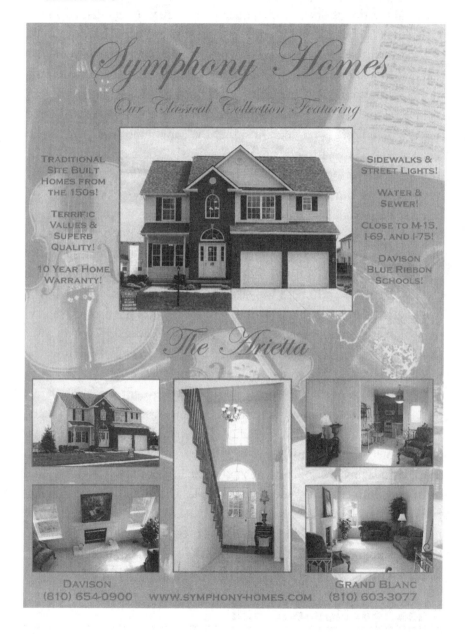

These neighborhoods represent where the average middle-class citizen lives. The ideal location is one in which most homes are well maintained and in an area that is not suffering from functional obsolescence. The area should be well established, have good schools nearby, and continue to have homes that sell in a shorter than average number of days compared with surrounding communities. Characteristics of this kind of neighborhood often include mature landscaping, pristine lawns, and homes that are well cared for. Although there is no guarantee that the community you purchase in today will be just as attractive to home buyers at some given point in the future, you nevertheless will improve your odds of being able to quickly resell when the time comes.

You also should take care to ensure that the house you buy fits in with the rest of the houses in the neighborhood. I have seen, for example, an ultracontemporary house in a mostly traditional neighborhood sit on the market for much longer than other houses in the same neighborhood. Be careful also not to purchase the largest or most expensive house in the neighborhood unless it can pass both requirements of the financial analysis, which are the sales-comps test and the cash-flow test. You can't wait to make these kinds of decisions when it's time to sell. They must be made, of course, before you even buy the rental property.

Finally, your investment property should be presented to prospective buyers in its most favorable condition. Common sense requires that the house be neat and clean in appearance. This includes items such as mowing the lawn, applying a fresh coat of paint, and cleaning up any debris that may be lying around. Furthermore, the interior of the house should be just as clean as the exterior. This includes cleaning the floors, replacing worn carpet and vinyl as needed, applying fresh paint, and giving the house a thorough scrubbing. With a little preplanning before buying and a little sprucing up when it comes time to sell, you'll have a rental house that even the most particular buyers will be interested in.

Price Your House to Sell

If you did your homework before you purchased your rental property, you already should have a good idea of prices in your market. If you're selling several years after purchasing and haven't kept up with home prices, be sure to reacquaint yourself with the market. Otherwise, if the house is priced too low, you will have given the buyer a great deal, but at your expense. On the other hand, if the house is priced above that of your competitors, chances are that it will take longer to sell, and even then you may end up reducing the price. I recommend making your house available for sale at a price just below market.

If the rental property happens to be vacant when it is time to sell, keep in mind that you will have ongoing carrying costs such as interest, taxes, and insurance. The quicker you sell, the quicker you can relieve yourself of those obligations, and the more money you will make. In addition, you have a lost opportunity cost, meaning that as long as your investment capital is tied up in one property, you are limited in your ability to take advantage of other opportunities. Remember, therefore, that when it comes time to sell your investment property, be sure to price it right because in the long run, doing so will save you both time and money.

Sweeten the Pot

If you are like most people, chances are that you're motivated by money. Your prospective buyers will be motivated by money, too. You can use a number of different types of incentives that have some monetary value to encourage prospective buyers to purchase your house instead of one of the many others they have to choose from. You may want to offer the buyer a credit at closing, for example, to be used for general improvements. This would enable buyers to use their discretion and make whatever improvements they wanted to their new home shortly after moving in. For many buyers, especially those who are first-time home buyers, it takes everything they have financially just to buy the house, so they would greatly appreciate having the benefit of a credit at closing for general improvements.

Whether the credit the buyer receives is used for landscaping, painting, or any other purpose is really not relevant. As the seller, your objective is to give them a reason to purchase your house now rather than to continue shopping around. Other incentives include agreeing to pay the buyer's closing costs (or a portion of them), offering to throw in a free appliance package, or giving them a gift certificate from a local moving company to help offset their moving expenses. Most mortgage companies, but not all, will allow the seller to give the buyer a credit of up to 3 percent to be used to apply toward closing costs, property improvements, or whatever else the buyer wants to use the money for.

As an investor in rental houses, the time eventually will come for you to sell your properties. Whether you choose to sell your houses after just 2 or 3 years or you decide to sell them 50 years from now, you nevertheless inevitably will sell them at some point in your lifetime. Regardless of when you sell, by using the five methods outlined in this chapter—beginning with the end in mind, maximizing your property's exposure, selling what the buyer wants to buy, pricing your rental property to sell, and sweetening the pot—you're certain to sell your house for more money and in less time.

I thank God for my handicaps, for through them, I have found myself, my work, and my God.
—HELEN KELLER

13

Six Smart Ways to Negotiate for the Best Price and Terms

The term *negotiate* refers to the process of conferring with another individual or party to bring about a mutually acceptable agreement by all the parties affected. To negotiate involves the exchange of two or more items that all parties agree to be of equivalent value, such as exchanging money for real estate. Learning to become an artful and effective negotiator is similar to learning any other skill. With the proper training, you can learn to become an expert negotiator skilled in the art of successfully consummating almost any real estate transaction. The more you understand about the psychology of interactions with others, the more likely you are to achieve a mutually acceptable agreement.

In this chapter I describe six techniques that when executed properly will enable you to negotiate the best possible price and terms for a rental house regardless of whether you're buying or selling. In time, you will come to know that many of the buyers and sellers you negotiate with are amateurs, meaning that they do not buy or sell real estate with any degree of frequency. They are, therefore, unskilled in the methods and techniques a master negotiator such as yourself might use. Amateurs participate in the real estate market out of necessity. Smart investors, on the other hand, have mastered the six steps of successful negotiations and use them to their advantage at every opportunity. While I am not suggesting that you take unfair advantage of anyone, I am suggesting that you study and apply the techniques listed in the following box and discussed in this chapter and become proficient in their use. As you will see, doing so can enable you to save literally thousands of dollars on your future real estate transactions.

Six Steps to Successful Negotiations

1. Psychology 101
2. Market knowledge is key
3. The trial balloon
4. The blame game
5. Put it in writing
6. The chess player

Psychology 101

One of the most important things to remember when negotiating with others is that you are dealing with people, many of whom develop an emotional attachment to their property somewhere along the way. Most of the buyers and sellers you deal with are not professionals and often find it difficult to separate their emotions from the rational, clear thinking that is required to conduct business. After a certain point in the sales process, people become emotionally engaged, which causes them to act in a manner they otherwise wouldn't. This is true for both buyers and sellers.

The easiest way to illustrate this technique is by using an example. Often when buyers come to one of our communities, they have already looked at a number of different houses in just as many communities and therefore have a difficult time making up their minds. After all, buying a new home is one of the most substantial financial decisions a person will make in his or her entire lifetime. Since we understand that a very real emotional and psychological transition must occur in the mind of the prospective buyer, we are prepared to deal with it through a process of encouraging the buyer to take a series of baby steps. That's right—baby steps. Before an infant can learn to walk, he first must become comfortable with crawling. Once his tiny little body has mastered that feat, he is then ready for the next stage of progression. He takes first one step, then a second step, and perhaps even a third one. Meanwhile, his parents, who are as excited as can be, sing songs of praise and encouragement, cheering him on each step of the way. After two or three months, the baby has mastered the task of "taking baby steps" and begins to walk rather quickly at times, which eventually turns into running. Before you know it, he is all over the place, just as busy as can be, and you find yourself saying, "That kid is wearing me out. I wish he would slow down long enough for me to catch my breath!"

Believe it or not, people buy houses in a similar stage of progression. The primary difference, however, is that these stages of advancement occur in the human psyche as opposed to the physical world. The Symphony Homes sales agents recognize that very few people purchase a house on the spot. This isn't to say that it doesn't happen, but that tends to be more the exception than the rule. Buyers come up with more reasons than you could imagine for postponing their decision. They want to think about it, or sleep on it, or pray about it, or consult with their attorney or accountant, or have their Uncle Joe look at it. All these reasons to delay making a decision are perfectly legitimate in the mind of the buyer, and if you are the seller, you must be prepared to deal with these reasons. If you are not, someone else who understands the process better than you do will make the sale that you just missed. The key to your success lies in getting your prospective buyer to take baby steps, that is, one step at a time, toward making a larger decision.

If a buyer tells me, for example, that she wants to think about it, I might reply with something like, "I understand your need to think it over. This is a very big decision, and you want to be absolutely certain that you are making the right decision. I'll tell you what. I know that you really like this beautiful new home. How would it be if we do a simple hold on the home, which will give you seven days to think it over? It's only $250. During the seven days, you can bring your parents by, or your attorney, or anyone else to look at your new home with you. If by the end of the seven days you have changed your mind for any reason at all, we'll gladly refund your $250. This really is a risk-free way for you to take the time you need before purchasing your new dream home, wouldn't you agree?" Of course she would.

This baby step provides the buyer with an opportunity to make a small, risk-free commitment to you. Even though he or she has not officially purchased the house, the buyer has taken an incremental step toward doing so. Taking this baby step is much more powerful than you may be inclined to think. What happens is that a transition begins to take place in the mind of the buyer. Although the buyer in this example only gave a deposit of $250, in her mind, that magnificent new home now belongs to her. A shift in her thinking has taken place. Now, instead of trying to decide if she should buy the house, the buyer is thinking about all the positive reasons to reinforce her decision. The buyer's intellect changes from one of fear and negativity to one of rationalization and justification. She more than likely will stop looking at other houses, which is exactly what you want him or her to do.

I'm happy to be able to report to you that even as I was writing this section, one of my sales agents called to inform me that she used this very technique to sell a house today. The buyers initially had wanted to put down $250 on the house to "think it over" for 30 days, but since the house was available for immediate occupancy, the agent told them that the deposit would be $1000 and that they could hold the house for seven days instead of the 30 days they had asked for. They wrote a check out on the spot for the full $1000 and are planning on bringing their parents out to see "their new home" tomorrow.

Although I have used purchasing a new home as an example, psychology is a vitally important component of the negotiating process. You must be able to understand the needs of the individuals you are dealing with to be able to work toward a common goal. When you work together to resolve problems and overcome objections, everybody comes out a winner.

Market Knowledge Is Key

To be successful in this business, you must have a comprehensive knowledge of the market you are dealing in. It is impossible to negotiate the best price without it. You must understand property values in your respective market as well as, or better than, the parties with whom you are doing business. You can use your market knowledge to make sound arguments to the parties you are dealing with to support the price and terms for which you are negotiating. By showing them what similar properties are selling for, you are presenting unbiased information that will enable them to feel more comfortable with the price differential.

I'm scheduled to meet with a family tomorrow morning that our sales agent has been working with for the past two months or so. This particular family has been concerned about finding the best lot on which to build their new home and has literally searched high and low in two bordering counties. The sales agent made every effort to convince them that for the money they wanted to spend and for the area they wanted to be in, they would not be able to find a better deal anywhere else than they could by purchasing a lot in one of our communities. Our sales agent had done her homework and knew the market well. Unfortunately she had a difficult time persuading this family that they weren't going to find a better deal. Some people are like that. They have to go through a process of discovery for themselves, and that's okay. As it turns out, the family has come full circle and is prepared to sign an agreement tomorrow in the very community we recommended to them to begin with.

Whether you are buying or selling vacant lots, rental houses, or apartment buildings, the need to thoroughly understand the market is exactly the same. You can't afford to pay too much for the rental property you are interested in buying, and you can't afford to sell for too little when it comes time to sell. As a professional real estate investor, you must be intimately familiar with the market you are dealing in and possess a comprehensive knowledge of it in order to be truly successful. Without this key information, you will discover all too soon that you cannot survive in the real estate business.

The Trial Balloon

The term *trial balloon* originated with the launching of hot air balloons that initially were unmanned. The history of hot air balloons extends back to 1782, when two brothers, Joseph and Etienne Montgolfiere, first began experimenting with balloon flight near Paris, France. Joseph had conceived the idea of using balloons to penetrate by air the impregnable fortress of Gibraltar. His intent was to use the balloons to carry an entire army right above the heads of the English to quickly defeat them. In 1783 several unmanned trial balloons were launched to test this novel idea. Finally, on August 27, 1783, a perfected trial balloon was launched, flying a distance of approximately 12 miles. Unaware that such a thing even existed, the French peasants in Gonesse, where the balloon descended from its lofty flight, were taken by surprise. Fearing that some monster had fallen from the heavens, the peasants quickly attacked the balloon with pitchforks, rendering it useless. On September 14 of that same year, another trial balloon was launched. In place of a man, a wicker cage containing a sheep, a chicken, and a duck was attached to the balloon to see if they would survive in the higher atmosphere. The flight was deemed a success because all three animals returned safely to earth, unharmed but perhaps a bit shaken by their history-making flight.

Although the term *trial balloon* is still used widely today, it seldom refers to a hot air balloon. The term does, however, share a similar meaning in that when it is used, it most often refers to a trial or a test of something. Politicians are said to float trial balloons on a regular basis. For example, a senator may have one of his administrative assistants leak an idea or a story to the press about increasing the sales tax to raise money for educational purposes. The senator is in reality attempting to gauge his or her constituents' reactions to determine if they will accept or reject the idea. Floating the unmanned trial balloon through a leak to the press affords the senator the opportunity to "test the waters" without exposing himself. If the public reacts favorably, the senator can then personally "man" the balloon and make known his intentions to increase taxes. Otherwise, he will remain safely silent with his reputation secure.

The trial balloon technique as it applies to real estate can be an extremely effective negotiating tool. Throughout the course of your dialogue with the other party, whether a buyer or seller, you can launch a series of your own trial balloons. The technique works by subtly floating a suggestion from time to time to test what the other party may be willing to do. Through observation, you can gauge the other party's reaction by how he responds to the suggestion.

Recall from Chapter 4 the example I used about the seller with the lake-view property on which I wanted to build condominiums for Symphony Homes. The seller's original asking price was $370,000. My analysis revealed that the cash flow from renting his house out would not support a value of his full asking price, so I decided to launch a trial balloon. I threw out the number $330,000 to see how he would react. To my surprise, he hardly seemed bothered at all by a price $40,000 less than his asking price. If the seller were at all opposed to that price, he would have signaled this one way or another to me. For example, he may have bristled at the low price by saying something like, "I've got to have more than that just to pay off the mortgage." Or he may have said something like, "That's ridiculous. I know my house is worth more than $330,000." Instead, he seemed calm and very comfortable with the lower price. In fact, he seemed so comfortable with it that I thought perhaps I had not yet reached his bottom line. I decided to leave it at that for the time being and let him become comfortable psychologically with the lower price.

After meeting with the seller, I visited with the city manager about the number of condominium units that would be allowed to be built on the property according to the existing zoning regulations. She indicated that up to eight units could be approved and possibly as many as 10. I experimented with both those numbers in a construction model I created to determine the financial feasibility of the project. Using a value of $330,000 and eight condominiums gave me a unit cost of $41,250, a number higher than I wanted to pay.

A few days later, I arranged another appointment with the seller so that I could bring my partner, Don, back with me to view the property. Remembering the seller's rather calm reaction to the last trial balloon I had floated, I sensed that there might be room for further negotiation of price. I sensed that he might even be comfortable all the way down to $300,000 and resolved to make that price point my objective. To do this, I decided to float another trial balloon, but I thought I would do so below my true objective. I explained to the seller that the going rate for a vacant lot in the area for a single-family house was about $70,000 and that for condominium units it was about half that. I then told him about my meeting with the city manager and that she felt very comfortable approving eight units but was unwilling to commit on any number greater than that. I then remained silent to see how he would react. I could see him quickly doing the math in his head. "Half of $70,000 is $35,000, and $35,000 times eight units is $280,000." Although the seller didn't say anything to me, I sensed I had struck a nerve and that he wasn't comfortable with the lower price. After all, why should he be? It was only a ridiculous $90,000 less than his asking price. I was just thankful he didn't punch me and throw me out of his house. He actually was very polite but obviously somewhat shaken by the lower price. I decided to leave it at that because I wanted that lower price point to sink in for a few days to soften him up. He now knew that I would not be willing to pay the $330,000 we talked about several days before and may have been feeling that all hope was lost with me as a buyer for his property. My objective was to leave him with a feeling of despair so that in the event that we were somehow able to reach a higher price, say, $300,000, that we could both agree on, both of us would end up feeling satisfied with the outcome.

As has been illustrated by this example, you can see just how effective the trial balloon technique can be when negotiating with buyers and sellers of real estate. You can float all kinds of trial balloons. For example, you can test the other party's willingness to negotiate on the interest rate, the down payment, carrying back a second mortgage, the date of closing, and a host of other things as well. For the conclusion of the example used here, be sure to read the negotiating technique I refer to as the *chess player*.

The Blame Game

The blame game technique does exactly as its name implies by diverting blame or fault in another direction. The technique is used to shift or transfer the blame from you as the investor to someone or something else. You probably are wondering what it is you might get blamed for when negotiating with others. The answer is, nothing if you use this technique.

Six Smart Ways to Negotiate for the Best Price and Terms

A primary key to successful negotiations with another party is to establish a positive relationship with that person. You want to build rapport with that person by staying focused on the positive. Using this approach will build their confidence in you and create an atmosphere of trust, thereby allowing a discussion of price and terms to take place. I recall reading a number of years ago about a negotiating strategy that took exactly the opposite approach. The idea was to attempt to beat the seller down in price by criticizing everything about his house by pointing out all its many faults. All this approach does is insult the seller and make him not want to do business with you under any circumstances, regardless of how much you may offer. I'm sure you've heard the old saying about catching more bees with honey. The same principle holds true when it comes to buying and selling real estate. The blame game technique affords you the opportunity to negotiate for a more favorable price or terms by shifting the blame or fault to either an animate object such as a third party or an inanimate object such as a project.

Let's look at an example. Assume that you are walking through the seller's house and you notice that the carpet is worn out and needs to be replaced. You might say something like, "Mr. Seller, you have a very nice home. It's obvious you've taken good care of it over the years. I noticed, however, that the carpet looks a bit worn and probably will need to be replaced. My partner is very particular about flooring and will most likely want to replace it. I doubt if I could talk him into buying your house, as lovely as it is, without there being some kind of allowance given to replace the flooring. Mr. Seller, is that something you would be willing to consider?"

Can you see how this approach might be more effective than directly finding fault with the seller's house? Instead of alienating the seller, you have complimented him. The partner mentioned here could be anyone. It could be a bona fide partner from your company, or it could simply be a spouse, a friend, or a relative. It doesn't really matter who it is. The point is that you are transferring or shifting the fault finding to another person who is not present. You can blame your partner for practically anything you can think of. If you don't like the yard, blame your partner. If you don't like the roof, blame your partner. If you don't like the paint, blame your partner. You get the idea.

There are many variations to this technique. You don't always have to blame your partner. You might express concern over the price and mention to the seller that based on the comparable sales you have examined, you don't know if your appraiser can get the house to appraise for the value he is asking. If your financial analysis indicates marginal cash flow, you might mention to the seller that there is barely sufficient cash from the rents to pay the note and that your lender requires a minimum of a 1.20 cash-flow-to-debt-service ratio. Although the seller may not understand this, you can explain to him how the lender requires a certain amount of cash from the property before it will be comfortable making the loan. Other parties or persons you can blame include your real estate attorney, the city planning commission, or your property manager. Use your imagination, and you probably can figure out a way to blame even your mother-in-law.

Now let's look at an example using an inanimate object. Assume that you have inspected the seller's house and have completed your financial analysis. The results reveal marginal returns that can be improved only by lowering the price. In this case, you would explain to the seller while making a compliment about her beautiful lawn that you have examined this opportunity very closely; however, your analysis has disclosed that the project simply will not work at the current price. You explain to the seller that you are an investor and that each and every project or investment opportunity you consider must meet your rate-of-return criteria before you can invest any money in it. You then say something like, "Mrs. Seller, I really would like to try to find a way to make this work. Is there any flexibility at all in the price you are asking?" You must then remain silent and wait for her to respond. In this type of situation, silence truly is golden because if you don't speak and wait for the seller to respond, you might just end up with some extra gold in your pocket.

In this example, you are transferring the blame to a project or an investment opportunity. The project must generate a predetermined rate of return on your invested capital or it simply won't work. The seller will not take your comments personally and, even more important, may in fact be willing to accommodate you by lowering the price.

After floating a couple of trial balloons on the lake view property for Symphony Homes, I used the blame game technique to formally present an offer. Here's how it went: I met the seller at his home with my offer ready to go. Seated in the kitchen, I began to implement the technique. I spent a couple of minutes telling him what a fine home he had and all the things I liked about it. Then I began to blame everyone and everything I could think of for the low offer I was about to present to him. I said something like the following, "Mr. Seller, my partner and I have analyzed this project very carefully. I've already mentioned to you that the city manager will only allow me to build eight units on the land you have here. I've also spoken with my lender, who insists on the property cash flowing properly before loaning money on it. After having taken everything into consideration and weighing all the facts, my partner and I are prepared to offer you $34,000 per unit for a total of $272,000." As you may recall, his original asking price was $370,000. I kept a close eye on him as soon as I said $272,000 for fear that he might reach across the table and punch me. After all, I was offering him $98,000 less than his asking price. I then assured him that although he had a very nice home, my offer was based on a sound and objective financial analysis and asked him to please think it over carefully for the next two days before getting back with me.

Although I came in with a very low offer, the seller clearly understood that my offer was based on all the different factors that affected his property. I initially transferred the blame to my partner, then to the city manager who would only allow eight units to be built, and then to my lender who might not loan money on the project if it didn't cash flow properly. Finally, I shifted the blame for such a low offering price to the overall financial analysis of the project. While visibly shaken, the seller promised me he would get back with me within the next two days. The very fact that he didn't tell me to go jump in the lake, which was only right across the street, gave me reason to hope.

Put It in Writing

This negotiating technique is used more appropriately as a closing technique and more particularly for sellers. The put-it-in-writing technique is to be used as a defensive measure against potential buyers who would float trial balloons as part of their strategy. As a seller of newly constructed homes for Sym-

How to Sell Rental Properties the Smart Way

phony Homes, I have clients float trial balloons all the time. For example, they may say something to one of our sales agents like, "We really like the house, but Builder XYZ down the street is offering a free landscaping package with his homes. Can you throw in a landscaping package to match what he is offering?" Sounds like a typical trial balloon floated by a prospective buyer trying to beat us on price. Hardly a day goes by that we don't get a setup question like this. How do you think we should respond to this type of question? How would you respond?

If the sales agent were to reply by stating that, yes, we would consider including a landscaping package at no additional charge, the buyer would assume that if he buys the house, he is going to get the free landscaping package. By even suggesting that we will consider it, we have just relinquished a portion of our bargaining power. Furthermore, once we agree verbally without a commitment from the buyer, he will float another trial balloon, and then another, and another, and so on. As the seller, you cannot afford to surrender control of the sales process to the buyer.

The appropriate response by the sales agent goes something like this. "Mr. Buyer, I can see that you really like the house, but I know from my experience with the builder that he will not consider any offer unless it is in writing. If you are really serious about purchasing this beautiful home, and I believe that you are, then let me suggest that we sit down together and include the landscaping package at no additional charge as part of your offer. Afterwards, I'll present the offer, along with your earnest money deposit, to the builder. I can't promise you that he will accept it, but we can certainly give it a try."

Can you see how effectively this method can be used to negotiate yourself right into a sale? Rather than give the buyer any indication verbally that you may be flexible, you get him to make a commitment to you by putting it in writing. This lets you know that the buyer is serious. My company gets tire kickers every day, many of whom are out looking at houses because they have nothing better to do. My sales agents know better than to give anything away through a simple question and answer dialogue. Instead, they use the buyer's trial balloon as an opportunity to write up the sale. If a buyer wants you to negotiate on price, simply tell him to put it in writing, and you'll be happy to consider it.

The Chess Player

The game of chess is played by two opponents who systematically move their respective chess pieces around the board in a strategic fashion and execute a series of well-planned moves. While being ever cognizant of the opponent, the chess player carefully places each piece in position in a setup-like fashion, waiting for just the right opportunity to strike. Although each piece is moved with precise deliberation, the players make every effort to contain all signs of outwardly visible emotion that potentially could reveal their underlying motives. Then, at just the right moment, on detecting an area of weakness or vulnerability, the player quickly moves the appropriate piece and announces, "Checkmate!"

The smart investor knows that negotiating for rental properties is similar to playing a game of chess. Each and every action is executed with deliberate precision. You begin the game by positioning your pieces so that they match those of your opponent. In a step-by-step fashion, you then begin to systematically move your pieces into position one at a time, until finally everything is just right. Throughout the process, you reveal only what the other player needs to know, being careful not to disclose information that may benefit her. Finally, when the moment is right and you detect an area of weakness, you quickly move into checkmate.

As mentioned previously, I used the blame game to formally present my offer to the seller of the lake view property on which I wanted to build condominiums. The blame game method was combined with the chess player technique so as to conceal as much as possible how much I would be willing to pay if the seller did not accept my offer. When I presented the offer to the seller of $34,000 per unit for each of the eight units for a total of $272,000, I did *not* say anything like, "Now Mr. Seller, I know that this price is a little low, and please keep in mind that it is only a starting point." On the contrary, just as a chess player is careful not to reveal his or her strategy, I was very careful not to even hint at the notion that I might be willing to pay more for the property. If I had, the seller would have known immediately that I was willing to pay more and surely would have rejected my offer. Instead, I deferred to the investment project and that the $34,000 per unit was how much we could justify for his property. Even though we could justify paying more, I had no intention of telling him that.

How to Sell Rental Properties the Smart Way

Remember that the seller's original asking price was $370,000. My intent was to make a low offer, knowing that he probably would not accept it, and end up expecting him to counter at a higher price, perhaps around $300,000 and as high as $330,000. If I could get the property for $300,000, I would be elated. By using a proprietary model in which a profit matrix was created, I determined that I could pay as high as $330,000 to no more than $340,000 for the property. Anything less than $330,000 would be a bonus.

I asked the seller to think it over for the next two days and then to please get back with me. I reminded him that my partner and I were well qualified to purchase his property and that we could cash him out in 30 days if he accepted the offer. He could have his bags packed and be on his way to Colorado in just a few short weeks if he so desired. He said that he would give the offer serious consideration and get back with me the following day. I knew that the seller would think it over very carefully just as he said because otherwise he would have rejected it on the spot. If he had felt really insulted by the low offer, he may have even told me to go jump in the lake, which was right across the street. In fact, he even may have given me some help getting there.

Late the next afternoon the seller called to tell me that he was respectfully declining my offer. That didn't surprise me. What would have surprised me is if he had called to tell me that he would accept the offer. I began to probe and to ask him questions such as, "What do you need to get out of the property to meet your needs?" He responded by telling me that $330,000 was a good number. I replied with something close to, "Mr. Seller, I know you would like to get $330,000 for your property, but if I were able to cash you out at $300,000, would you be comfortable with that? I don't know yet if my partner would be willing to pay that much, but if $300,000 is acceptable to you, then I will talk to him and see if I can get him to go that high." The seller replied by telling me that $300,000 sounded pretty good to him and that he thought he would be comfortable with that price. Just as a chess player would conceal her excitement immediately prior to the moment of moving in to declare checkmate, so did I conceal my enthusiasm by stating, "Mr. Seller, I'll talk it over with my partner and get back to you in the next day or so." I then hung up the phone and shouted, "Yahoo!"

Six Smart Ways to Negotiate for the Best Price and Terms

I immediately called my partner and informed him that we had just saved ourselves $70,000 on this excellent piece of lake view property. I kept my word to the seller by doing exactly as I had told him I would do—I talked it over with my partner. Although there wasn't much to talk over, we nevertheless did talk it over and quickly agreed that we should proceed with the transaction. Knowing that the seller was going out of town for the weekend on Friday, I called him late in the afternoon on Thursday to inform him that my partner would be willing to pay the $300,000 he was requiring and asked if it would be okay if I stopped by to drop off a revised purchase agreement to reflect the recent changes. The seller replied that it would be okay to drop off the agreement but that he wouldn't have time to review it completely and sign off on everything because he was preparing for his trip out of town the next day. I took the revised purchase agreement to him and asked that he sign off on it and fax it back to me when he returned from his trip, which he agreed to do.

I left the seller's house feeling a little anxious about whether or not he would change his mind over the weekend. As I write this very paragraph, it is Monday, the day I was supposed to hear back from him. As of 4:45 P.M. today, since I had not heard from the seller, I decided to give him a call. I casually asked how his weekend went and eventually worked my way into inquiring about the purchase agreement. He explained that he had decided to stay an extra day on his weekend excursion and that he had just returned home a few minutes prior to my calling. By 6:00 P.M. the seller had faxed over the revised agreement to my office, complete with his signature, for the agreed-on purchase price of $300,000. Checkmate!

I believe that the greatest compliment a man can receive is when his wife expresses her respect and admiration for him. I shared the good news about the lake view property with my wife, Nancy, who has been following this story. After having given the matter some thought, she told me that she knew I possessed good business skills but that she really had her doubts about this one. She was genuinely impressed with my ability to shave $70,000 off the asking price on a prime piece of lake view property. It is with humility and graciousness that I received the adoration she so kindly expressed to me. After all, a man's got to do something to be able to impress his wife, right?

In summary, the six smart ways to negotiate included in this chapter are just a sampling of the many techniques available to real estate investors. I encourage you to study and review each one of them and to apply these methods in your negotiations with both buyers and sellers. As indicated by the example here, these techniques just saved me $70,000 on one transaction alone. By carefully studying these negotiating techniques, I am confident that you can learn to master them and then execute them skillfully and artfully to your advantage in the many real estate transactions that await you. When the time comes, like me, you too will be able to declare "Checkmate!"

I hope I shall always possess firmness and virtue enough to maintain what I consider the most enviable of all titles, the character of an honest man.

—George Washington

14

Five Golden Rules for Success

In Chapter 10, the final chapter of *The Complete Guide to Buying and Selling Apartment Buildings*, I wrote about the five keys to your success as follows:

> The central focus of this book is on arming you with the specific tools necessary to identify potential acquisition candidates, to acquire and manage those properties once identified, to implement sound techniques for creating value, and finally, to capture all of that value, or as much of it as possible, through various exit strategies. The process by which all of this can be accomplished rests, I believe, on five keys that are crucial to success. These keys do not deal with the mechanical processes involved in buying and selling apartment buildings but are grounded in principles fundamental to life itself. These laws deal with the human psyche. They govern our thoughts, which, in turn, direct our actions. The failure to understand these keys—which can provide the foundation of happiness, and ultimately of success—will almost certainly guarantee your defeat.

The Five Keys to Success

1. Understanding risk
2. Overcoming fear of failure
3. Accepting responsibility
4. Willingness to persevere
5. Defining your sense of purpose

After completing the book on apartments, I wrote *The Complete Guide to Flipping Properties*. In Chapter 11, the concluding chapter, I wrote about the three principles of power as follows:

In this chapter, I will discuss what I refer to as the three principles of power. These three principles have absolutely nothing to do with real estate in particular, yet everything to do with your success in it. For that matter, the three principles of power can be applied to any business or profession and are not just limited to real estate. These laws can furthermore be utilized in your personal life and when properly applied, can be a source of great joy and happiness to you and to those with whom you associate.

Although I have a passion for investing in real estate, the things that I write in this chapter are far more important to me than finding the next house to buy or sell. These principles lie at the very core of my belief system. They are an integral part of who I am. They are what compel me each and every day to strive for that perfection which I know I will never achieve in this life. It is my hope to inspire you to incorporate these three principles of power into your belief system. Doing so will enable you to reach the highest level of achievement of which you are truly capable. You will be empowered to fulfill the measure of your creation, to reach your potential, and to enjoy the abundant gifts life has to offer.

The Three Principles of Power

1. The principle of vision
2. The principle of passion
3. The principle of autonomy

By now you are probably beginning to get the idea. The first 13 chapters of this book have been devoted to the topic of investing in real estate—how to buy it, how to manage it, how to sell it, and most important, how to make money by participating in these activities. In this chapter I want to give you something more than just the how-tos of real estate, just as I did in the concluding chapters of my previous books. It is my sincere belief that each of us needs to understand a body of knowledge outside our chosen profession that deals more specifically with various factors that can help to prepare us to become successful. If I can offer even one bit of advice that will help you to achieve your goals, whatever they may be, then the time I have taken to write this chapter will have been worth every minute of it.

The Five Laws of Gold

In his classic book *The Richest Man in Babylon* (New York: Hawthorn/Dutton, 1955), George S. Clason tells a fascinating tale using "Babylonian parables" to instruct others in the fundamental principles of finance. One such parable reveals the five laws of gold, which, if followed according to the counsel given, can enable you over time to amass great wealth. The storyteller in this chapter is a wise, old gentleman named Kalabab. He begins his story by relating the following:

"A bag heavy with gold or a clay tablet carved with words of wisdom; if thou hadst thy choice, which would thou choose?"

By the flickering light from the fire of desert shrubs, the sun-tanned faces of the listeners gleamed with interest.

"The gold, the gold," chorused the twenty-seven.

Old Kalabab smiled knowingly.

"Hark," he resumed, raising his hand. "Hear the wild dogs out there in the night. They howl and wail because they are lean with hunger. Yet feed them, and what do they do? Fight and strut. Then fight and strut some more, giving no thought to the morrow that will surely come.

"Just so it is with the sons of men. Give them a choice of gold or wisdom—what do they do? Ignore the wisdom and waste the gold. On the morrow they wail because they have no more gold.

"Gold is reserved for those who know its laws and abide by them" [p. 71].

Kalabab then recounts the story of Arkad, the richest man in Babylon, and of Arkad's son, Nomasir, whom he sent out to prove himself. Arkad gave to Nomasir two things—a bag of gold and a clay tablet on which were carved the five laws of gold. Arkad gave his son these instructions:

My son, it is my desire that thou succeed to my estate. Thou must, however, first prove that thou art capable of wisely handling it. Therefore, I wish that thou go out into the world and show thy ability both to acquire gold and to make thyself respected among men. . . . Ten years from this day come thou back to the house of thy father and give account of thyself. If thou prove worthy, I will then make thee the heir to my estate. Otherwise, I will give it to the priests that they may barter for my soul the kind consideration of the gods.

And so it was that Nomasir soon discovered that proving himself worthy to inherit his father's estate would be much more difficult than he had imagined. It didn't take long for the foolish young man to part company with the bag of gold that had been so generously given to him. Much of Nomasir's wealth was squandered on a scheme designed to bet on horses, and what was left was lost to an unwise business partner who spent the money foolishly. Nomasir then sold his slaves, his robes, and all that he had, except for one thing, just to eat. It was then that he remembered the clay tablets his wise father, Arkad, had given to him. Inscribed on the tablets were the five laws of gold.

The Five Laws of Gold

1. Gold cometh gladly and in increasing quantity to any man who will put by not less than one-tenth of his earnings to create an estate for his future and that of his family.
2. Gold laboreth diligently and contentedly for the wise owner who finds for it profitable employment, multiplying even as the flocks of the field.
3. Gold clingeth to the protection of the cautious owner who invests it under the advice of men wise in its handling.
4. Gold slippeth away from the man who invests it in businesses or purposes with which he is not familiar or which are not approved by those skilled in its keep.
5. Gold flees the man who would force it to impossible earnings or who followeth the alluring advice of tricksters and schemers or who trusts it to his own inexperience and romantic desires in investment.

Over the next several years, Nomasir committed to applying earnestly each of the five laws of gold in his quest for wealth, lest he return to his father ashamed and disgraced because of his earlier loss. As Nomasir grew in wisdom, so did he grow in wealth. He eventually determined that the clay tablets were far more valuable than the bag of gold his father had originally given him, for with his wisdom came the ability to earn many bags of gold. Kalabab concluded his tale by conveying that Nomasir was able to report to his father, Arkad, that although he suffered a loss initially, he had now learned the lessons of the five laws of gold well and that while he had indeed grown in wealth, even more important, he had grown in wisdom.

The First Law of Gold

Gold cometh gladly and in increasing quantity to any man who will put by not less than one-tenth of his earnings to create an estate for his future and that of his family.

Kalabab proceeds to share his own experience with the first law of gold by proclaiming

> Any man who will put by one-tenth of his earnings consistently and invest it wisely will surely create a valuable estate that will provide an income for him in the future and further guarantee safety for his family in case the gods call him to the world of darkness. This law also sayeth that gold cometh gladly to such a man. I can truly certify this in my own life. The more gold I accumulate, the more readily it comes to me and in increased quantities. The gold which I save earns more, even as yours will, and its earnings earn more, and this is the working out of the first law [p. 82].

While Kalabab's counsel to save 10 percent of all you earn is unquestionably sound advice, it is in all actuality most difficult to apply. I'm sure many of you believe that it's all you can do just to pay your bills, much less set aside 10 percent each month. Establishing a consistent savings plan often means giving something up now that you might otherwise enjoy. It means making a sacrifice, such as holding off on the new car and making do with the one you have that is already paid for. To sacrifice continuously over time requires a disciplined approach. I might add, however, that although sacrificing now may at first seem difficult, it becomes easier over time. Each month as you set money aside for investment purposes, you are forming a habit. Once the habit is formed, it becomes easier and easier to apply. In fact, the habit in time will become difficult to break. Yes, I know that saving 10 percent each month will be next to impossible for many of you, but I also firmly believe that you have the power and strength within you to govern your choices.

I remember years ago when I first started attending college the sacrifice that it required of me. Since I joined the U.S. Air Force right out of high school, I didn't go to college until I was in my midtwenties. In retrospect, that turned out to be a mistake. Joining the Air Force and serving my country was not at all a mistake, but choosing not to attend night school was. I was fortunate enough to have served during peacetime and therefore had ample opportunity to take college courses at night but instead chose not to. By the time I decided to begin attending school, my tour of duty in the military was long over, and I was working full time and had family and financial responsibilities of my own.

Just as many as you have, I eventually chose the road less traveled and took the plunge by signing up for just one college course, which happened to be an English class. I've always enjoyed English, and my success in that class gave me the confidence I needed to sign up for two more courses. What felt at first like a tremendous sacrifice was already becoming a way of life. I was forming habits that would carry me throughout my studies over the course of the next seven years. I determined at that time that I would set a goal to get an associate degree in business, which is a two-year degree for students attending full time. My disciplined approach, along with the sacrifices I was making, was finally paying off. Although it took me about two and one-half years to complete the program because I also was working full time, it is with deep humility that I am able to report that I had the honor of graduating first in my class.

After earning an associate degree, I set another goal to earn a bachelor's degree in business finance, which is a four-year degree for students attending full time. By this time I no longer felt like I was sacrificing anything. Spending time with family, attending church, going to work, dabbling in real estate, and studying at school had become a way of life. Before I knew it, another two and one-half years had passed, and I was awarded a bachelor's degree and had the good fortune of graduating cum laude.

I remember quite vividly during those years the difference between the life I was living and the lives most of my friends and work associates were living. While some of them had earned degrees long ago, many of them had not. I recall that while I was in school, almost every evening and weekend my coworkers were out enjoying some type of leisure activity. While I had my nose buried in the books, they were out living it up on their boats or on the golf course and enjoying the good life. While I used vacation days and holidays to catch up on my studies, they were enjoying trips to Disney World, Six Flags, and the beach. In some ways I envied the leisure time my friends and coworkers enjoyed. After all, who wouldn't want to relax and enjoy the good life? I also recall, however, that although I was somewhat envious of them, I didn't ever, not even for a single moment, regret my decision to pursue a college degree. I had long since formed the habits required of discipline, and sacrifice had become a way of life. I knew that by investing my time in my studies, I also was investing in my future, and I knew that this investment in myself eventually would pay many dividends.

Now that I had achieved two goals with respect to my education, it was time to set a third goal. Several months before receiving my bachelor's degree, I applied to Rice University for enrollment into its MBA program. For those of you who may not have heard of Rice, it is a moderately sized private school with a matriculation of about 4000 students. The school was established by a wealthy merchant named William Marsh Rice in 1891 when the initial charter was drafted. Rice is located in Houston, Texas, and is situated on a magnificent 285-acre campus with buildings designed using an early twentieth-century neo-Byzantine style of architecture. While many people refer to Rice University as the "Harvard of the South," we, in turn, referred to Harvard as the "Rice of the North."

Although acceptance into Rice's graduate school of management came as welcome news, attending the program would demand an even greater sacrifice than that which had been required of me previously. The MBA program was designed around a fairly rigid two-year curriculum that would require me to attend on a full-time basis in order to complete the mandatory 64 semester hours. The only way I could do that would be to quit my job completely and to relinquish some of my other responsibilities. To give up my job and my primary source of income meant that I would have to sell my house, which at the time was one of the finest homes in all of Pasadena.

I recall with vivid detail standing in front of Lovett Hall, one of the original main buildings located near the east entrance, with my wife, Nancy. It was a beautiful spring morning colored by thousands of azaleas blooming in all their splendor and beauty. I was confronted with a decision that potentially could have a significant impact on my life. By the grace of God, I had been granted an opportunity to attend one of the best universities in the nation. Doing so, however, would require a tremendous personal sacrifice. Nancy and I held hands as we walked across the plush green grass contemplating this momentous decision that lay before us. We talked about the demands attending a rigorous program would place on us, the sacrifices that would be required, and the investment of time and energy and money. We also talked about the many doors that would be opened and the opportunities made available to us after I completed the program successfully. Together, Nancy and I concluded that any short-term sacrifices we made would be well worth it in the long run. We decided to go for it!

Shortly thereafter, we sold our home and paid cash for a small two-bedroom mobile home in order to alleviate as much debt as possible and minimize our living expenses. After I resigned from work, we weren't quite as poor as church mice, but it certainly felt like it at times. We lived off of love, our savings, and student loans. Two years later, with diploma in hand, I was ready to conquer the world! Since that time, we have never once regretted our decision for me to attend graduate school. Our investment of time and money had finally begun to pay dividends.

I do not share this experience with you to boast of my accomplishments but rather to help you to understand more fully the principles outlined in the first law of gold. I'm sure that many of you have made similar choices that have required great personal sacrifices. Also like many of you,

I come from a very humble upbringing and not one of affluence. This is not to say that I ever went hungry, because we always had plenty to eat. The reason I know that we always had plenty to eat is because when I used to ask for a second serving of roast beef or meat loaf, my dad would often tell me, "No son, you've already had plenty to eat!" I don't recall ever being told that, however, when I asked for seconds on the vegetables, which I didn't eat much of anyway. The point is that whether you give one-tenth of your income or a portion of your time, you are exercising the discipline of sacrificing now so that you may enjoy the fruit of your labors at a later time.

The Second Law of Gold

Gold laboreth diligently and contentedly for the wise owner who finds for it profitable employment, multiplying even as the flocks of the field.

Again, Kalabab shares his insight of this second law of gold. He states

Gold, indeed, is a willing worker. It is ever eager to multiply when opportunity presents itself. To every man who hath a store of gold set by, opportunity comes for its most profitable use. As the years pass by, it multiplies itself in surprising fashion [p. 82].

Remember the magic of compound interest described in Chapter 1? The principle described by Mark O. Haroldsen in his book, *How to Wake Up the Financial Genius Inside You,* is exactly the same as the one described in the second law of gold by Kalabab. As you recall, Mr. Haroldsen presented two choices. The first choice was to work for him and be compensated at the rate of $1000 per day for 35 days. The second choice was to be compensated with only 1 cent the first day and having the wage double every day thereafter for 35 days. Although the first choice resulted in a very respectable wage of $35,000 after just 35 days, the second choice resulted in excess of a phenomenal $342 million.

The smart investor knows that in order to maximize the utility of capital, he or she must put his or her capital to work. Time is a finite constraint on your earning ability because there are only so many hours in a day. One of the most effective ways to overcome this constraint, however, is to employ whatever savings you have. That's right. Each ounce of gold, each dollar bill, is like a little worker bee. As the employer, you must put your employees to work so that "as the years pass by," it will "multiply itself in surprising fashion." There is much truth in the adage that states, "It's not how hard you work, but how smart you work."

The Third Law of Gold

Gold clingeth to the protection of the cautious owner who invests it under the advice of men wise in its handling.

Of the third law of gold, Kalabab has this to say:

Gold, indeed, clingeth to the cautious owner, even as it flees the careless owner. The man who seeks the advice of men wise in handling gold soon learneth not to jeopardize his treasure, but to preserve in safety and to enjoy in contentment its consistent increase [p. 83].

Kalabab's counsel to seek the advice of wise men is well founded. Often people think that they can save money by circumventing the services of a person who is skilled in a particular profession. Remember the for-sale-by-owner (FSBO) approach in Chapter 3? The owner who sells FSBO assumes that he knows just as much about selling a house as a licensed real estate agent does. What the FSBO lacks, however, is access to the Multiple Listing Service (MLS), a pool of prospective buyers the agent may already be working with, and exposure through various other media, such as commercial publications and a network of agents. Also, an unskilled FSBO may not be able to price his home properly, nor will he typically have the negotiation skills required to complete a transaction successfully. All these shortcomings may cost the FSBO both time and money in the long run. Kalabab's advice applies equally to investments other than real estate, such as stocks, bonds, precious metals, or a small business. Regardless of what you are planning to invest in, seek the expertise of individuals already skilled in the respective area. The smart investor will take every precaution to preserve her investment capital by not permitting the careless use of it.

The Fourth Law of Gold

Gold slippeth away from the man who invests it in businesses or purposes with which he is not familiar or which are not approved by those skilled in its keep.

Of the fourth law of gold, Kalabab reveals this sage advice:

To the man who hath gold, yet is not skilled in its handling, many uses appear most profitable. Too often these are fraught with danger of loss, and if properly analyzed by wise men, show small possibility of profit. Therefore, the inexperienced owner of gold who trusts to his own judgment and invests it in businesses or purposes with which he is not familiar, too often finds his judgment imperfect, and pays with his treasure for his inexperience. Wise, indeed, is he who investeth his treasures under the advice of men skilled in the ways of gold [p. 83].

The fourth law of gold, much like the third law, maintains that individuals should exercise caution when investing in businesses or purposes with which they are not familiar. A lack of experience when venturing into a new endeavor can be very costly if you are not careful. This is not to suggest that you cannot accept new challenges and new opportunities. After all, if you don't try a particular thing, how will you ever gain experience in it? The key is to seek the advice of those who have gone before you and to learn from their mistakes. Although you can learn by trial and error, it is better to learn from experienced professionals who can guide you through the process. Professional advice can be sought through various media, including reading books, listening to tapes or CDs, searching for information on the Internet, being tutored by mentors, or hiring a professional for personal one-on-one training. An alternative to doing it yourself, of course, is to hire a professional to represent you in the appropriate capacity.

The Fifth Law of Gold

Gold flees the man who would force it to impossible earnings or who follows the alluring advice of tricksters and schemers or who trusts it to his own inexperience and romantic desires in investment.

How to Sell Rental Properties the Smart Way

Of this, the fifth law of gold, the wise old Kalabab declares

> Fanciful propositions that thrill-like adventure tales always come to the new
> owner of gold. These appear to endow his treasure with magic powers that will
> enable it to make impossible earnings. Yet heed ye the wise men for verily they
> know the risks that lurk behind every plan to make wealth suddenly. Forget not
> the rich men of Nineveh who would take no thought of losing their principal or
> tying it up in unprofitable investments [pp. 83, 84].

The fifth law of gold is perhaps more relevant today than the other
four laws combined. If you are like most people, your mailbox probably
gets flooded with all kinds of offers about how to make millions in this
thing or that thing. These get-rich-quick schemes all have a common
theme—they promise untold wealth with only a small investment and
very little effort. It's easier than you might think to get caught up in
believing such stories. Think of the millions of people who invested in an
overinflated stock market on the advice of some stock market guru only
to lose a significant portion of their life savings. Kalabab aptly describes
these seemingly lucrative investment opportunities as a treasure endowed
with "magic powers that will enable it to make impossible earnings." You
must exercise caution when following the fourth law of gold—to seek the
advice of professionals—by making certain that the individual whose
advice you are seeking is truly qualified to give it. Although the huckster
on the telephone guarantees you that an investment in Stock XYZ will
double over the next six months, he in reality may be churning your
investment account to generate commissions, or he may be unloading
the firm's inventory of junk stocks to anyone who will buy them. The
Enron story is a perfect example of the many shareholders who got taken
for a ride by false promises made by the unscrupulous people in charge.
Most of these shareholders, and especially the employees, lost much of
their savings in what was thought to be a sound investment. Remember
the age-old advice that if it sounds too good to be true, it probably is.

Kalabab concludes his instruction regarding the five laws of gold by
revealing that these same five laws largely have been responsible for his
own success. He asserts that anyone schooled in these fundamental principles of finance likewise can enjoy great success. Kalabab maintains that

all one has to do is follow the five laws as prescribed on the ancient clay tablets given to Nomasir by his wise father, Arkad, to be equally successful. He submits the following to his attentive audience:

> Ten years from this night, what can you tell about this gold?
>
> If there be men among you, who, like Nomasir, will use a portion of their gold to start for themselves an estate and be thenceforth wisely guided by the wisdom of Arkad? Ten years from now, 'tis a safe wager, like the son of Arkad, they will be rich and respected among men.
>
> Our wise acts accompany us through life to please us and to help us. Just as surely, our unwise acts follow us to plague and torment us. Alas, they cannot be forgotten. In the front rank of the torments that do follow us are the memories of the things we should have done, of the opportunities which came to us and we took not.
>
> Rich are the treasures of Babylon, so rich no man can count their value in pieces of gold. Each year, they grow richer and more valuable. Like the treasures of every land, they are a reward, a rich reward awaiting those men of purpose who determine to secure their just share.
>
> In the strength of thine own desires is a magic power. Guide this power with thy knowledge of the five laws of gold and thou shalt share the treasures of Babylon [pp. 84, 85].

Although Arkad's tablets were made only of clay, the tablets were indisputably worth far more than their weight in gold, for the wisdom contained in the five laws of gold is capable of empowering anyone who will apply them to amass untold wealth. In the words of Kalabab, I pose the following questions to you: "A bag heavy with gold or a clay tablet carved with words of wisdom; if thou hadst thy choice, which would thou choose? . . . Ten years from this night, what can you tell about this gold?"

The Light of Integrity

The soul is dyed the color of its thoughts. Think only on those things that are in line with your principles and can bear the full light of day. The content of your character is your choice. Day by day, what you choose, what you think, and what you do is who you become. Your integrity is your destiny. . . . It is the light that guides your way.

—HERACLITUS, GREEK PHILOSOPHER

Afterword

For More Information

Current ordering information for the Value Play Rental House Analyzer and other real estate products can be found at www.thevalueplay.com.

For information regarding Symphony Homes, one of Michigan's premier builders, please log on to www.symphony-homes.com.

A copy of the Property Inspection Checklist and other forms can be found at www.thevalueplay.com.

Glossary

Real estate investors will find this glossary helpful for understanding words and terms used in real estate transactions. There are, however, some factors that may affect these definitions. Terms are defined as they are commonly understood in the mortgage and real estate industry. The same terms may have different meanings in another context. The definitions are intentionally general, nontechnical, and short. They do not encompass all possible meanings or nuances that a term may acquire in legal use. State laws, as well as custom and use in various states or regions of the country, may in fact modify or completely change the meanings of certain terms defined. Before signing any documents or depositing any money preparatory to entering into a real estate contract, the purchaser should consult with an attorney of his or her choice to ensure that his or her rights are protected properly.

Abstract of Title A summary of the public records relating to the title to a particular piece of land. An attorney or title insurance company

Glossary

reviews an abstract of title to determine whether there are any title defects that must be cleared before a buyer can purchase a clear, marketable, and insurable title.

Acceleration Clause A condition in a mortgage that may require the balance of the loan to become due immediately in the event regular mortgage payments are not made or for breach of other conditions of the mortgage.

Accretion An addition to one's land by the gradual and almost undetectable deposit of soil by natural causes, usually due to the flow of water, such as around a lake or by a river.

Acre A measure of land equaling 160 rods, or 4840 square yards, or 43,560 square feet, or a tract of land approximately 208.71 feet by 208.71 feet.

Ad Valorem Designates an assessment of taxes against property in a literal sense according to its value.

Adverse Possession A possession that is inconsistent with the right of possession and title of the true owner. It is the actual, open, notorious, exclusive, continuous, and hostile occupation and possession of the land of another under a claim of right or under color of title.

Agency The relationship that exists by contract whereby one person is authorized to represent and act on behalf of another person in various business transactions.

Agreement of Sale Known by various names, such as contract of purchase, purchase agreement, or sales agreement, according to location or jurisdiction. A contract in which a seller agrees to sell and a buyer agrees to buy under certain specific terms and conditions spelled out in writing and signed by both parties.

Amortization A payment plan that enables a borrower to reduce a debt gradually through monthly payments of principal, thereby liquidating or extinguishing the obligation through a series of installments.

Appraisal An expert judgment or estimate of the quality or value of real estate as of a given date. The process through which conclusions of property value are obtained. It also refers to the formalized report that sets forth the estimate and conclusion of value.

Appurtenance That which belongs to something else. In real estate law, an appurtenance is a right, privilege, or improvement that passes as an incident to the land, such as a right of way.

Assessed Value An official valuation of property most often used for tax purposes.

Assignment The method or manner by which a right, a specialty, or a contract is transferred from one person to another.

Assumption of Mortgage An obligation undertaken by the purchaser of property to be personally liable for payment of an existing mortgage. In an assumption, the purchaser is substituted for the original mortgagor in the mortgage instrument, and the original mortgagor is to be released from further liability in the assumption. The mortgagee's consent is usually required.

The original mortgagor always should obtain a written release from further liability if he or she desires to be fully released under the assumption. Failure to obtain such a release renders the original mortgagor liable if the person assuming the mortgage fails to make the monthly payments.

An assumption of mortgage is often confused with *purchasing subject to a mortgage.* When one purchases subject to a mortgage, the purchaser agrees to make the monthly mortgage payments on an existing mortgage, but the original mortgagor remains personally liable if the purchaser fails to make the monthly payments. Since the original mortgagor remains liable in the event of default, the mortgagee's consent is not required for a sale subject to a mortgage.

Both assumption of mortgage and purchasing subject to a mortgage are used to finance the sale of property. They also may be used when a mortgagor is in financial difficulty and desires to sell the property to avoid foreclosure.

Beneficiary A person for whose benefit property or funds are placed in trust or the recipient of funds from an insurance fund or annuity contract.

Glossary

Bill of Sale A written document or instrument that provides evidence of the transfer of right, title, and interest in personal property from one person to another.

Binder or Offer to Purchase A preliminary agreement, secured by the payment of earnest money, between a buyer and a seller as an offer to purchase real estate. A binder secures the right to purchase real estate on agreed terms for a limited period of time. If the buyer changes his mind or is unable to purchase, the earnest money is forfeited unless the binder expressly provides that it is to be refunded.

Blanket Mortgage A single mortgage that covers more than one piece of real estate. It is often used to purchase a large tract of land that is later subdivided and sold as individual parcels.

Bona Fide Made in good faith; good, valid, without fraud, such as a bona fide offer.

Bond Any obligation under seal. A real estate bond is a written obligation, usually issued on security of a mortgage or deed of trust.

Breach The breaking of law or failure of a duty either by omission or commission; the failure to perform, without legal excuse, any promise that forms a part or the whole of a contract.

Broker One who is engaged for others in a negotiation for contacts relative to property, with the custody of which they have no concern.

Broker, Real Estate Any person, partnership, association, or corporation that, for a compensation or valuable consideration, sells or offers for sale, buys or offers to buy, or negotiates the purchase or sale or exchange of real estate or rents or offers to rent any real estate or the improvements thereon for others.

Building Code Regulations established by local governments setting forth the structural requirements for buildings.

Building Line or Setback Distances from the ends and/or sides of a lot beyond which construction may not extend. The building line may be

Glossary

established by a filed plat of subdivision, by restrictive covenants in deeds or leases, by building codes, or by zoning ordinances.

Capital   Accumulated wealth; a portion of wealth set aside for the production of additional wealth; specifically, the funds belonging to the partners or shareholders of a business, invested with the express purpose and intent of remaining in the business to generate profits.

Capital Expenditures   Investments of cash or other property or the creation of a liability in exchange for property to remain permanently in a business; usually pertaining to land, buildings, machinery, and equipment.

Capitalization   The act or process of converting or obtaining the present value of future incomes into current equivalent capital value; also the amount so determined; commonly referring to the capital structure of a corporation or other such legal entity.

Caveat Emptor   The phrase literally means "let the buyer beware." Under this doctrine, the buyer is duty bound to examine the property being purchased and assumes conditions that are readily ascertainable on view.

Certificate of Title   A certificate issued by a title company or a written opinion rendered by an attorney that the seller has good marketable and insurable title to a property that he or she is offering for sale. A certificate of title offers no protection against any hidden defects in the title that an examination of the records could not reveal. The issuer of a certificate of title is liable only for damages due to negligence. The protection offered a homeowner under a certificate of title is not as great as that offered in a title insurance policy.

Chain of Title   A history of conveyances and encumbrances affecting the title to a particular real property.

Chattels   Items of movable personal property, such as animals, household furnishings, money, jewelry, motor vehicles, and all other items that are not permanently affixed to real property and which can be transferred from one place to another.

251

Glossary

Closing Costs   The numerous expenses that buyers and sellers normally incur to complete a transaction in the transfer of ownership of real estate. These costs are in addition to the price of the property and are items prepaid on the closing day. The following is a common list of closing costs.

Buyer's expenses:
- Documentary stamps on notes

- Recording fees for deed and mortgage

- Escrow fees

- Attorney's fee

- Title insurance

- Appraisal and inspection fees

- Survey charge

Seller's expenses:
- Cost of abstract

- Documentary stamps on deed

- Real estate commission

- Recording fee for mortgage

- Survey charge

- Escrow fees

- Attorney's fee

The agreement of sale negotiated previously between the buyer and the seller may state in writing who will pay each of these costs.

Closing Day   The day on which the formalities of a real estate sale are concluded. The certificate of title, abstract, and deed generally are prepared for

Glossary

the closing by an attorney, and this cost is charged to the buyer. The buyer signs the mortgage, and closing costs are paid. The final closing merely confirms the original agreement reached in the agreement of sale.

Cloud on Title An outstanding claim or encumbrance that adversely affects the marketability of a title.

Collateral Security A separate obligation attached to a contract to guarantee its performance; the transfer of property or of other contracts or valuables to ensure the performance of a principal agreement or obligation.

Commission Money paid to a real estate agent or broker by the seller as compensation for finding a buyer and completing the sale. Usually it is a percentage of the sale price ranging anywhere from 6 to 7 percent on single-family houses and 10 percent on land.

Compound Interest Interest paid on the original principal of an indebtedness and also on the accrued and unpaid interest that has accumulated over time.

Condemnation The taking of private property for public use by a government unit against the will of the owner but with payment of just compensation under the government's power of eminent domain. Condemnation also may be a determination by a governmental agency that a particular building is unsafe or unfit for use.

Condominium Individual ownership of a dwelling unit and an individual interest in the common areas and facilities that serve the multiunit project.

Consideration Something of value, usually money, that is the inducement of a contract. Any right, interest, property, or benefit accruing to one party and any forbearance, detriment, loss, or responsibility given, suffered, or undertaken may constitute a consideration that will sustain a contract.

Contract of Purchase See *Agreement of Sale.*

Contractor In the construction industry, a contractor is one who contracts to erect houses, buildings, or portions of them. There are also contractors for each phase of construction, such as heating, electrical, plumbing, air conditioning, road building, bridge and dam erection, and others.

Glossary

Conventional Mortgage A mortgage loan not insured by the Department of Housing and Urban Development (HUD) or guaranteed by the Veterans' Administration. It is subject to conditions established by the lending institution and state statutes. The mortgage rates may vary with different institutions and between states. (States have various interest limits.)

Cooperative Housing An apartment building or a group of dwellings owned by a corporation, the stockholders of which are the residents of the dwellings. It is operated for their benefit by their elected board of directors. In a cooperative, the corporation or association owns title to the real estate. A resident purchases stock in the corporation, which entitles him to occupy a unit in the building or property owned by the cooperative. While the resident does not own his unit, he has an absolute right to occupy the unit for as long as he owns the stock.

Covenant An agreement between two or more persons entered into by deed whereby one of the parties promises the performance of certain acts or that a given state does or shall or does not or shall not exist.

Deed A formal written instrument by which title to real property is transferred from one owner to another. The deed should contain an accurate description of the property being conveyed, should be signed and witnessed according to the laws of the state where the property is located, and should be delivered to the purchaser on the day of closing. There are two parties to a deed—the grantor and the grantee. (See also *Deed of Trust, General Warranty Deed, Quitclaim Deed,* and *Special Warranty Deed.*)

Deed of Trust Like a mortgage, a security instrument whereby real property is given as security for a debt; however, in a deed of trust there are three parties to the instrument—the borrower, the trustee, and the lender (or beneficiary). In such a transaction, the borrower transfers the legal title for the property to the trustee, who holds the property in trust as security for payment of the debt to the lender or beneficiary. If the borrower pays the debt as agreed, the deed of trust becomes void. If, however, she defaults in payment of the debt, the trustee may sell the property at a public sale under the terms of the deed of trust. In most jurisdictions where the deed of trust

Glossary

is in force, the borrower is subject to having her property sold without benefit of legal proceedings. A few states have begun in recent years to treat the deed of trust like a mortgage.

Default   Failure to make mortgage payments as agreed to in a commitment based on the terms and at the designated time set forth in the mortgage or deed of trust. It is the mortgagor's responsibility to remember the due date and send the payment prior to the due date, not after. Generally, 30 days after the due date if payment is not received, the mortgage is in default. In the event of default, the mortgage may give the lender the right to accelerate payments, take possession and receive rents, and start foreclosure. Defaults also may come about by the failure to observe other conditions in the mortgage or deed of trust.

Depreciation   Decline in value of a house due to wear and tear, adverse changes in the neighborhood, or any other reason. The term is most often applied for tax purposes.

Documentary Stamps   A state tax, in the form of stamps, required on deeds and mortgages when real estate title passes from one owner to another. The amount of stamps required varies with each state.

Down Payment   The amount of money to be paid by the purchaser to the seller on the signing of an agreement of sale. The agreement of sale will refer to the down payment amount and will acknowledge receipt of the down payment. Down payment is the difference between the sales price and maximum mortgage amount. The down payment may not be refundable if the purchaser fails to buy the property without good cause. If the purchaser wants the down payment to be refundable, she should insert a clause in the agreement of sale specifying the conditions under which the deposit will be refunded if the agreement does not already contain such clause. If the seller cannot deliver good title, the agreement of sale usually requires the seller to return the down payment and to pay interest and expenses incurred by the purchaser.

Duress   Unlawful constraint exercised on a person whereby the person is forced to perform some act or to sign an instrument or document against her will.

Glossary

Earnest Money The deposit money given to a seller or his agent by a potential buyer on signing of the agreement of sale to show that he is serious about buying a house or any other type of real property. If the sale goes through, the earnest money is applied against the down payment. If the sale does not go through, the earnest money will be forfeited or lost unless the binder or offer to purchase expressly provides that it is refundable.

Easement Rights A right of way granted to a person or company authorizing access to or travel over the owner's land. An electric company obtaining a right of way across private property is a common example.

Economic Life The period over which a property may be profitably used or the period over which a property will yield a return on the investment over and above the economic or ground rent due to its land.

Economic Obsolescence Impairment of desirability or useful life arising from economic forces, such as changes in optimal land use, legislative enactments that restrict or impair property rights, and changes in supply and demand relationships.

Eminent Domain The superior right of property subsisting in every sovereign state to take private property for public use on the payment of just compensation. This power is often conferred on public service corporations that perform quasipublic functions such as providing public utilities. In every case, the owner whose property is taken must be justly compensated according to fair market values in the prevailing area.

Encroachment An obstruction, building, or part of a building that intrudes beyond a legal boundary onto neighboring private or public land or a building extending beyond the building line.

Encumbrance A legal right or interest in land that affects a good or clear title and diminishes the land's value. It can take numerous forms, such as zoning ordinances, easement rights, claims, mortgages, liens, charges, a pending legal action, unpaid taxes, or restrictive covenants. An encumbrance does not legally prevent transfer of the property to another. A title search is all that is usually done to reveal the existence of such encumbrances, and it is up to the buyer to determine whether he wants to purchase with the encumbrance or what can be done to remove it.

Equity The value of a homeowner's unencumbered interest in real estate. Equity is computed by subtracting from the property's fair market value the total of the unpaid mortgage balance and any outstanding liens or other debts against the property. A homeowner's equity increases as she pays off the mortgage or as the property appreciates in value. When the mortgage and all other debts against the property are paid in full, the homeowner has 100 percent equity in the property.

Escheat The reverting of property to the state by reason of failure of persons legally entitled to hold or when heirs capable of inheriting are lacking the ability to do so.

Escrow Funds paid by one party to another (the escrow agent) to hold until the occurrence of a specified event, after which the funds are released to a designated individual. In Federal Housing Administration (FHA) mortgage transactions, an escrow account usually refers to the funds a mortgagor pays the lender at the time of the periodic mortgage payments. The money is held in a trust fund provided by the lender for the buyer. Such funds should be adequate to cover yearly anticipated expenditures for mortgage insurance premiums, taxes, hazard insurance premiums, and special assessments.

Estate The degree, quantum, nature, and extent of interest that one has in real property.

Execute To perform what is required to give validity to a legal document. To execute a document, for example, means to sign it so that it becomes fully enforceable by law.

Fee Simple The largest estate a person can have in real estate. Denotes totality of ownership, unlimited in point of time, as in perpetual.

Fiduciary A person to whom property is entrusted; a trustee who holds, controls, or manages for another. A real estate agent is said to have a fiduciary responsibility and relationship with a client.

Glossary

Foreclosure A legal term applied to any of the various methods of enforcing payment of a debt secured by a mortgage or deed of trust by taking and selling the mortgaged property and depriving the mortgagor of possession.

Forfeiture Clause A clause in a lease enabling the landlord to terminate the lease and remove a tenant when the latter defaults in payment of rent or any other obligation under the lease.

Freehold An interest in real estate of not less than a life estate; either a fee simple estate or a life estate.

Functional Obsolescence An impairment of desirability of a property arising from its being out of date with respect to design and style, capacity and utility in relation to site, lack of modern facilities, and the like.

General Warranty Deed A deed that conveys not only all the grantor's interests in and title to a property to the grantee but also warrants that if the title is defective or has a cloud on it (such as mortgage claims, tax liens, title claims, judgments, or mechanic's liens against it), the grantee may hold the grantor liable.

Grantee That party in the deed who is the buyer or recipient; the person to whom the real estate is conveyed.

Grantor That party in the deed who is the seller or giver; the person who conveys the real estate.

Ground Rent The rent or earnings paid or attributable for the right of use and occupancy of a parcel of unimproved land; that portion of the total rental paid that is considered to represent a return on the land only.

Hazard Insurance Protects against damages caused to property by fire, wind storms, and other common hazards.

Highest and Best Use That use of or program of utilization of a site that will produce the maximum net land returns over the total period comprising the future; the optimal use for a site.

Glossary

Homestead   Real property owned by a person under special legal restrictions and exemptions from claims of creditors under the Constitution.

HUD   U.S. Department of Housing and Urban Development. Office of Housing and Federal Housing Administration within HUD insures home mortgage loans made by lenders and sets minimum standards for such homes.

Implied Warranty or Covenant   A guaranty of assurance the law supplies in an agreement, even though the agreement itself does not express the guaranty or assurance.

Injunction   A writ or order of the court to restrain one or more parties to a suit from committing an inequitable or unjust act in regard to the rights of some other party in the suit or proceeding.

Interest   A charge paid for borrowing money. (See also *Mortgage Note.*)

Joint Tenancy   Property held by two or more persons together with the right of survivorship. While the doctrine of survivorship has been abolished with respect to most joint tenancies, the tenancy by the entirety retains the doctrine of survivorship in content.

Judgment   The decision or sentence of a court of law as the result of proceedings instituted therein for the redress of an injury. A judgment declaring that one individual is indebted to another individual when properly docketed creates a lien on the real property of the judgment debtor.

Lease   A species of contract, written or oral, between the owner of real estate (the landlord) and another person (the tenant) covering the conditions on which the tenant may possess, occupy, and use the real estate.

Lessee   A person who leases property from another person, usually the landlord.

Lessor   The owner or person who rents or leases property to a tenant or lessee; the landlord.

Lien   A claim by one person on the property of another as security for money owed. Such claims may include obligations not met or satisfied, judgments, unpaid taxes, materials, or labor. (See also *Special Lien.*)

Glossary

Marketable Title   A title that is free and clear of objectionable liens, clouds, or other title defects. A title that enables an owner to sell his property freely to others and which others will accept without objection.

Market Value   The amount for which a property would sell if put on the open market and sold in the manner in which property is ordinarily sold in the community in which the property is situated. The highest price estimated in terms of money that a buyer would be warranted in paying and a seller would be justified in accepting, provided both parties were fully informed and acted intelligently and voluntarily, and furthermore that all the rights and benefits inherent in or attributable to the property were included in the transfer.

Meeting of Minds   A mutual intention of two persons to enter into a contract affecting their legal status based on agreed-on terms.

Metes and Bounds   A term that comes from the Old English word *metes* meaning "measurements" and *bounds* meaning "boundaries." It is generally applied to any description of real estate; describes the boundaries by distance and angles.

Mortgage   A lien or claim against real property given by a buyer to a lender as security for money borrowed. Under government-insured or loan-guarantee provisions, the payments may include escrow amounts covering taxes, hazard insurance, water charges, and special assessments. Mortgages generally run from 10 to 30 years, during which the loan is to be paid off.

Mortgage Commitment   A written notice from a bank or other lending institution saying that it will advance mortgage funds in a specified amount to enable a buyer to purchase a house.

Mortgage Insurance Premium   The payment made by a borrower to the lender for transmittal to HUD to help defray the cost of an FHA mortgage insurance program and to provide a reserve fund to protect lenders against loss in insured mortgage transactions. In FHA-insured mortgages this represents an annual rate of one-half of 1 percent paid by the mortgagor on a monthly basis.

Glossary

Mortgage Note   A written agreement to repay a loan. The agreement is secured by a mortgage, serves as proof of an indebtedness, and states the manner in which it shall be paid. The note states the actual amount of the debt that the mortgage secures and renders the mortgagor personally responsible for repayment.

Mortgage (Open-End)   A mortgage with a provision that permits borrowing additional money in the future without refinancing the loan or paying additional financing charges. Open-end provisions often limit such borrowing to no more than would raise the balance to the original loan figure.

Mortgagee   The lender in a mortgage agreement.

Mortgagor   The borrower in a mortgage agreement.

Net Income   In general, synonymous with net earnings, but considered a broader and better term; the balance remaining after deducting from the gross income all expenses, maintenance, taxes, and losses pertaining to operating properties except for interest or other financial charges on borrowed or other forms of capital.

Net Lease   A lease in which, in addition to the rental stipulated, the lessee assumes payment of all property charges such as taxes, insurance, and maintenance.

Nonconforming Use   A use of land that predates zoning but is not in accordance with the uses prescribed for the area by the zoning ordinance. Because it was there first, it may be continued, subject to certain limitations.

Note   An instrument of credit given to attest a debt; a written promise to pay money that may or may not accompany a mortgage or other security agreement.

Nuisance Value   Although not having true value, it is the amount that someone other than the owner of a property is willing to pay for it, not for any intrinsic value, but because in its present ownership it is an annoyance or is actually damaging to the prospective buyer.

Offer   A proposal, oral or written, to buy a piece of property at a specified price with specified terms and conditions.

Glossary

Option The exclusive right to purchase or lease a property at a stipulated price or rent within a specified period of time.

Percentage Lease A lease of commercial property in which the rent is computed as a percentage of the receipts, either gross or net, from the business being conducted by the lessee, sometimes with a guaranteed minimum rental.

Personal Property Movable property that is not by definition real property and includes tangible property such as moneys, goods, and chattels, as well as debts and claims.

Planned Unit Development (PUD) Residential complex of mixed housing types. Offers greater design flexibility than traditional developments. PUDs permit clustering of homes, sometimes not allowed under standard zoning ordinances, utilization of open space, and a project harmonious with the natural topography of the land.

Plat A map or chart of a lot, subdivision, or community drawn by a surveyor showing boundary lines, buildings, improvements on the land, and easements.

Points Sometimes referred to as *discount points*. A point is 1 percent of the amount of a mortgage loan. For example, if a loan is for $250,000, one point is $2500. Points are charged by a lender to raise the yield on a loan at a time when money is tight, interest rates are high, and there is a legal limit to the interest rate that can be charged on a mortgage. Buyers are prohibited from paying points on HUD or Veterans Administration guaranteed loans (sellers can pay them, however). On a conventional mortgage, points may be paid by either buyer or seller or split between them.

Prepayment Payment of mortgage loan, or part of it, before the due date. Mortgage agreements often restrict the right of prepayment either by limiting the amount that can be prepaid in any one year or charging a penalty for prepayment. The FHA does not permit such restrictions in FHA-insured mortgages.

Principal The basic element of a loan as distinguished from interest and mortgage insurance premium. In other words, principal is the amount on

Glossary

which interest is paid. The word also means one who appoints an agent to act for and on behalf of; the person bound by an agent's authorized contract.

Property The term used to describe the rights and interests a person has in lands, chattels, and other determinate things.

Purchase Agreement An offer to purchase that has been accepted by a seller and has become a binding contract.

Quiet Enjoyment The right of an owner of an interest in land, whether an owner or a tenant, to protection against disturbance or interference with his or her possession of the land.

Quitclaim Deed A deed that transfers whatever interest the maker of the deed may have in a particular parcel of land. A quitclaim deed is often given to clear a title when the grantor's interest in a property is questionable. By accepting such a deed, the buyer assumes all the risks. Such a deed makes no warranties as to the title but simply transfers to the buyer whatever interest the grantor has. (See also *Deed.*)

Real Estate Agent An intermediary who buys and sells real estate for a company, firm, or individual and is compensated on a commission basis. The agent does not have title to the property but generally represents the owner.

Real Estate Investment Trust (REIT) An entity that allows a very large number of investors to participate in the purchase of real estate, but as passive investors. The investors do not buy directly but instead purchase shares in the REIT that owns the real estate investment. REITs are fairly common with the advent of mutual funds and can be purchased for as little as $10 per share and sometimes less.

Real Property Land and buildings and anything that may be permanently attached to them.

Recording The placing of a copy of a document in the proper books in the office of the register of deeds so that a public record will be made of it.

Redemption The right that an owner-mortgagor or one claiming under him has after execution of a mortgage to recover back his title to the mortgaged property by paying the mortgage debt plus interest and any other costs or penalties imposed prior to a the occurrence of a valid foreclosure. The payment discharges the mortgage and places the title back as it was at the time the mortgage was executed.

Refinancing The process of the same mortgagor paying off one loan with the proceeds from another loan.

Reformation The correction of a deed or other instrument by reason of a mutual mistake of the parties involved or because of the mistake of one party caused by the fraud or inequitable conduct of the other party.

Release The giving up or abandoning of a claim or right to the person against whom the claim exists or against whom the right is to be exercised or enforced.

Release of Lien The discharge of certain property from the lien of a judgment, mortgage, or claim.

Renewal Taking a new lease after an existing lease expires.

Rent A compensation, either in money, provisions, chattels, or labor, received by the owner of real estate from a tenant for the occupancy of the premises.

Rescission of Contract The abrogating or annulling of a contract; the revocation or repealing of a contract by mutual consent of the parties to the contract or for other causes as recognized by law.

Restrictive Covenants Private restrictions limiting the use of real property. Restrictive covenants are created by deed and may run with the land, thereby binding all subsequent purchasers of the land, or may be deemed personal and binding only between the original seller and buyer. The determination of whether a covenant runs with the land or is personal is governed by the language of the covenant, the intent of the parties, and the law in the state where the land is situated. Restrictive covenants that run with the land are encumbrances and may affect the value and marketability of title. Restrictive covenants may limit the density of buildings per acre; regulate size, style, or price range of buildings to be erected; or

Glossary

prevent particular businesses from operating or minority groups from owning or occupying homes in a given area. This latter discriminatory covenant is unconstitutional and has been declared unenforceable by the U.S. Supreme Court.

Revocation The recall of a power or authority conferred or the vacating of an instrument previously made.

Right of Survivorship Granted to two joint owners who purchase using this particular buying method. Stipulates that one gets full rights and becomes the sole owner of the property on death of the other. Right of survivorship is the fundamental difference between acquiring property as joint owners and as tenants in common.

Sales Agreement See *Agreement of Sale.*

Security Deposit Money or things of value received by or for a property owner to ensure payment of rent and the satisfactory condition of the rented premises on termination of the written or oral lease.

Security Interest An interest in property that secures payment or performance of an obligation.

Setback The distance from a curb or other established line within which no buildings or structures may be erected. A setback ordinance prohibits the construction of buildings or structures within the defined setback areas.

Special Assessment A special tax imposed on property, individual lots, or all property in the immediate area by a public authority to pay the cost of public improvements, such as for the opening, grading, and guttering of streets; the construction of sidewalks and sewers; or the installation of street lights or other such items to be used for public purposes.

Special Lien A lien that binds a specified piece of property; unlike a general lien, it is levied against all of one's assets. It creates a right to retain something of value belonging to another person as compensation for labor, material, or money expended in that person's behalf. In some localities it is called *particular lien* or *specific lien.* (See also *Lien.*)

Glossary

Special Warranty Deed A deed in which the grantor conveys title to the grantee and agrees to protect the grantee against title defects or claims asserted by the grantor and those persons whose right to assert a claim against the title arose during the period the grantor held title to the property. In a special warranty deed the grantor guarantees to the grantee that she has done nothing during the time she held title to the property that has or might in the future impair the grantee's title.

Specific Performance A remedy in court of equity whereby the defendant may be compelled to do whatever she has agreed to do in a contract executed by her.

State Stamps See *Documentary Stamps.*

Statute A law established by the act of legislative powers; an act of the legislature; the written will of the legislature solemnly expressed according to the forms necessary to constitute it as the law provides.

Subdivision A tract of land divided into smaller parcels of land or lots usually for the purpose of constructing new houses.

Sublease An agreement whereby one person who has leased land from the owner rents out all or a portion of the premises for a period ending prior to expiration of the original lease.

Subordination Clause A clause in a mortgage or lease stating that one who has a prior claim or interest agrees that his interest or claim shall be secondary or subordinate to a subsequent claim, encumbrance, or interest.

Survey A map or plat made by a licensed surveyor showing the results of measuring the land with its elevations, improvements, boundaries, and relationship to surrounding tracts of land. A survey is often required by a lender to ensure that a building is actually sited on the land according to its legal description.

Survivorship The distinguishing feature of a tenancy by the entirety, by which on the death of one spouse the surviving spouse acquires full ownership.

Glossary

Tax As applied to real estate, an enforced charge imposed on persons, property, or income to be used to support the state. The governing body, in turn, uses the funds in the best interests of the general public.

Tax Deed A deed given where property has been purchased at public sale because of the owner's nonpayment of taxes.

Tax Sale A sale of property for nonpayment of taxes assessed against it.

Tenancy at Will An arrangement under which a tenant occupies land with the consent of the owner but without a definite termination date and without any definite agreement for regular payment of rent.

Tenancy in Common Style of ownership in which two or more persons purchase a property jointly but with no right of survivorship. Each tenant in common is the owner of an undivided fractional interest in the whole property. They are free to will their share to anyone they choose, a primary difference between this form of ownership and joint tenancy.

Tenant One who holds or possesses land or tenements by any kind of title, either in fee, for life, for years, or at will. The term is used most commonly as one who has under lease the temporary use and occupation of real property that belongs to another person or persons. The tenant is the lessee.

Time Is of the Essence A phrase meaning that time is of crucial value and vital importance and that failure to fulfill time deadlines will be considered to be a failure to perform a contract.

Title As generally used, the rights of ownership and possession of particular property. In real estate usage, title may refer to the instruments or documents by which a right of ownership is established (title documents), or it may refer to the ownership interest one has in the real estate.

Title Insurance Protects lenders or homeowners against loss of their interest in property due to legal defects in title. Title insurance may be issued to a mortgagee's title policy. Insurance benefits will be paid only to the named insured in the title policy, so it is important that an owner purchase an owner's title policy if he desires the protection of title insurance.

Glossary

Title Search or Examination A check of the title records, generally at the local courthouse, to make sure that a buyer is purchasing a house from the legal owner and that there are no liens, overdue special assessments, or other claims or outstanding restrictive covenants filed in the record that would adversely affect the marketability or value of title.

Trust A relationship under which one person, the trustee, holds legal title to property for the benefit of another person, the trust beneficiary.

Trustee A party who is given legal responsibility to hold property in the best interest of or for the benefit of another. The trustee is one placed in a position of responsibility for another, a responsibility enforceable in a court of law. (See also *Deed of Trust.*)

Unimproved As relating to land, vacant or lacking in essential appurtenant improvements required to serve a useful purpose.

Useful Life The period of time over which a commercial property can be depreciated for tax purposes. A property's useful life is also referred to as its *economic life.*

Usury Charging a higher rate of interest on a loan than is allowed by law.

Valid Having force or binding forces; legally sufficient and authorized by law.

Valuation The act or process of estimating value; the amount of estimated value.

Value Ability to command goods, including money, in exchange; the quantity of goods, including money, that should be commanded or received in exchange for the item valued. As applied to real estate, value is the present worth of all the rights to future benefits arising from ownership.

Variance An exception to a zoning ordinance granted to meet certain specific needs, usually given on an individual case-by-case basis.

Void That which is unenforceable; having no force or effect.

Waiver Renunciation, disclaiming, or surrender of some claim, right, or prerogative.

Glossary

Warranty Deed A deed that transfers ownership of real property and in which the grantor guarantees that the title is free and clear of any and all encumbrances.

Zoning Ordinances The acts of an authorized local government establishing building codes and setting forth regulations for property land usage.

Index

Index

Index

Index

Index

Investment strategies, 3
  for building $10 million retirement portfolio, 21–25
  leverage in, 10–18
Investor (equity) financing, 12
IRS (Internal Revenue Service), 6

J

Jefferson, Thomas, 192

K

Keller, Helen, 216
King, Martin Luther, Jr., 170
Kitchens, 180–182
Knowledge, investment, 253

L

Landscaping, 174–175
Lead-based paint disclosure, 166–167
Leaks:
  in plumbing, 33
  in roof, 32
  in walls, 31–32
Lease agreements, 158–170
  abandonment clause in, 167–168
  additional provisions section in, 168
  assignment and subletting in, 164
  default agreement in, 169
  entire agreement section in, 168–169
  entry and inspection rights in, 165
  fixed-term, 158, 159
  indemnification section in, 169–170
  lead-based paint disclosure in, 166–167
  limits on use and occupancy in, 160–161
  locks provision in, 166
  maintenance of dwelling/property in, 164–165
  month-to-month, 158–159
  parties to, 160
  payment of rent in, 161–162
  penalties in, 162
  possession section in, 166
  property address in, 160
  and rent increases, 198
  right to quiet enjoyment section in, 165–166
  security deposit in, 162–163
  term of, 161
  termination of tenancy in, 167

Lease agreements *(Cont.)*
  utilities payment in, 164
  validity of each part section in, 169
Lease applications, 146–149
Lease options, 108–109, 111–112
Leveling of houses, 31
Leverage, 10–18
  and debt financing, 11
  effect of price appreciation on, 13–15
  and equity financing, 12
  and other people's money principle, 10, 11
  and return on investment, 12–13
Levitt, Theodore, 154
Lighting, 180
Limited-liability corporations (LLCs), 12
Limits on use and occupancy, 160–161
Lincoln, Abraham, 112, 132
LLCs (limited-liability corporations), 12
Loan origination fees, 94
Loan-assumption addendum, 125–126
Loans, 11
  amount of, 88–91
  fees with, 92–97
  interest rates on, 81
  reductions in principal, 6
  term of, 90–91
  (*See also* Financing)
Local bank financing, 104–105
Locating rental properties, 37–51
  from billboards/signs, 41–42
  classified advertisements for, 38–39
  Internet searches for, 40–41
  methods for, 37–38
  real estate magazines for, 39–40
  for sale by owners, 48–51
  scouts for, 45–47
  through professional affiliations, 47–48
  through real estate agents, 42–45
Location of property, 27–28
  in classified ads, 140
  as consideration for selling, 211, 214
  ten-point checklist for, 28
Locator services, 144–146
Locks provisions (lease agreements), 166
Lombardi, Vince, 182

M

Maintenance (in lease agreement), 164–165
Management:
  hiring individual for, 191–192

274

Index

Index

Index

Index

About the Author

Steve Berges is a real estate investment professional with over 25 years of experience. As principal of Symphony Homes, he is an active investor specializing in creating value through various real estate mechanisms, including single-family houses, multifamily apartment complexes, and the development and construction of single-family and condominium housing communities. Berges holds an MBA degree in finance and marketing from Rice University and is the author of *The Complete Guide to Buying and Selling Apartment Buildings* and *The Complete Guide to Flipping Properties*.